SEXUAL
VIRTUE

Dear Kyle,

Life has a funny way of surprising us.
One of the better surprises for me was having the chance
to meet you and become good friends. And to think
it happened in Erie, PA -- after we both left the
Midwest.

You have a very sharp mind and a great
sense of humor. Both have helped me more
than you know. I look forward to many more
years of friendship + adventures!

My best,
Roth

SEXUAL VIRTUE

An Approach to Contemporary Christian Ethics

Richard W. McCarty

Published by State University of New York Press, Albany

© 2015 State University of New York

For information, contact State University of New York Press, Albany, NY
www.sunypress.edu

Production, Jenn Bennett
Marketing, Kate Seburyamo

Library of Congress Cataloging-in-Publication Data

McCarty, Richard W., 1975–
  Sexual virtue : an approach to contemporary Christian ethics / Richard W.
McCarty.
        pages cm
  Includes bibliographical references and index.
  ISBN 978-1-4384-5429-0 (hc : alk. paper) 978-1-4384-5428-3 (pb : alk. paper)
  E-ISBN 978-1-4384-5430-6 (ebook)
  1. Sex—Religious aspects—Christianity. 2. Sexual ethics. 3. Christian
ethics. I. Title.

BT708.M415 2015
241'.664—dc23   2014003520

10 9 8 7 6 5 4 3 2 1

Dedicated to
Jesse Vedder Edwards-Borowicz
In all that leads to unconditional love and human flourishing,
we remember you.

Contents

Skip :)

Preface

This is a book on sexual ethics, and one that advances an argument about redefining sexual virtue for Christian ethics. In particular, I will argue that prudential reflection on sexual morality—when informed by contemporary critical insights—allows for a more inclusive understanding of sexual virtue than what traditional views have permitted. While my argument about sexual virtue comes from academic study in religion and sexual ethics, the seeds for thinking anew about sexual ethics were planted long ago by real-life questions, experiences, curiosities, pleasures, pains, and anxieties—and all of these stemming from simply living in a culture where the categories "sex" and "religion" (especially "Christianity") often ignite fires of controversy, or shine spotlights of shame. Along the way, I decided it was a good thing to study and write on these issues. My journey would lead me to see new possibilities for conceiving sexual morality, which is expressed here as a work of constructive sexual ethics. My hope is that the argument of this book is one that has practical implications for how people might actually talk about sex and sexuality, whether in academic settings, religious communities, or the public square. Thus, my goal is not only to make a small contribution to the academic fields of religious studies and sexual ethics, but also to create a safe intellectual space for people's real-life concerns about sexual morality.

I hope what I've written helps you on your journey, as it has mine.

Whether you are engaging in the field of sexual ethics as a scholar or a student of the liberal arts, or as a person engaged in confessional Christian discourse; or even if you are unconvinced by the various arguments in these pages because you have other commitments, philosophically or theologically, I am hopeful that I can get you to consider the merit of engaging Christian sexual ethics through an ethic of virtue. Admittedly, I also hope that a byproduct of this book is the promotion of sexual liberation and human flourishing. But as a work of *ethics*, I want first to promote moral discourse on sexuality, through the perspective of *virtue*, in order to encourage new proposals about the relationship between human sexuality and human happiness. Even so, it is not my intention to "settle the issue" once and for all.

You see, my colleague Keiko Takioto Miller—a specialist in Japanese language and culture—once taught me about the concept of *hara-hachibu*. The term literally means "eight-tenths-of-a-belly." As Keiko explains it, her Japanese grandmother taught her about *harahachibu* so that Keiko would learn some moderation when eating. Keiko's grandmother suggested that we need to leave at least 20 percent of our plates free, so that we're not "stuffed" and burdened down by "too much." Allegorically, Keiko believes that *harahachibu* applies to intellectual discourse, and I agree. We need to leave some "free space" in our intellectual work, especially in our writing. That "free space" amounts to certain questions left unanswered, in order to focus in on particular ideas worth savoring for themselves. I believe it is good, then, to put forward our ideas to encourage ongoing moral and theological discourse, but also to recognize that no one work of ethics will anticipate or respond to every possible objection or disciplinary perspective.

The argument set forth in this book, then, is *harahachibu*. It is the start of what I hope can be a renewed discourse on sexual virtue. However, I do not pretend to preserve established interpretations about virtue ethics. Much of what has been said about virtue ethics—especially virtue ethics in Christian discourse—has come from scholarship on Aristotle and Thomas Aquinas. But it is not my intention to rehearse an argument about how best to interpret these philosophical figures. Instead, I am intrigued by concepts of virtue, and specifically how the concept of *sexual virtue* might be reimagined for contemporary use. Thus, what I offer here is only a *sketch* of how sexual virtue might be reimagined. To those scholars who have spent their careers studying the virtue ethics of Aristotle or Aquinas, what I "leave out" from your library of study may register as an incomplete description of virtue (or a limited conversation with your academic community). But my analysis of sexual virtue is not about representing Aristotle or Aquinas. As I will say in the book, I draw on their work like a painter's palette in order to think new thoughts about sexual virtue—especially new thoughts about sexual virtue in a Christian framework.

Even so, the interpretive and analytical works of Aristotelian and Thomistic scholars such as Charles Curran, Jean Porter, Stephen Pope,

Diana Cates, James Kennan, and so many others have been invaluable to my own study. Such scholars have probed the philosophical and religious dimensions of virtue ethics with a rigor I can only hope to one day acquire. For readers not familiar with these scholars, their work considers how best to read and interpret the teachings of Aristotle or Aquinas. I, however, am seeking to accomplish something different. I wish to draw on the theoretical framework of virtue ethics, in a Christian context, to try out *new* definitions of sexual virtue, without at the same time being tied down by the specific moral conclusions reached by either Aristotle or Aquinas. If for no other reason, I am convinced that we can appropriate virtue ethics more generally, so that we can then turn to conceive sexual virtue in light of new information about sexuality and religious sources of moral authority—the kind of information that was unavailable to even great thinkers such as Aristotle and Aquinas. Doing so, I believe this book will be of interest to the reader who seeks out new intellectual models for thinking about sexuality, ethics, and religion. But it will also be of interest to the reader who has dismissed Christian moral discourse on sexuality as "out of touch." Namely, I believe I can suggest why contemporary reflection on Christian sexual ethics might yet contribute interesting moral insights that actually help us to think more carefully about sex and sexuality. I ask, then, that a wide variety of readers remain open to the possibility that an exploration of Christian virtue ethics—informed by the natural and social sciences, as well as critical moral and religious discourses—can provide a compelling alternative to the rote condemnations we are used to associating with Christian sexual ethics.

Even with these qualifications, I accept that there will always be incomplete aspects to any argument, including my own. There is always something to dispute about a moral perspective. Some ethicists see "disputed claims" where others see "settled issues." Some see "assertions" where other see "inferential conclusions." Some insist on one canon of scholarship over another. Thus, there is always something to revise. We can be anxious about that, or, we can accept that our limitations and our "weak" spots are really moments of *harahachibu*—open space, and yes, perhaps even unintended incompletions. But these allow us to come back another day, with another project, or, to allow *someone else* to try again. And why do we try? Why do I? Because I still believe that there are identifiable goods that contribute to our flourishing as the kind of creatures that we are (now)—and I believe there are multifaceted goods about *sexuality* that have much to do with our flourishing as human beings.

Acknowledgments

I offer many thanks to everyone who helped to make this book a reality. To my mentor, Diana Fritz Cates, who first encouraged me to think about sexual morality through an ethic of virtue: your wisdom and friendship have inspired me to believe in the possibility of human goodness, and the hope for a better world. To Dallas Brede, for our profound solidarity in friendship and spirit—without which, life would not be the same. To Dave Merry: you have seen this project from its first stirrings years ago, to where it is today. You follow the light of reason, and it serves you well—as has your friendship to me. To Mercyhurst University: for granting me successive research contracts in order to plan, write, and revise this book. To Tom Forsthoefel, for encouraging me through some truly trying years in the writing of this manuscript—you helped me to believe that writing an academic book can also be an effort of love. Your friendship during those difficult years was truly a grace. To Alice Edwards, for reminding me that the humanities must be humane. Together, now, we work for the vision of the world Jesse dreamed. To Brigitte Owen Kucharski, Donna Malzewski, and Amanda Langer-Williamson: for preparing countless drafts of this manuscript, and for all of our impromptu celebrations! To all of my colleagues at the 2010 *Religion and Sexuality Seminar* at Emory University, but especially to Mark Jordan for hosting me during a research trip to Harvard Divinity; to Laurie Jungling for reminding me why normative works in ethics still matter; and to Patrick Cheng, for our ongoing dialogue and friendship. To the community at The Church Within (Indianapolis, IN) for offering a symposium on the subject material of this book in 2012, as well as for your continued support of me and my ongoing work. To the Reverend Dr. John Harper for faithfully checking in and encouraging the completion of this particular project, and for hosting and/or meeting for retreats in Palm Springs and Toronto.

I am also grateful for my readers of the revised version of this manuscript: Abbylyn Helgevold, Christine Darr, Jodi Shay, Rodney Haveman, and Matthew van Maastricht. Each of you contributed to the final version of this manuscript in so many helpful ways (tangible and intangible). Likewise, to those anonymous scholars who reviewed and critiqued this manuscript for publication at SUNY Press: thank you! Your insights were valuable, and I was able to integrate many of your comments. Thank you, also, to my acquisitions editor at SUNY Press, Nancy Ellegate, who guided me through the review process and to publishing—your generosity is greatly appreciated. Thank you also to my family, especially my parents Richard and Jeannette, for encouraging me in my academic work.

But most of all, I want to give thanks to my loving partner, Ryan Graber. Ryan, I am in awe of who you are. I love you and I am grateful to share life with you.

Introduction

To Reclaim Sexual Virtue

A graciously contrarian posture on sex values is probably the surest route to ill-treatment at the hands of the guardians of morality in any culture.

—Raymond Lawrence

Sexual Liberation, Sexual Virtue

The desire for sex is nearly universal. But what we desire of it is rather complex. We want sex to be pleasurable, but pleasure is not all we seek. At certain times we want it to be exhilarating, playful, or perhaps an episode of emotional and physical release. We like it, also, for its capacity to express intimacy and feelings of affirmation. We are mindful of its reproductive powers, both in anticipation of new offspring, but also in our withholding of that potentiality. What is more, we sometimes seek it to fulfill certain fantasies, and to expand horizons of sexual creativity.

For as much as sex and sexuality are often said to be personal, these are far from private matters. Sex and sexuality are constantly on display: by the way we dress, the stories we read, the movies we watch, and the lyrics to any given top ten song on the pop charts. Television commercials advertise erection-enhancing drugs for men, and women are promised mindblowing orgasms if they purchase specially designed lubricants "for her." In most urban settings in the Euro-American West, sex stores offer creative adult toys for adventurous people seeking new pleasures; and for the tech savvy, smart phone apps now help people to find willing sex partners, providing photos, chat options, and even information about the distance one must travel to rendezvous (from miles, to feet).[1] And so, when sexual desire stirs, there is little question

1

that we actually have *a lot* to think about when seeking to enjoy the pleasures of sex. Namely, we have to think about what, of all of our sexual options, is valuable to pursue, not only for ourselves, but for our sexual partners too.

Such thinking is the subject of sexual ethics.

Whether we think we do, or not, we all engage the ethics of sex. Even the moral relativists among us recognize that it is necessary to think carefully about how we enjoy sexual activity, so as not to exploit or maliciously harm one another. What is more, sexual communities from mild to wild usually have codes of sexual ethics. For example, the BDSM community advances the moral standard of being "safe, sane, and consensual."[2] On a completely other hand, the Vatican tells us that we need to be in a heterosexual pairing, lovingly married, *and* aiming at procreation if we are to enjoy sexual pleasure in light of our status as creatures of God.[3] A range of moral positions exist with respect to human sexuality—certainly, many of us already know this. But if we have a concern for living and doing well as sexual beings, and if we also care about the value and treatment of people as sexual partners, then we have good reasons for thinking about the quality of our sexual lives, and to encourage others to think carefully about sex and sexuality too. Conceived this way, sexual ethics is about our empowerment and flourishing as sexual beings.

Of course, it is understandable if one associates sexual ethics with the authoritarian arm of a religious or social hierarchy. All too often, manuals on sexual ethics have been used to control and chastise. For example, when we trace the history of sexual ethics in Europe and the European colonized Americas, we find that concepts of sexual morality are often rooted in medieval/religious norms of "natural" and "unnatural" sex (having everything to do with what does and does not lead to procreation).[4] Likewise, we find marriage and family arrangements still influenced by Victorian era and premodern patriarchal concepts of social order.[5] And yet, we are not stuck in the past. A lot has changed: religiously, morally, and socially.

Like the Copernican shift that reset our understanding of the Earth's relationship to the Sun, new insights into sexuality, ethics, and religion have significantly challenged—and for some, transformed—the old patriarchal and procreative frameworks for sexual morality.[6] The change is one of principled sexual liberation: promoting social, political, religious, and moral freedom from the imposition of patriarchal, heterosexual, marital, and procreative norms (to name a few).[7] Heralds of sexual liberation tend to believe that advancing reasonable ideas about sexual liberty will one day allow human beings to truly flourish as sexual beings.

Sexual liberation, as a movement of social and moral transformation, may mark one of humanity's greatest conversions. If successful, the last reservoirs of patriarchy will be replaced with the mutuality of egalitarian care, and heterosexism with respect for all sexualities and sexual performances that promote genuine human well-being. Of the evidence we have that the principles of sexual liberation are transforming ideas about sexuality, the moral reforms taking place within religious communities are noteworthy.[8] These religious reforms are significant because organized religion has often functioned to guard moral convention and to accept change only gradually.[9] Therefore, when we see that the keepers of convention are beginning to change their minds about sexual morality, it signals that there must be larger ideological shifts at play.

The imagined chasm between "sexual liberation" and "religious morality" has largely been bridged by critical reflection on human sexuality, in conversation with analytical studies of religion and religious ethics. Even across religious and denominational lines, many people are finding that sexual liberation is *not* an enemy of religion or morality. To the contrary, it has been a welcomed discovery that sexual liberation (well-defined) has much to contribute to serious moral discourse, even as it is also about freedom from certain ideological constraints on sexual identity and expression.[10] Through careful analysis aided by contemporary insights into human sexuality—insights that were unavailable to a number of history's venerated ethicists and theologians—scholars of religion and ethics, as well as theologians in a wide variety of traditions, are finding and naming the qualities of virtue where once only accusations of sexual vice prevailed.[11]

It is worth noting, however, that many of these new arguments about virtue and sexuality have tended to focus on sexual justice.[12] Justice is indeed a cardinal virtue, and explorations of sexual justice have rightly exposed a variety of injustices—especially those that have denied the moral agency of women and the legitimacy of same-sex relationships. But even as we have a number of inclusive arguments about sexual justice, we have not yet heard much about how contemporary insights into sexuality might reshape our understanding of sexual virtue itself.[13] This is a matter having to do with what sexual goods we pursue—the reasons why we pursue these—and the contribution of our sexual activities and relationships to our living and doing well. To pursue a definition of sexual virtue, then, we must have an adequate definition of virtue itself. To be clear: virtue is not a generic term for morality.

Shaped by the Greek philosopher Aristotle, an ethic of virtue is one that concerns cultivating good habits. These habits, or virtues, dispose people to seek wisdom and moral excellence according to the light of reason, in order that we might experience human happiness (or human flourishing), which the philosopher defined as the enjoyment of a whole human life well-lived. Virtues provide for human happiness, in that they dispose us to be the kind of people who reflect and choose well in the course of our everyday living. We do so, in part, by learning to identify, and avoid, the extremes of excess and deficiency, whether in our social relations, our pursuits of pleasure, or in our aversions to pain. We do this not by following a list of static rules, but by carefully considering the particularities of our individuality, as well as the context of a situation, allowing reason to apprehend what is best for us to pursue, or, how best to respond to others, as well as how best to respond to a wide variety of our natural inclinations and feelings.

Not a "one rule fits all"/cookie cutter approach to morality, virtue ethics takes seriously that life consists of individual nuances and contextual differences. It also presumes our requirements for well-being (health, basic needs, care for individual complexity, our sociality, and so forth). It does so, but then shifts to discern, morally, what is best for us to pursue in a given situation, in order to promote our genuine happiness. Virtue ethics thus seeks to help people actualize their unique potential for living life well. Although virtue ethics originated as a philosophical moral theory, when it is appropriated within a religious framework (as it has been, especially in Christianity), virtue ethics can also provide a way of functioning morally in relationship to one's highest end (whether one conceives that as God, enlightenment, or some other supernatural object or goal).

When it comes to sexual morality, sexual virtue illuminates human desires for the pleasures of sex. The realization of sexual virtue requires the coordination of at least two virtues. The first is the virtue of prudence. This is the virtue of knowing the right reason of things to be done, and of knowing accurately (as possible) about the truth of things. Cultivating the virtue of prudence is a matter of learning to reason as a wise person, and choosing as a wise person would choose.[14] Described this way, prudence is not something we stumble upon, but is something we acquire by refining the mind. We pursue prudence so that we might discern what contributes to our happiness, and then, to make it so.

Thus, prudence allows us to apprehend the "ends" in life that genuinely contribute to human happiness. We seek this intellectual clarity, not through solitary effort, but in the company of wise community. Those who are midwives of prudence help us to think carefully, contextually, and in light of wider social issues. Such midwives chastise us when we would prefer the comfort of rote response, instead of right reason. As a matter of sexual virtue, the virtue of prudence allows us to apprehend what "ends" of sex contribute to our genuine happiness.

But we are not simply rational creatures. We are *sensual* creatures having physical bodies, with sensory powers of apprehension and inclination. We act and feel in light of reason, but we do so in coordination with our bodily desires and feelings, not the least of which is our enjoyment of pleasure and our reactions to pain. Thus, when considering sexual virtue, we not only need the virtue of prudence to think well about how sex contributes to human happiness, but we also need to practice virtue when responding to our sexual desires and engaging in sexual activities. It is one thing to "know" what is best to pursue, sexually, it is another thing to actually dispose ourselves to enjoy sexual activities that result in genuine happiness. With respect to acting on our desires for sex, the virtue of temperance comes into play.

The virtue of temperance illuminates human desires for the pleasures of touch.[15] We cultivate this virtue in order to best enjoy the tactile pleasures of food, drink, and sex. In particular, temperance enlightens us so that we are not reduced to the brutish pursuit of food, drink, or sexual activity according to the simple want for physical pleasure. Of course, there's nothing wrong with enjoying a tasty meal, a fine drink, or a pleasurable sexual experience with a well-skilled lover. But we also know that there is nothing about the immediate experience of pleasure (of itself) that helps us to realize how best to enjoy it. For example, one piece of chocolate cake may make you feel divine, but the whole pan, another story. Likewise, any number of sexual experiences may yield great feelings of pleasure. But the feeling of sexual pleasure (which manifests as complex physical and psychological sensations) does not, of itself, help us to discern what it means to enjoy (well) a sexual experience. Such discernment is important because sex acts involve people. Whether solo, in duet, or in group, each person has meaning and value. Thus, while our sexual partners may provide us pleasurable experiences, they (and we) still retain our capacity—whether in approaching sexual encounters, during sexual encounters, or after sexual encounters—to respect one another as people, who generally have a desire to flourish as human beings. Failing to do so, we turn ourselves (and others) into mere instruments for gratification—and where humans are seen merely as instruments, it may follow that their (and our) happiness, or flourishing, is no longer a conscious concern.

To pursue sexual virtue, then, is to mindfully identify (and realize) those good "ends" of human sexuality that help us to enjoy sexual pleasure in ways that promote genuine happiness. I argue that there are at least three ends of sexual virtue that should be named in light of contemporary insights from the sciences and critical moral discourse: *recreation, relational intimacy,* and *selective acts of procreation.* While these ends can be mutually coordinated, my proposal is that sexual virtue need not be limited to heterosexual, or marital, or procreative expressions.

Individually, recreation, relational intimacy, and selective acts of procreation are important human goods, and they should not be undervalued. Recreation, for example, is not something having to do only with the pursuit of "pleasure." Broadly speaking, recreation is a human good that we pursue to restore positive affective states, to reduce stress, and to engage in creative pursuits (of mind and body) that renew our personal resources.[16] We do so that we might be refreshed to better engage the world, our work, and the people in our lives. To pursue recreation as an end of sexual virtue, then, requires creative thinking about what it means to play well with others, whether we do so with sexual friends, short-term lovers, or long-term partners and spouses. Recreational sex, well-described, realizes a human good that is often lost on critics who equate recreation with an adolescent pursuit of pleasure, or with excessive hedonism. As we shall see, suspicions about recreation (and recreational sex) have largely kept us from exploring in what ways we might live and do well as creatures that need "play" (in many forms) to maintain a balanced and happy life.

Likewise, relational intimacy is a human good that can be supported by sexual activity. But as specialists will tell us, relational intimacy requires the coordination of many other intimacies too, such as commitment, communication, mutual support, and so forth.[17] To pursue the good of relational intimacy—as an end of sexual virtue—is to approach sexual relations as a means of deep disclosure and a symbolic expression of other relational commitments. It is not merely to have "physical intimacy" in the sense of describing the basic "knowing" of others, borne through the intercourse of revealed sexual bodies. Thus, relational intimacy (well-defined) is not something sought or achieved in every mutual sexual encounter (for example, in short-term sexual relationships ordered more toward recreation). But I suggest it can be realized within intentional relationships that integrate sexual relations into the overall goal of relational flourishing.

Of course, we also know that we can choose to exercise our reproductive capacity (if available) through the intentional use of our genitals. Unlike many other animals, human beings do not have to wait for a mating season to instinctually compel us to perpetuate the species. Ideally, we choose the persons with whom we want to share in reproduction and/or procreation (whether in the sharing of reproductive cells, or outright co-parenting). When parenting is intentional and mutual, we approach it through biological generation borne of intercourse, surrogacy, in vitro fertilization, or adoption. But some ethicists have privileged the biological potential for reproduction over all other human goods that can be realized in sexual relations. I do not. I take it that the choice to procreate an offspring is a long-term commitment requiring serious thought and preparation. It requires selective acts of procreation. That is not to deny that certain unexpected pregnancies have led to many a happy family. But "surprises" ought not to be the idealized norm, nor should they be romanticized, especially given the incredible burdens placed upon any number of women in such cases. Given the wide variety of circumstances in which women find themselves with an unexpected pregnancy, it will do the moral community great service to prudentially reflect on when the pursuit of biological reproduction contributes to the genuine happiness of women, to women's families, as well as to particular societies and the global community.

However, even as I will suggest that sexual virtue can support multiple "ends," some religious arguments about prudence and temperance—especially Christian ones—have advanced the idea that the desire for sexual pleasure needs chastising unto its narrow expression in heterosexual, marital, procreative sex. In fact, the chastising of sexual desire toward this end is precisely why many Christians have cited "chastity" as the specific title for sexual virtue.[18] But to suggest that reproduction (and thus procreation) is the end with which all other sexual goods must be coordinated preferentially conceals the multivalent nature of human sexuality. What is more, it fails to respect that we can pursue other goods in and through our sexual capacities—and that we can realize these goods completely, without also realizing our biological powers of reproduction. As we shall see, naming recreation, relational intimacy, and selective acts of procreation as the ends of sexual virtue will allow us to realize the potentiality of living and doing well (as sexual beings), whether in our playfulness, our deepest intimate relations, or in our responsible parenting—and that we can affirm these "ends" even within a Christian framework.

In fact, I wish to show how moral reflections on sexuality can actually help sexually active adults (young and old), of many varieties of sexualities, live with both integrity and freedom—even when we situate such moral reflection in a Christian framework. Admittedly, because Christian ethics has long been controlled by heterosexist, marital, and procreative norms, my suggestion that Christian ethics might still have something meaningful to say to the "sexually active" of "many varieties of sexualities" may seem implausible, or absurd. I acknowledge that we live in a time when many people have jettisoned (sometimes for good reasons) the idea that Christian reflections on sexuality have anything meaningful to offer. But we also live in times in which the rejection of "traditional" norms has sometimes meant retreating to the lowest common denominator of morality—the kind of moral norm that only advances an ethic of non-maleficence. "Do no harm" is a good start, but such a norm fails to speak to a whole host of moral issues related to our character, or how we value ourselves and others as human/sexual beings. "Do no harm" keeps us from hurting one another—and rightly so—but it does not help us to imagine how sex and sexuality can contribute in distinct ways to the overall goal of human flourishing (or happiness). Non-maleficence is good, but it does not (of itself) help us to consider why sexuality matters—to us or to others—especially in terms of what sexual activities can (qualitatively) communicate or facilitate between people. Likewise, "do not harm" only scratches the surface of the many interesting connections (or conversation points) between sexuality and religion. Resisting this kind of moral minimalism as the standard of sexual ethics, I suggest we dig deeper into sexuality precisely at the intersection of religion and morality. Challenging the view that Christian perspectives are categorically unhelpful for reflection on sexuality, I propose another look at these issues. In particular, I suggest that when we revisit the Christian philosophical traditions of virtue ethics and natural law (a hallmark of Catholic thinking), and when we pair that with careful study of Christian scripture (a central emphasis in Protestantism), then we will actually find that Christian sexual ethics can be remarkably open to ideas about sexual liberation, precisely through the promotion of sexual virtue.

Some Upfront Admissions

Analyzing moral debates about sexuality continues to be a relevant endeavor in the twenty-first century. Christian debates about sexual morality are particularly interesting, given their prolific place in American public discourse. A number of Christian judgments about sexual morality have carried over from the churches into contemporary social discourse (and back again). Many of these Christian judgments are premodern in origin, grounded in ancient concepts of "nature," or from scriptures written millennia ago in very foreign contexts, and then, with relatively unusual concerns about sexual relationships when compared to our own. This reliance on premodern norms has reified, for some Christians, a vision of moral authority that advances limited sexual liberties. Because premodern views on sexual morality prevail in a variety of churches (both domestic and international), a number of difficult situations have arisen.

As a matter of fact: people are being excluded from churches, cut off from their ancestral or chosen communities of faith (and support) because their sexual lives do not conform to church teaching—whether because they are lesbian, gay, bisexual, or transgender (LGBT)—or because they are divorced and remarried, or even because they use birth control. What is more, religious moralities have inspired political efforts to curtail access to contraceptives for women, as well as to deny LGBT people the basic legal/civil rights of protection and accommodation. Likewise, Christian arguments are being used to support narrow legal rulings about who can be a family, whether that concerns civil marriage privileges, parenting rights, or both.[19] Academic freedom and scholarly careers have been threatened where critiques of traditional sexual moral norms have been published and circulated.[20] Clergy have been hauled before ecclesiastical courts, losing ordained status (and thus employment) over issues of sexual ethics, especially if they love and include LGBT people (or because they "come out" themselves).[21] Women continue to have to fight for unburdened access to reproductive choice, often in the face of an all-male clergy, who see no reason why women cannot abide by church teachings. HIV/AIDS continues to ravage heterosexual communities in Africa where certain Christian condemnations of contraception are favored over the prevention of real human suffering. Parents have used their religious beliefs to reject (and exile) their LGBT children—which, according to some reports, has led to a near-epidemic of LGBT teen homelessness.[22] And without question, friendships have been deeply wounded where religious and political allegiances have been tested over one's belief, or voting record, on matters of sexuality.[23]

These realities motivate me to write about sexual morality not only within the confines of academic discipline, but also as a moral agent who has an ethical responsibility to intervene in the moral debates that are shaping the quality of life now. I believe that the moral gravity of these real-life disputes over religion, morality, and sexuality deserves a practical ethic that empowers people to confront disputed issues of sexual morality, and to do so seriously from the perspective of ethics. These issues also call forth the need to provide a voice of advocacy for those not empowered yet to speak. Admitting as much may distress some scholars who work very hard not to show any sign of personal participation in these issues. However, the intersection of religion, ethics, and sexuality excludes no one. At some point we all have a stake in these issues. We do well, therefore, not to feign any kind of privileged objectivity, but to admit our perspectives, and then to show why our views are compelling, and how they hold together in philosophical and/or religious frameworks.

Disputations

Seeking an ethic to navigate the intersection of sexuality, religion, and ethics, I have chosen an ethic of virtue. But to meaningfully speak of virtue requires at least some knowledge of it as a moral theory. Even if we do not agree about how virtue is best construed, we cannot simply use this term rhetorically. And yet there are certainly those in society who do just that. For example, traditionalists love dressing up their moral codes and policy platforms with the language of virtue.[24] But many of them do so without explaining what virtue is, or how it is rightly defined and recognized. As a result, concepts of virtue have been skewed in our society toward socially conservative definitions. This need not be the case.

At the same time, there are those who understand moral theories of virtue and who come to certain conclusions about it that seem (to many of us) largely disputable. For example, Vatican statements on sexuality (dispensed throughout the Catholic Church) draw on very articulate definitions of virtue in order to promote heterosexual, marital, procreative sex as *the* definition of sexual virtue for those who are engaged in sexual relationships. However, they do so through particular interpretations of scripture, nature, and church teaching. These interpretations have received significant critique from theologians, ethicists, and biblical scholars alike. Therefore, while certain church officials (whether Catholic or Protestant) may regard their own teachings as established and irrefutable, many of us still approach them under the heading of "disputed questions."[25] Such disputes open the door for us to suggest other formulations of sexual virtue to put in conversation with existing definitions of it. Our effort, then—whether it is with politicians, Vatican officials, Protestant traditionalists, or with any other institution or thinker—is to evaluate the strength of their argument(s) about sexual morality, and when we disagree with them in good conscience, to reply with what we take to be stronger moral claims.

I advance an ideal of sexual virtue realized by the three "ends" that I have named: recreation, relational intimacy, and selective acts of procreation. However, I anticipate that stating this moral proposal at the outset will likely set off a reader's moral intuition with some emotional charge. Some will surely recoil from such a statement, morally and theologically. Others will tend toward it with a kind of moral resonance. Moral intuitions are important markers of our individual convictions, and so I ask the reader (especially those readers being *introduced* to the study of sexual ethics) to continue to reflect on that initial moral sense as the book proceeds. In particular, I invite readers to consider how they came to their intuitions about sexual morality. Did it arise from careful reflection? Or does it more reflect the teachings one has accepted from custom (maybe even prejudice)? Or does it come from other inherited authorities, such as family or religious community? While thinking about that, I also ask the reader to create the intellectual space to examine the reasons for holding such position(s) and to imagine if any other articulation of sexual morality is reasonable and worth considering. I ask this not only of readers who may hold more traditional views about sexuality, but also of those readers who have settled for "do no harm" as their primary sexual ethic (a good place to start, but in my view, not a good place to finish). I ask it also of liberal thinkers who may be quick to affirm "sexual diversities" (which I also affirm), but who do so without an ability to articulate strong moral arguments about these matters.

While I admit that my sense of what counts as sexual virtue will be contested, what I hope the reader will find is that my argument will reveal important moral dimensions to human sexuality that are sometimes neglected. Namely, I will encourage people to think not only about sexual activities and pleasures, but also about how our pursuit of these reveal what we value of ourselves and others as sexual beings. We will explore this together by considering the strengths of character that sexual virtue can yield. Because I am interested in Christian concepts of sexual virtue, I will not only advance specific normative moral claims, but I will also engage in moments of imaginative theological reflection. I do this so that readers might have an example of how a renewed view of sexual virtue might be articulated from a Christian perspective. But in no way do I mean to indoctrinate from such imaginative statements. I simply find it helpful to occasionally speak in the voice of the religious context being discussed (albeit broadly) in order to be meaningful to a diverse readership.

The Social, Moral and Political Importance of Virtue

Of course, some may wonder if constructing an argument about sexual morality within a Christian framework is a worthwhile endeavor what-soever. Certainly much has been said about Christian sexual ethics from both progressive and traditionalist perspectives. What is more, theorists have thoroughly critiqued heterosexist views of sexual morality that have been sustained by various Christian communities. And yet, explicit argu-ments about inclusive definitions of sexual virtue are largely missing. For this reason—along with the sense that virtue ethics can reveal some real, meaningful human/sexual goods—I believe that the effort to give a new definition of sexual virtue is an important one to make.

We live in times in which we cannot afford to be apathetic or ignorant about what counts as sound moral reasoning. If for no other reason, moral perspectives are often the grounding for particular positions on social issues, as well as the foundation upon which some political candidates (and pundits) rally their troops.[26] More often than not, these moral perspectives are dressed as religious concerns. Therefore, as we engage in the debate over sexual morality in the public square—and where we find that these debates lead us back to the churches—being able to define and defend sexual virtue will be a key strategy in order to convince a wide variety of people that generous and inclusive thinking on sexual morality is a matter that contributes to both genuine human happiness and sexual liberation.

A demonstrable concern for morality is what many people are looking for when they consider an issue such as sexuality. Many also want to be sure that their moral positions do not violate their religious sensibilities, or at the very least, acknowledge their religious concerns. As the philosopher and ethicist Martha Nussbaum has noted, "It would be weird and tyrannical to ask religious people to accept the idea that moral principles are utterly 'separate' from their religious principles."[27] Nussbuam's insight should be well heeded, especially by those seeking to advance progressive social/sexual liberties.

Critics of "tradition" who refuse to cultivate strong moral arguments, as well as those who ridicule the influence of religious perspectives on civil and moral issues, fail to speak the kind of cultural language that is necessary for meaningful social discourse to occur.[28] That is not to say that we should concede moral debates, or social policies, to the whim of anyone with a particular religious or moral ideology. Such a path would set a dangerous precedent for sectarian rule according to the unchecked religious and moral beliefs of the majority. While that may sound good to those belonging to a majority now, history reminds us that those in majorities do not persist indefinitely. What we need, then, is a way to better communicate between communities holding divergent moral perspectives. By appropriating a true concern for sexual morality through a careful study of virtue, we might be able to dialogue more effectively with religious and political communities who are interested in the cultivation of virtue, but who have not been able to imagine inclusive sexual values as a part of that moral picture.

Part I

Getting Situated

One

Sexual Positions

Twists and Turns

. . . once the erotophobic Christian ideologies were removed, the other resources were able to become powerful tools for recognizing the original blessing of sexuality.

—Robert Shore-Goss

Traditionalists Versus Sexual Liberation

Whenever the call for change includes reform to codes of sexual morality, there is almost always resistance. In our time we especially hear this resistance coming from particular and well-established traditionalist Christian leaders and institutions. Appeals to the Bible, to church teaching, and to nature have all been used to prop up the argument that sex is only for marriage, narrowly defined as between a man and a woman, with a strong emphasis on procreation. Christians who hold to this norm are convinced that it alone allows sexual activity to realize sexual virtue. Admittedly, it is not difficult for such Christian traditionalists to accessorize this view with examples and arguments from antiquity, attempting to show us that "this is the way it has always been." Such Christians usually insist that the heterosexual and marital norm is a sacred and well-preserved tradition, warning that any departure from it is a dangerous step on a slippery slope toward sexual and social anarchy. When one listens carefully to their concerns, there is no question that these religious traditionalists appear ready to fight to keep this the norm not only for themselves or their given religious communities, but for all people.

With a particular view of sexuality and morality in mind, a con-
federation of resistance cells in this country (and elsewhere) wage a
struggle that they call a "culture war." They do so under the banners of
"traditional morality" and "defending the traditional family." This they
champion, not only in their churches, but also in society through ballot
measures or acts of legislation. They tell us that the heterosexual and
marital norm was established by God, affirmed by Christ, and therefore
is not only good for personal morality, but for the ordering of society
through law. Never mind that American democracy is constitutional
(not theocratic), this religiously informed norm, they say, is the standard
of sexual morality (and thus virtue) for all people.[1]

The facts, however, get in the way of their narrative.

The heterosexual and marital norm was actually *not* the preferred
definition of sexual morality for many Christians. History clearly demonstrates that a number of the early Christian movements grew in the
direction of sexual asceticism.[2] This fostered deeply negative views not
only about sexual activity, but sexual desire as well—especially the desire
for sexual pleasure. There is a certain irony, then, when some Christians
(today) praise heterosexual marriage as the grounding of good society, or
the place to fulfill "God-given" sexual desires. What many of them do
not know is that they stand apart from a number of their Christian predecessors. To some early Christian leaders, today's traditionalists would
likely seem sexually permissive.[3]

For example, when St. Gregory of Nyssa interpreted the biblical Eden narrative (Genesis 2–3), the theologian argued that sexuality was alien to the human creature before the "fall" of humankind
into sin. As Phil Sherrard describes it, Gregory believed that life before
the fall was defined by "immortality and incorruptibility"; and thus St.
Gregory assumed that "the presence of these two qualities [required] the
absence of sexuality."[4] In Gregory's view, the perfect image of God in
the human being could not also include a sexual dimension. But this
ancient Christian ideal is remarkably absent when we contrast it with
many contemporary Christian views on marriage and family, including
conservative Christian views. For example, Focus on the Family (a conservative evangelical American-based ministry) goes so far as to declare
that God "made" sex for humans. In one advice column, Focus on the
Family celebrates sexuality this way:

> God created it—sex is remarkably sacred and ultimately about
> seeking that which God made us for. We must understand
> that God's interest in human sexuality is so much more than

merely making sure people behave themselves. . . . God, and
those who follow Him, take sex very seriously, and the Christian picture of sexuality is much more serious, vibrant, and
well . . . sexy . . . than any other view held in the larger culture.
As a result it's far more fulfilling.[5]

This conservative evangelical teaching is very far removed from St.
Gregory of Nyssa. What is more, even contemporary Vatican teachings
disagree with Gregory about the nature of human sexuality. What this
example reveals, then, is that Christians (even conservative Christians)
have a track record of revising views on human sexuality, given different
theological or moral perspectives.[6]

And so, while many contemporary traditionalists claim to defend
"Christian sexual morality"—as if it is one monolithic thing—it is more
accurate to say that the definition of sexual morality has always been
in an ongoing state of redefinition. That is not to say that longstanding
views on sexual virtue failed to develop and remain in place. They did.
However, it would be incorrect to suggest that Christians have only
ever agreed on one definition of sexual morality. When we pull back
the covers on just some of the sexual norms and practices in Christian
history, what we find will likely encourage us to reassess our assumptions and expectations about sexual morality, as well as our definitions
of sexual virtue. What is more, when we take a short look at what used
to be prevailing Christian views on sexual morality it may very well give
some people the permission that they need to ask critical questions about
certain teachings today.

I invite us, then, to make a short side trip through history. It will
be selective, and it will be brief. It will not include everything in the
archives that one might include. But it will nevertheless demonstrate
that amending religious and moral teachings about sexuality is not of
itself alien to Christianity. In fact, when we take a closer look into these
issues, I would wager that a good number of today's Christians (both
traditionalist and progressive) will be glad that their predecessors went
about the business of redefining sexual morality.

An Unfortunate Truth:
Christianity's Legacy of Sexual Suspicion

Christian concern for sexual morality has been present ever since groups
began organizing around the teachings of Jesus. For example, between

the years 55 and 57 CE, a convert to the way of Jesus wrote to a Christian community in the city of Corinth. His name was Paul. He told the Christians of Corinth that in light of some "impending crisis" and "the passing away of this present world," it was best for them not to marry, unless they were aflame with sexual passion. He even told them that it was better to be a virgin, or become celibate, as he was (or had become).[7] Within the same set of years, this Paul would write to another Christian community, this time to a group of Christians in Rome. He wrote that polytheism had disordered God's creation. He cited the example of polytheistic men and women going "in excess of their nature" by engaging in unnatural sex acts (whatever those turned out to be) as well as same-sex activities (which in first century Rome often included rape and/or the instrumental sexual use of slaves and prostitutes).[8] Within these letters (and others), Paul also warned Christians to avoid "sexual immorality," but without ever providing a detailed explanation of what qualified sexual vice from sexual virtue. Centuries later, these letters were canonized as scripture and Christians were charged with the difficult task of interpreting them well.[9]

Paul was not the only early Christian to weigh in on sexual matters in an ascetic leaning way. As the religion and sexuality scholar Rosemary Radford Ruether has well documented: some second and third-century Christian leaders taught that marriage (and thus marital sex) was actually a threat to the Christian lifestyle. The theologian Tatian is notable. In 150 CE, Tatian converted and studied under the influential theologian Justin Martyr. In his own ministry, Tatian began teaching that true Christians must renounce sexual activity in order to be baptized and to walk best in the way of Christ. Tatian's teachings were not out of place among his contemporaries in the various Christian sects. With Tatian, many other Christian teachers denigrated sexual desire and assigned sexual activity no place (or low place) in the Christian life.[10]

The early centuries of Christianity were certainly a peculiar time for Christian views on sexual morality. But they were also a tumultuous period in which a wide range of theological differences between the various Christian movements sponsored competition for legitimacy and authority. Some of these became recognized as "orthodox" (meaning, of the right belief). The "others" were labeled as heterodox or heretics, teaching outside of the authorized tradition. The scholarship of Ruether (and others) shows us that when we step into the third and fourth centuries, a number of "orthodox" teachers were addressing the moral and religious status of sexuality in the Christian life. One such theologian,

Clement of Alexandria, said that sexual activity did have a place in the Christian life, but only insofar as it was ordered toward procreation early in marriage, and then with "dignified motions" (whatever those turned out to be).[11] He even encouraged Christians to give up sexual activity as marriage progressed in years so that the spouses might better contemplate God.[12] The idea that sex—in and of itself—somehow disrupts a person's relationship with God might seem unsubstantiated now, but its broad acceptance by early orthodox church leaders fertilized the ground that would grow the tradition of required celibacy for religious leaders.

Within this current of sexual asceticism the influential theologian Augustine emerged. As part of his legacy, Augustine solidified a low view of sex as the preferred Christian view. After engaging in a life of sexual hedonism in his early adulthood, as well as exploring a number of religious and philosophical traditions, Augustine converted to Christianity and pursued the life of a cleric and theologian. He too found sexual desire—and much about sexual activity—to be a thorn in the side of Christian living. In his authoritative role as a bishop, Augustine affirmed that the best Christian life was the one lived in virginity and celibacy. But he could not bring himself to deny that procreation was a natural good in God's creation, and so he named it the "one worthy fruit" of intercourse, even if sexual activity was motivated by less than righteous sexual desires. Augustine provided space for the married-sexual life, but awarded it second place in the "kingdom of God."

At the same time, Augustine evaluated marital *companionship* a very good thing insofar as it provided social order (albeit, patriarchal order) and mutual care between spouses. Nevertheless, the theologian still insisted that those who pursue marriage do so—in particular— because they cannot control their sinful sexual desires for sensual pleasure. Indeed, the writings of Augustine even imagine a world in which all are celibate: bringing the generations of the human race to an end and Christ's return hastened. But this ideal, he realized, would not likely resonate with the lived experiences of most people. Therefore, Augustine maintained celibacy and marital procreation as the paradigm of sexual morality for the Christian community. His view was upheld as orthodox teaching among members of the emerging church hierarchy. Indeed, Augustine's marital norm and procreative priority have been preserved in many Christian communities to this day.[13]

Drawing on the teachings of Augustine and theologians like him, the tradition of clerical celibacy was championed by many in the church hierarchy. Although it was resisted by many priests (and their wives!), required clerical celibacy was formalized in the twelfth century.[14] In 1139 the First Lateran Council established that priestly ordination was a sacrament that could be received only in celibacy.[15] As a result, the belief was institutionalized in Western Christianity that the holiest people cannot *also* be sexual people. Yes, the church continued to allow for married, sexual lives among the laity, but such people were not regarded with the same measure of spiritual purity as those who remained virgins, or celibate. For them, sex was indeed *dirty*.

The medieval scholar and theologian Thomas Aquinas pushed back a bit on this enduring sexual asceticism by reframing sexual pleasure and activity as natural to the human condition—albeit as part of our "lower" nature. Sex (and sexual pleasure), Aquinas said, participated in our animal nature and required reason and church teaching to be well ordered.[16] However, he could not deny his predecessors' teachings that human sinfulness permeated all things, including sexuality. As a result, he taught that sexual desire was especially difficult to chastise, and that sexual virtue was practiced (when engaged in genital contact) only by married partners who ordered sexual desires and activity in such a way that procreation was not contravened. Aquinas's fellow scholastic theologians agreed, and subsequent manuals on sexual morality further secured the procreative norm (or celibacy) as a matter of attending well to Christian sexual morality.

Thus, in its first millennium of formation, institutional Christianity was clearly dominated by an evolving synthesis of sexual asceticism and what we would now call *heteronormativity*. It fixed a notion in many Christian minds that sexual desire and activity are especially related to sin, potentially scandalous, and in need of severe restraint—whether by celibacy or obedience to the marital/procreative norm. In short, the Christian narrative for sexual morality idealized celibacy and tolerated heterosexual marriage, so long as the goal of procreation redeemed the "immodest" pleasures of sex. Apart from these options, all other forms of sexual expression and relationships were regarded (by the church) as unnatural and sinful. And by certain civil standards, "unnatural" sex acts were punishable by death.[17]

Against the celibate church hierarchy the Protestant Reformation would rise, but even the Reformation did not wrest sexual shame and suspicion away from church teachings. Sixteenth-century Protestant reformers such as Luther and Calvin were willing to challenge the tradition of clerical celibacy, and yet they largely preserved procreation as the moral norm of sexual activity. They would even retain a number of suspicions about sex as spiritually polluting.[18] In fact, it would not be until 1930 that certain Protestant denominations would begin to officially consider contraception as an exercise of prudence, freeing people to consider other valuable reasons for engaging in sexual activity.[19] Where Protestants took the lead on contraceptive use, some Catholic theologians hoped to follow. In 1963, a special commission was appointed by Pope John XXIII to study contraception.[20] Many of those appointed to this commission came to the conclusion that the Catholic Church should also permit the use of some contraceptives by married couples, as a matter of family planning.[21] But the hierarchy of the Catholic Church would ultimately disagree.[22]

The Vatican reacted strongly against contraceptive-using Christians, declaring through papal encyclicals (and other official statements) that procreation was still the finality of sexual union that had to be respected and pursued only in sanctioned marriages.[23] But even as official Roman Catholic teachings on sexual morality rejected artificial birth control, the Catholic Church did accept that marital love is a valid end to pursue in sexual relations—but only as an indissoluble end with procreation.[24] The Catholic Church would even learn to accept natural family planning (i.e., the rhythm method) as a way for couples to enjoy sexual intimacy at a time when conception is not likely. Namely, the church (now) accepts that God designed the natural rhythms of fertility and infertility, in the ovulation cycle, such that heterosexual spouses can plan *when* to enjoy sexual activity for its contribution to marital intimacy (and not reproduction), while at the same time avoiding a "contraceptive will."

But contraception would be just one of many disputed liberties.

In the face of almost two thousand years of narrow Christian teaching on sexuality, the nineteenth and twentieth centuries yielded new moral and theological discourses on gender roles and human sexuality.[25] First-wave feminism inspired the campaign to secure women's right to vote and to acquire property rights too. This, in turn, illuminated moral and social questions about the autonomy of women, especially matters having to do with reproductive choice and socioeconomic equality.[26] As second-wave feminism gave voice, and fight, for women's moral, social, reproductive, and political rights, and third-wave feminism advanced critical analyses of essentialist views on "femininity," so too a variety of social movements and organizations began to give voice, and fight, for the acceptance of homosexuality, and in turn, acceptance of diverse sexual/social identities.[27] Given the prolific sexual asceticism in the churches, a spotlight on women and gay and lesbian issues was destined to ignite schism, if not scandal too.

And it did.

Twentieth-century Catholic and Protestant churches were forced to wrestle morally and theologically with constructions of gender and moral anthropology. They also had to face (sometimes begrudgingly) new understandings about sexual orientations that were emerging from the social, medical, and psychological sciences. They also had to contend with a multifaceted women's' rights movement, which worked tirelessly (though unsuccessfully) for a constitutional Equal Rights Amendment. At the same time, the churches could not hide from the growing "gay rights" movement in the United States and elsewhere.[28] It included lesbian, gay, bisexual, and transgender (LGBT) people—as well as straight allies—brought together in order to resist the discrimination suffered by the LGBT community.

The fight would not be a purely secular or political one. When the Universal Fellowship of Metropolitan Community Churches (MCC) was organized in 1968 by the Rev. Troy Perry, it was an effort to give LGBT people a welcoming spiritual home. With the rise of the MCC it became impossible to say, as some wanted to, that the LGBT movement was opposed to the things of God.[29] Theologically speaking, God found a home among the LGBT community through churches and groups like the MCC. As a result, a number of LGBT people found that the struggle for acceptance need not be conceived as a battle against religion. This was a realization that would become all the more pronounced, especially as the Unitarian Universalists, Reform Judaism, and many mainline Protestant groups and churches would come to find that one need not reject the divine to embrace sexual diversity.

As social and moral norms were being challenged in the churches and in the public square, scholars of religion, ethics, and sexuality emerged more boldly, investigating the integrity of the traditional sexual norms in Christianity. Feminist philosophy exposed patriarchal privilege. The Augustinian tradition of sexuality and marriage came under severe criticism. Careful study of the Bible punctured "certainties" that the churches had been holding about sexual morality. Between the 1980s and the turn of the millennium serious questions about sexual ethics were reiterated or given new voice. Greater numbers of scholars, clergy, and theologians emerged who challenged the narrow procreative and marital norms in both Catholic and Protestant churches.[30]

But in spite of these critical insights, a number of Christian churches advancing conservative, or traditionalist, views on sexuality would strike back. For example, in confrontation with cultural acceptance of homosexuality, the Catholic Church advanced the position that homosexuality is an "objective disorder"—a disorder that inclines people toward "intrinsic moral evil."[31] In the same document that condemns homosexuality this way, the Vatican author went on to write these haunting words:

> [W]hen homosexual activity is consequently condoned, or when civil legislation is introduced to protect behavior to which no one has any conceivable right, neither the Church nor society at large should be surprised when other distorted notions and practices gain ground and irrational and violent actions increase.[32]

The author was none other than Cardinal Joseph Ratzinger.

Ratzinger was elected pope in 2005 and is now well known as Pope Benedict XVI. As Mark Jordan noted about this Vatican statement on violence against gays, Ratzinger seemed to be saying that "it is only to be expected that gay activism will reap its own reward in gay bashing."[33] While Ratzinger acknowledged (in the same document) that nothing *justified* violence against LGBT people, his expectation of such violence left an enduring mark on LGBT folk, especially those of Christian faith who have been exposed to his teachings. Perhaps in an attempt to tend to the wound of Ratzinger's sting, the *Catechism of the Catholic Church* expressly denounces violence against gays, and calls all Catholics to treat gay and lesbian people with care and justice. Indeed, the church's recognition of "gay and lesbian persons" is notable. It represents a significant shift in the Catholic hierarchy's recognition of sexual orientations. Even so, the church has not yet reversed its negative teaching about the moral status of homosexuality, except to call some forms of it innate, albeit as a pathological condition.

According to the official teachings of the Catholic Church, the origin of this moral pathology can be traced to the fall of humankind into sin. Because of this diagnosis, LGBT people were (and are) told to "unite to the sacrifice of the Lord's Cross the difficulties they may encounter because of their *condition*."[34] And according to the church, if one should lay down that cross of sexual solitude for connection with another person, such an act exchanges the virtue of chastity for mortal sin—a weight so heavy it can drag a soul to hell. Indeed, even Pope Francis's more pastoral tones about sex and sexuality have not reversed the official teachings of the church.

Protestant traditions have fared better and worse in various ways. With the rise of the Religious Right among conservative evangelicals and fundamentalists in the last quarter of the twentieth century, gay and lesbian issues became a favorite moral, religious, and political target. But so too were feminists, single mothers, and straight nonmarried sexual partners.[35] Even so, some Protestant denominations rejected the theologically charged invective of the Religious Right and reformed their positions on sexual morality. Such churches came to articulate inclusive moral teachings, which now affirm a wide variety of sexual practices and relationships for people who are straight or LGBT.[36] Where this has happened, however, division has often followed, especially when the issue has concerned the inclusion of the LGBT community. When the Episcopal Church accepted its first out gay bishop, Gene Robinson, parishes broke off and allied themselves with conservative Anglican dioceses in Africa. When denominations such as the Evangelical Lutheran Church in America and the United Church of Christ opened their doors to LGBT people for church membership, ordination, and marital blessings, congregations broke away.

But let me not paint the picture too darkly. As I have been alluding all along, progressive-thinking churches have flourished. Insights can be taken from their successes. However, it is in light of the long and imposing history of narrow sexual morals onto Christian communities that many Christians (and churches) still struggle. Within this struggle there is a sense held by many people that Christianity could have included— and still might support—sexual liberation (at least of some kind). This is a view held not only by some of those who identify as Christian, but also by those who study Christian ethics professionally.[37] As we shall see in the next chapter, a number of influential Christian ethicists argue that the (now) traditional norms of conservative Christians need not persist as the standard of Christian sexual ethics—especially in light of new knowledge about sexuality, as well as new insights about scripture and church teachings.

Of course, the suggestion that we can revise ideas about sexual morality will strike some people as a matter of radical thinking, because it calls into question one's faithfulness to established religious principles. Proposals of reformation and change often elicit such concerns (remember the Protestant Reformation, and even the II Vatican Council!).

Some people simply like their religion "old," assuming that antiquity bequeaths truth and authority that couldn't possibly be present in new religious ideas. And yet, the history of Christianity itself suggests that Christians have always been about the business of revising codes of sexual morality. Thus, the question that Christian theologians, ethicists, and lay people must ask (now) is whether particular religious teachings about sexual morality are worth preserving.

Given the incredible pain, anxiety, and alienation experienced by so many people around matters of sexuality and religion, there is little question that we need fresh approaches to sexuality that genuinely uplift people as sexual and moral beings. We need this not only in communities of faith, but also in the wider society where religious narratives still hold serious moral weight. One way we can suggest new approaches to sexual morality is by engaging the field of sexual ethics—which, as we will see, requires both traditionalists and progressives alike to account for the moral proposals we make.

In the next chapter, I invite the reader to consider the field of sexual ethics in order to better understand *how* sexual ethics can help us to analyze Christian proposals about sexual morality. We will do so by looking at a selective sample of contemporary Christian sexual ethicists who, in some way, have offered challenges to traditional Christian norms. From these insights, we will then be able to launch into a more detailed exploration of sexual virtue.

Two

Sexual Ethics

Looking for Good Sex

It is harder, but more honest and of deeper social value, for us to engage one another's lives in a spirit of mutual respect and discovery. And what better definition of love?

—Carter Heyward

Humans as Sexual and Moral Beings

Human beings are sexual beings. This is not a controversial statement. Many biologists, psychologists, ethicists, and theologians agree that a core component of who we are—and how we define ourselves—is informed by our sexuality.[1] And yet, the sexual dimensions of our lives are quite complex. After all, we think sexual thoughts, we have creative sexual imaginations, and our sexual attractions are constantly alerting us to other people as potential sexual partners—whether or not we actually pursue physical sexual encounters with them. Socially speaking, we construct ideas about "proper" dress, touching, and physical proximity in association with what we take to be appropriate to our sexual boundaries (however conventionally or queerly defined). What is more, we sometimes sexualize our speech to suggest everything from flirtation to disdain, and our literature draws on sexual imagery to communicate the heights and depths of human experience. And in a complex arrangement that we have not yet been able to fully explain, our sexuality is a glorious tangle of biological and psychological grounding (in sexual inclination and orientation), social construction (according to public sexual identity), and personal choice (with respect to how we express ourselves sexually).

29

So far, so good; we can likely agree that there is no controversy in the statement that human beings are sexual beings. But it is a statement that is loaded with *moral* implications. To put it far too bluntly: we can be "good" or "bad" (to various degrees) in the sexual dimensions of our lives. By this I do not mean how we rate in our physical performance with others. We can leave the measure of our sexual proficiency to our own imagination or to the judgment of our sexual partners. "A well-skilled lover" is something we all might want on our resume of personal strengths. But how we perform physically in sexual relationships ends up being rather insignificant if we fail to consider our sexual partners as full moral persons, they us, and how our sexual lives contribute to our flourishing as human beings.

As moral agents we do this through mindful reflection, in which we take the time to ask questions about how our sexual lives contribute to (or detract from) a life well lived. The awareness that our choices (sexual or otherwise) have consequences to the quality of our lives reveals the moral horizons of human life. This awareness gives birth to moral discourse, which prompts us to voice (and listen for) what might help us to have a happier life, not only as human beings in general, but as individuals whose happiness requires particular reflection and contextual specificity. Because sexuality can contribute to human happiness (or suffering), it is not exempt from moral reflection. Sexual ethics is the formal vehicle by which we engage in such deliberation.

Sexual Ethics

To better understand what it is that sexual ethics seeks to accomplish, it is first necessary to appreciate the task of ethics itself, broadly speaking. People engage in ethics when we reflect carefully (or engage in critical thinking) on the moral realm. This includes discerning ideas and drawing conclusions with respect to what counts as the good and the bad (morally)—defined, in part, by what does (and what does not) contribute to our living and doing well (i.e., our flourishing or happiness as human beings). But ethics also has to do with showing why we hold to the moral conclusions that we do. On one level, then, ethics is about each of us cultivating reliable (and justifiable) moral frameworks—or narratives—that help us to live happy lives. These not only prepare us to choose well in our own navigation of life, but also to respond well to others in the moral community. However, for as much as ethical activity strengthens and matures our moral sensibilities, ethics also requires conversation with other people who, like us, are moral agents. Many ethicists will point out that we do not engage in ethics through the exercise of an inner monologue alone, but through dialogue between people; which is to say, we do ethics in community.[2]

Religious ethicist Diana Cates offers us illumination on the activity of ethics. She writes:

> Thinking well about a proposed morality requires considering that morality (or parts of it) in relation to our own. This requires bringing elements of our morality into explicit consciousness—thinking about what we take to be our rights, duties, and responsibilities, about what it means to be happy or liberated, about the character traits or virtues that are evident in the best human lives—and thinking about why we think these things. Thinking well about a proposed morality involves also becoming more aware of unsettled features of our current moral practices— nagging questions, possible inconsistencies, and inclinations to reject parts of the packaged morality in which we were raised. It requires making comparisons and assessments all along with an eye toward determining which moral point of view, if any, is the more compelling.[3]

This activity of making moral arguments, listening to others, and (likely) reformulating our own thinking requires real and sometimes difficult engagement with other people and their various points of view. To quote a familiar proverb: iron sharpens iron.

Notice how Cates guides us to think about the task of ethics: it is not merely to give words to moral intuitions, or to give an opinion (although these are important), or even to recite rote teachings from conventional or inherited authorities. Rather, the activity of ethics (including inquiry, debate, storytelling, and dialogue) requires that we show reasons for holding the positions that we do. It also requires that we as moral agents can show how these reasons hold together as logical, compelling, and reliable. This is evident in Cates's description of ethical activity. It is also shared by ethicist Jeffrey Stout, who says that ethics requires us to "give and demand reasons of one another" about our moral sensibilities, whether these concern our sense of the "good" and "bad," or virtue and vice.[4] That, however, does not mean that we lose our sense of civility or our openness to truth in the arguments of others. As much as ethics demands reasons for our moral sensibilities, so too I suggest that ethics requires generosity, openness, and humility. The activity of ethics ought not to be conceived as drawing battle lines and defending them at all costs. Rather, the activity of ethics admits to give and take as argumentation and insights aid us in the hearing and understanding of what is truly good and wise.

The activity of ethics also requires that we possess an appreciation for the moral realm. No matter how different we are in our approach to moral theory, we come to the activity of ethics agreeing on a basic level (and with a substantiated conviction) that there are justifiable reasons for "drawing the moral line." We do so recognizing that it is right to promote the good, and where we can, to resist immorality. This, however, is not a matter of simply preserving conventional codes of morality. The activity of ethics "draws the moral line" and promotes "the good" heuristically, on the basis of sound principles, and then in order to promote genuine happiness. Thus, ethics is also a matter of liberation from all that would oppress. Those who care to engage in ethics, then, are prepared to surrender long-held moral perspectives if in the end those fail to contribute to our flourishing as human beings.

Ethical discourse also calls for a measure of good faith among its participants. Namely, faith that all who come to the table of ethics agree that we do so because we truly do care about the proliferation of human happiness, and the restraint of all that diminishes human flourishing. If we find ourselves engaged in the actual activity of ethics (as opposed to mere ranting or fighting), then the ones who disagree with us are not our enemies, but are people who need to be reimagined as much-needed companions on a common journey—who we hope have a similar goal of promoting a good life, possessing mindfulness of people's worth and a commitment to human flourishing. The degree to which we spar or disagree with other moral agents in the activity of ethics might only suggest to us the degree to which we all (whether conservative or liberal, religious or secular) take seriously the task of living and doing well. At the very least, a generous view of our critics will foster the kind of civility and respect between persons that is so often lacking.

Perhaps it is unnecessary to say, then, that in public and political debates, as well as in major media outlets, we quite often fail to engage in the activity of ethics. We are more accustomed, it would seem, to catch phrases, clichés, and heated emotional exchanges as the substance of our disagreements. That is not the fruit of ethics, but is instead the poison of simple diatribe. And yet, I do not mean to suggest that ethics is void of emotion or personal conviction. Ethical inquiry and dialogue can certainly incite passion out of the convictions we hold as moral agents. This is rightly so as people who actually care about the promotion of human flourishing. However, the activity of ethics demands that we curb our proclivities to be harsh or rash. Unbridled, these may make for entertaining exchanges between political candidates and talking heads, but at the table of moral discourse such excesses strip ethical activity of much of its rational integrity.

Of the many moral issues before us, sex and sexuality often elicit strong emotional reactions. But to truly engage the ethics of sex, we must do more than simply register our feelings or repeat rote teachings. Having seen that ethics amounts to careful reflection on the moral realm, by which we "give and demand reasons of one another" for our thoughts about the "good" and the "bad" in relation to human happiness or suffering, then sexual ethics can be understood as careful reflection (or critical thinking) about the moral dimensions of sexuality—in particular, what of human sexuality contributes to our happiness, or flourishing, as human beings.[5] In this, we give and demand reasons of one another for our thoughts about sexual morality and immorality, sexual virtue and sexual vice.

Curiously, however, I encounter a number of people who resist engaging in the task of sexual ethics. Some have told me that matters of sexual morality are already firmly established by the decrees of God, by the commands of certain scripture, or by millennia of venerated human tradition. For people such as these, the act of coming to the table of sexual ethics (so as to be shaped and reshaped) amounts to a compromise of faith, or a surrender of certainty. Others have told me that sexual ethics is an oxymoron: that there are no ethics in sex if it is to be enjoyable whatsoever. Clearly, people such as these have been exposed to only narrow definitions of sexual morality, which in turn have shaped in them a belief that anything creative or enjoyable about sex has little in common with anything we might call "good." Consequently, this generates a belief that much of sexuality has little to do with morality (an unfortunate conclusion). Still others have told me that the task of sexual ethics—especially where it is prescriptive—becomes too invasive and often is a vessel for moral authoritarianism.

Little about these responses is very helpful for thinking about the real-life navigation of sexual morality. Our sexual activities and relationships, our thoughts and our feelings—even our curiosities—are all capable of contributing to our happiness as human beings. Thus, I find it difficult to accept that anyone would believe themselves to hold infallible teaching on sexual morality that is without need of further reflection. Likewise, I am unconvinced by those who claim to be content with apathy toward sexual morality, and I am concerned about those who insist upon radical moral isolation.

With respect to those who are suspicious of prescriptive projects in sexual ethics, I admit that such have been used to control (hierarchically) and narrowly condemn. I resist this as well. I also admit that there is moral complexity (and sometimes ambiguity) in human sexuality. Namely, sometimes what we experience sexually doesn't fit neatly into our moral theories. But there are also moments of moral clarity, and these help us to better confirm what we value about ourselves and others as sexual beings—precisely in terms of what does and does not contribute to genuine human happiness. Therefore, to make an argument about what we might count as sexual morality or immorality is not necessarily an effort to control other people's sexuality. To the contrary, it can be regarded as an effort to explore the meaning and value we have as sexual beings, and to attend to these issues as a matter of tending and caring for human flourishing.

Let me press the importance of sexual ethics a bit further.

Rape, sexual assault, manipulation, coercion (explicit or subtle), vicious degradation, insensitivity, cold objectification, and hurtful shaming are all examples in a short list of the kind of ways in which we have failed to live and do well as sexual beings.[6] All of these realities carry with them a certain moral weight that requires us to acknowledge that there are sexual scenarios that are appropriately categorized as "bad," because they result in real human suffering—and thus, they do not improve our character if we pursue them. But we need not harp on the negative to suggest the importance of sexual morality. There is also moral weight in all of our potentialities for sexual flourishing. The enjoyment of sexual pleasures, the cultivation of a wide variety of mutual sexual relationships, the capacity for love and deep relational intimacy, the possibility of children, and the connections between sexuality and spirituality are but a few positive examples that also reveal the reasons why sexual morality matters. Namely, there are identifiable sexual "goods" that are not only pleasing to experience "in the moment," but which can also be appreciated for their contribution to our overall flourishing as human beings. Conceived this way, sexual ethics is about our liberation and happiness, not an exercise ordered entirely to restriction.

Sexual Ethics and Christian Ethics

Nevertheless, when we turn to engage sexual ethics in a Christian context, we do face considerable complications. The first is that Christian views on sexual morality are shaped by interpretations of religious sources of moral authority (e.g., the Bible, church teachings, and natural law). We will address these sources more specifically in later chapters. However, because many of these religious sources of moral authority come from (or are based in) antiquity, Christian sexual ethics is further complicated by historical-contextual issues. This complication might best be described as a matter of acknowledging and/or reconciling disparate worldviews. If for no other reason, the sacred texts and theological traditions from which many churches seek to address modern issues of sexual morality were constructed in times and places that understood (or imagined) sex and sexuality quite differently than we do today.

Those engaging in Christian ethics, then, must be historically and contextually vigilant. What a biblical author (or church theologian) wrote millennia (or centuries) ago may have meant something quite different than what we are talking about *now*. For example, in the New Testament there is a negative reference to male-male sexual activity in Romans 1:27. This verse is often used (now) as a general condemnation of any kind of sexual activity between men. And yet, the negative reference may have been describing what was often seen in first century Rome—in particular, to the Roman free-man, who could rape or use a male slave sexually as an expression of patriarchal dominance (i.e., penetration), or to the use of the slave's male body (instrumentally) for sexual gratification. If so, the biblical text is hardly a reflection on modern men who engage in mutual sexual activity. Indeed, there are many other texts in the Bible that reference sexual matters, but do so in light of ancient contexts and worldviews, quite foreign to our own. Therefore, recognizing that context matters, Christian ethics should never be a matter of simply applying surface readings of ancient texts or traditions to contemporary moral issues.

That being said, many Christians already practice such contextual vigilance. For example, a number of Christians (today) would never sell a daughter into slavery so that she might become the wife (and the property) of a polygamous man. The Bible permits it.[7] The Bible also permits the stoning of women who are raped.[8] Surely, this is something many modern Christians would never accept as morally licit. Recall, also, the theological perspectives of the Christian sexual ascetics—many of whom claimed that sexual desire itself came from the fall of humankind into sin. And yet, contemporary Christians—even traditional or conservative ones—tend not to share these views.

In fact, many contemporary Christians (especially those in the West) explain away things such as polygamy or slave-wives as matters of "ancient cultural context." Christians do so when they recognize that religious teachings are articulated within (and indebted to) particular worldviews—some of which are no longer worth sustaining (e.g., owning slave-wives, or exacting capital punishment on rape victims). What is more, both traditional and progressive Christians have argued that biblical and theological resources have been taken out of context throughout Christian history, whether by various churches or by particular church leaders. To suggest, then, that we should pay attention to differences between contemporary and ancient worldviews is not to utterly disregard religious teachings. But it is to examine, very carefully, how ancient worldviews informed religious sources of moral authority. This is especially important given that many of us embrace worldviews that are informed by data that our most venerated theologians did not possess.

For example, with respect to sexuality, we can speak in terms of statistical variations of sexual inclinations, qualitative/diagnostic review of our sexual orientations, health advantages and risks in our sexual expressions, and the correlation between sexuality, basic affectional needs, relational development, and so forth.[9] This information must inform our reasoning about sexual morality, especially if we are concerned with the promotion of well-being and human happiness. Without this data, we would continue to think about sexuality with the constructs of antiquity—constructs that can be flawed, not because they are old, but because they are incomplete, or, are referring to something culturally specific that we are not talking about (now), or, because certain ancient ideas about sex and sexuality are arguably false.

In other words, it is important for Christians to recognize that sometimes what has been said about sexuality in the past (by other Christians) has less to do with the principles of Christianity, and more to do with the worldviews in which those Christians lived. As human institutions, churches spring forth from the times, places, and cultures in which their people exist. Each church, then, (past or present) draws upon and responds to the worldview of its given culture. In doing so, a church declares what (of the worldview it participates in) resonates or contrasts with the enduring principles of their religion. This is a matter of interpretation. In our time, Western Christian churches participate in worldviews that almost always include insights from nonreligious sources. For example, Mark Jordan has noted that communities of faith (both traditional and progressive) now discuss sexual orientation and sexual identity with the vernacular of the natural and social sciences, drawing on new categories of sexuality that were unknown by premodern Christians.[10] What is more, contemporary Christian faith communities also talk about the relationship between sexual intimacy and psychological health—encouraging couples to seek helpful counseling in order to promote relational growth. But these are concepts not explicitly found in sacred scripture or the sacred traditions of antiquity. They originate, instead, from "secular disciplines of knowledge."[11]

The sexual ethicist Margaret Farley notes that secular disciplines of knowledge "give us a kind of 'access' to reality—to the world and the universe, to human persons and the meanings of sexuality, to tragic or beneficial consequences of action," and thus, she says, "they are necessary for the doing of sexual ethics."[12] That is to say, secular disciplines of knowledge help us to know, in part, what is possible for us as sexual beings according to our creaturely nature and various natural capacities. As secular disciplines of knowledge fill in the details of what is possible for us as sexual beings, we can consider (anew) concepts of sexual morality through ethical inquiry.

And yet, science alone does not tell us what is right or good to pursue. We must be careful not to confuse what "is" with what "ought to be" (morally). But that does not mean that we lack a bridge between secular disciplines of knowledge and ethics. Secular disciplines of knowledge describe what is possible for human beings, according to the kind of creatures that we are (or are now). Upon this information we can engage in ethical inquiry with more accurate descriptions of our subject matters. Prudence thus hovers over the assemblage of scientific knowledge and illuminates the moral imagination.

I suggest that such scientific knowledge also informs the religious imagination. Namely, scientific knowledge allows religious thinkers to reflect on how religious principles are best applied, given more accurate descriptions of our creaturely nature, if not also the world we live in. This is a matter with which Christians have been wrestling for some time. For example, thanks to science, Christians no longer believe in a flat Earth at the center of the universe. What is more, with the advent of modern medicine, many religious communities do not diagnose mental illness as demonic possession, but instead, recognize such as a treatable (or manageable) disease. Thus, many Christians have learned to accept that we need not think of religion and science as enemies. We can imagine them instead as potential partners—in an ongoing dialectical relationship.

It is only when we ideologically weld ourselves to certain world-views (especially if we weld ourselves to ancient worldviews) that we become blind to the larger horizons of truth. As the old saying goes, *We do not see things as they are, but as we are.*[13] It is good, therefore, to move around a bit and to have the heart of an explorer in our consideration of morality and human flourishing. We can do that without abandoning the moral convictions or commitments that we have valued or found trustworthy. But if we are truth seekers, we must be prepared to reorganize (or even lay down) certain perspectives if they end up being less reliable than we once imagined them to be.

This includes how we interpret and apply religious principles to human sexuality.

In fact, so as not to ordain ancient worldviews about sex and sexuality as the final authority on sexual morality, many faith communities now acknowledge that what is *described* in ancient religious teachings (about sexual and/or gender relations) might best be buried with its ancient social context. Indeed, in later chapters we will hear from a wide variety of scholars and theologians who will tell us that some religious teachings are more indebted to ancient cultural norms than they are to sustainable moral and religious principles. That kind of careful reading of religious text and tradition will serve us well when considering the subject of sexual morality from religious perspectives. In particular, it will allow us to ask anew whether Christians are best served by clinging to notions of "traditional sexual morality" derived from particular worldviews, or, if it is better to reform traditional views in light of contemporary insights into human sexuality—as well as from new insights into religious sources of moral authority.

Approaches to Sexual Ethics

As I noted at the beginning of this book, I am inviting readers to revisit sex and sexuality from an ethic of virtue, and then within a broad Christian framework. Recall that I have set out to emphasize the virtues of prudence and temperance, and to argue that recreation, relational intimacy, and selective acts of procreation are three "ends" of sexual virtue that can be prudently pursued and happily enjoyed.[14] Chapters 3 and 4 will lay out a framework for thinking about sexual virtue, and chapters 10, 11, and 12 will defend the ends of sexual virtue that I have proposed. But before the reader turns to consider the theoretical aspect of my argument, it is important to identify some streams of thought that have influenced my own moral imagination.

The religious ethicist Mark Jordan once noted that "[e]very new speech about Christian sexual ethics comes out of a library of older speeches."[15] Indeed, they do. For example, to talk about sexual virtue it will be necessary for me to glean from the scripts of the philosopher Aristotle and the theologian Thomas Aquinas. That will be the work of the next two chapters. But I am also trying to advance ideas about sexual virtue that neither Aristotle nor Aquinas dared to propose. I do so, because I have studied the works of other scholars in the field of Christian sexual ethics, and I have come to agree with those who argue that sexual morality should not be limited by heterosexual, marital, or reproductive norms. Thus, some of my speech about sexual morality comes from the library of these contemporary Christian sexual ethicists, especially the "speeches" that consider how to live a happy life, unconstrained by patriarchal or heterosexist norms. And yet, I am also trying to say something that even these thinkers have not—in particular, that definitions of sexual virtue can liberate people from narrow moral norms, while at the same time encouraging moral excellence and human happiness.

Thus, while it is correct to say that arguments about sexual morality derive from "libraries of older speeches," before anyone can "speak," the library must first be assembled. We (i.e., you and I as choice makers) are the ones who put the libraries together. We decide which of the speeches (or scripts) we find illuminating, or authoritative. Recognizing that we are the ones who assemble (or accept) the authoritative "speeches" about sexual morality (whether from scholarship, scriptures, cultural teachings, personal experiences, and so forth) greatly explains why people disagree with each other—so much—on these issues. We're simply not speaking from the same library of texts. But in order to engage in sexual ethics well—the act by which we give and demand reasons for holding the positions that we do—it is important to consider a variety of approaches to sexual morality and to think about them in relation to one another.

When we compare approaches to sexual ethics we give ourselves the opportunity to consider the various strengths and weaknesses of any given argument. Comparing different approaches to sexual ethics helps us to see that what was once a settled issue according to one approach, is unsettled by important insights from another. For the remainder of this chapter, I invite the reader to consider four different approaches to sexual ethics. These four perspectives are in various shades of agreement and disagreement with one another, and I draw on them to show the reader the (contemporary) philosophical contexts out of which I seek to offer a new definition of sexual virtue. Allow me to introduce these, briefly.

The first and second approaches I will mention concern whether or not normative moral claims are defensible when subjected to postmodern critiques. The proposal that sexual morality is possible to define (and practice) is predicated on the belief that there are real and knowable goods that human beings can identify and pursue. Such a view is in profound tension with approaches to ethics that are steeped in postmodern commitments to moral relativism. I will defend normative ethics from the perspective of critical realism, but I will also suggest that postmodern critiques are helpful for testing the strength of moral norms; and I will further suggest that queer theory is particularly helpful in order to test any normative proposals about sexual morality. Upon exploring critical realism and postmodern relativism, we will next consider the ethics of justice, and especially the need for justice as a central criterion for sexual morality. Namely, for those of us who are concerned with issues of mutuality, equality, and fair treatment of human beings, what we aim at in sexual relations (whether procreation, recreation, intimacy, or pleasure) means very little if how we engage in sexual relations violates basic requirements of the just treatment of human beings. Finally, I will invite the reader to consider the moral utility of sexual pleasure. In particular, we will consider an argument that supports sexual pleasure as a good, to pursue for its own sake. Admittedly, this is something that institutional Christianity has largely rejected. And yet, for many of us, there is nothing wrong with enjoying sexual pleasure. On the other hand, it is difficult to defend the pursuit of "pleasure" (for its own sake), without some qualifications. Pleasure, well enjoyed, requires reasonable standards for sexual relating, such as consent, boundaries, accountability, and so forth. What is more, we know that people have taken unseemly pleasure in any number of vicious activities that we would never call praiseworthy. Thus, when it comes to the moral evaluation of sexual pleasure we are caught between not wanting to perpetuate erotophobia (the fear of sexual pleasure), while at the same time not treating pleasure as an unqualified good.

And so, like friends gathered around a table in meaningful conversation, I invite the reader to listen in on just a few approaches to sexual ethics—a few "speeches"—that can inform our understanding of sexual morality (and certainly have informed mine). Without disrupting the conversation too much, I will point out, now and then, where I find certain points to be persuasive. But constrained by the format of a book, I cannot stop and explain every aspect about these approaches to sexual ethics. All I can seek to accomplish—in the space of a relative few pages—is to highlight why I think these particular philosophical insights are worth considering. At the end of the chapter I will then describe why I think these four perspectives are relevant to my argument about sexual virtue.

A Principled Tension:
Critical Realism and Postmodern Theories

Critical realism is a theoretical perspective, which advances the idea that our natural faculties allow us to apprehend the world, particular objects, and people as real, knowable, and relatable. With respect to ethics, critical realism seeks to uncover what actually leads to our flourishing on the basis of what common goods we can discern from critical reflections on human living. The religious ethicist Lisa Sowle Cahill notes that from the perspective of critical realism, "[m]orality requires reasonable reflection on human existence, fine discrimination of goods whose possession truly constitutes happiness, and judgments about which activities lead to those goods and which do not."[16] We can only do this by starting with what we know to be true about human life and exploring outward from there. In particular, this requires inductive reasoning on the basis of our real-life experiences; making "fine discrimination of goods" in light of many reports of what contributes to human happiness, or suffering.

But because we are creatures that can err in our thinking, it is important that what we say about morality benefits from critical analysis, and then from multiple perspectives. As much as critical realism presumes the possibility of discerning human/moral goods, it does not deny that sometimes moral arguments fail to promote genuine human flourishing. Cahill notes that when moral arguments fail it is often because they "deliberately or inadvertently extrapolate conceptions of the good, of flourishing and of virtues and vices, from the preferences of circumscribed historical communities."[17]

Admittedly, thinking that is circumscribed, or simply preferential, can skew the whole project of discerning objective human/moral goods. But this potential for error does not mean that moral relativism wins the day. Generally conceived, moral relativism asserts that morality "like fashion, can vary from time to time and from person to person."[18] To a certain degree, it does. But many forms of moral relativism insist that these differences reveal that there really are no reliable norms, or common human goods; that morality is more or less "made up." But critical realists can (and should) resist the relativist's view of morality. As Cahill says so well:

> Although contentious relativists like to overestimate disagreement, we can and do sit down to discuss hunger or justice or the quality of women's lives with people from other parts of the world and we still find it "possible to proceed as if we are talking about the same human problem." Human experience can disclose goods which constitute a full human life, and practical reason can guide action toward them.[19]

While I agree with Cahill on this point, to embrace critical realism is not to also imply that arriving at a list of human/moral goods will be easy.

As we examine our experiences of happiness and suffering, surely there will be admissions of moral ambiguity and individual differences—especially where cultural differences are at play. Critical realism can withstand shades of grey, and it can engage difficult dialogues between diverse communities. But it is not content with excusing injustices in the name of personal, cultural, or moral relativism. The philosopher and ethicist Martha Nussbaum captures the prudential flexibility of critical realism quite well. In her discussion on justice, she writes:

> On the one hand, it seems impossible to deny that traditions, both Western and non-Western, perpetuate injustice . . . in many fundamental ways, [which] touch on some of the most central elements of a human being's quality of life—health, education, political liberty and participation, employment, self-respect, and life itself. On the other hand, hasty judgments that a tradition in some distant part of the world is morally retrograde are familiar legacies of colonialism and imperialism and are correctly regarded with suspicion by sensitive thinkers in the contemporary world. To say that a practice endorsed by tradition is bad is to risk erring by imposing one's own way on others, who surely have their own ideas of what is right and good. To say that a practice is all right whenever local tradition endorses it as right and good is to

risk erring by withholding critical judgment where real evil and oppression are surely present. To avoid the whole issue because the matter of proper judgment is so fiendishly difficult is tempting but perhaps the worst option of all. It suggests the sort of moral collapse depicted by Dante when he describes the crowd of souls who mill around in the vestibule of hell, dragging their banner now one way, now another, never willing to set it down and take a definite stand on any moral or political question.[20]

In response to this problem, Nussbaum says (and I agree): "[I]t is better to risk being consigned by critics to the 'hell' reserved for alleged Westernizers and imperialists—however unjustified such criticism would be—than to stand around in the vestibule waiting for a time when everyone will like what we are going to say."[21]

Thus, one of the dividing lines in ethics is between those who accept the idea that there are (at times) good reasons for advancing normative moral arguments and those who reject advancing norms for the moral community—typically, postmodern relativists. Postmodernists who emphasize moral relativism tend to argue that what one values is completely subjective (whether individually or culturally), and thus, definitions of the "good" should not be projected onto others who do not share similar values. In their rejection of advancing moral norms, postmodernists (described only generally here) have often treated sexual morality in terms of "whatever is consensual and 'feels right.'"[22]

Upon first glance, there is a welcomed kind of simplicity (if not generosity) in postmodern moral minimalism. But it is ultimately not convincing. Just as normative moral claims are at times problematic, so too we must admit that the postmodernist door is wide open to moral difficulties. For example, the moral relativist, or postmodernist, might tell us that sexual morality is best left to individual (subjective) consent. Admittedly, there are good reasons for holding this view, especially when respecting the importance of sexual and relational autonomy. However, even the basic standard of "consent" requires more moral specificity than what some postmodernists might initially anticipate. If for no other reason, subtle and explicit forms of coercion have led some people to vocalize consent to sexual activity that they otherwise deeply resist.[23] What is more, what "feels right," sexually is not always the best indicator of what we ought to pursue, especially with respect to various emotional, physical, and relational complexities and consequences.[24] Lisa Cahill has correctly critiqued postmodern moralities, noting two specific problems:

[M]ost postmodern thinkers count on a consensus about liberal
values which they do not theoretically defend. They work out
their practical programs in a context of cultural commitment to
liberal equality. Second, and implied by the first problem, is the
fact that cross-cultural "resistance" [to any forms of domination]
will be disabled if . . . equality as a critical social principle in
general, is not firmly enough implanted culturally and politically
to survive its philosophical discreditation.[25]

And so, even if postmodern thinking highlights important matters of
subjectivity, its theoretical foundations potentially destabilize morality
to unsustainable ends.

For example, if the postmodernist categorically dismisses moral
norms as mere "narrative frameworks" tantamount to fiction, we might
be moved to agree when various norms can be shown to result from pure
circumscription (e.g., philosophically and/or theologically). But consider
also poignant life moments, as when we describe incidents of emotional
and physical violence as "injustices." In the face of such human suffering we offer moral definitions of "justice" in order to promote human
flourishing. The postmodernist would be hard pressed in these cases to
suggest that concepts of "justice" are really just narrative fictions (tell that
to women suffering domestic abuse, or to LGBT teens daily harassed at
home or at school). The critical realist contends, then, that while moral
frameworks are indeed narratives, they are narratives that (if carefully and
critically constructed) can promote real human flourishing with a promis-
ing measure of reliability. I say this, however, not to trivialize postmodern thinking. In my view, postmodernists often make important cultural
and moral critiques, which they (seemingly) would like others to affirm.
However, such postmodernists have to resign themselves to the thin hope
that rhetoric alone will lead to a consensus of subjective affirmations.

That said, postmodern arguments can be fascinating studies into the
realm of moral, social, and political conscience. Postmodern arguments
often inspire individuals to wrestle with conventional norms, and when
this happens individuals can better evaluate, for themselves, matters of
oppression and liberation. And yet we are not simply individuals on our
own courses. We are that, but we are also social beings, interconnected.
Many of us find that while our individuality (and our individual choices)
ought to be respected, we also sense that we can help one another to
uncover common and recognizable goods that contribute to our flourishing as human beings. Postmodernism, on the other hand, usually refuses
to name many norms for the moral community, and thus relegates the

standard of morality to the lowest common denominator, such as "consent" or "do no harm," or what (at any given time) is personally desired or socially tolerated. However, abstaining from the articulation of moral norms largely entrusts persons and certain values to whatever subjective principles are, as Cahill says, "implanted in culture." But that is not to say that postmodern frameworks will always undermine living and doing well. To be clear, not all postmodernists agree about moral reasoning—which is to say, not all moral postmodernists conceive of morality as discursive fiction. Indeed, many postmodernists are more concerned about the epistemological claim to "objective" moral norms, and this concern is philosophically warranted. But if postmodernists abdicate, ignore, or dispose themselves of practical or empirical insights about human happiness, then I think they are not being wholly truthful about what we can actually say about living and doing well as human beings.

In my view, this weakness of postmodern thinking raises far more concerns about postmodernism as the foundation of one's moral compass than does the inherent potentiality for flawed thinking when engaging in critical realism. If for no other reason, critical realism admits that we must engage in ongoing critical reflection (and dialogue) on all subjects related to human living. It does so not only with the goal that we become critical thinkers, but that we might also uncover human goods that allow us to enjoy genuine happiness and diminish human suffering.[26]

The potential ethical deficiency of postmodernism, however, does not mean that it is altogether valueless. Indeed, I think we do well to hold critical realism and postmodernism in a principled tension. The postmodern critique provides for us avenues of critical analysis, by which the strength of a given norm is tested. Thus, while there is certainly a philosophical "tug of war" between critical realism and postmodernism, my sense is that when we listen to the best insights of both approaches, these perspectives might actually lead to "fine discrimination" about morality—especially sexual morality. I am particularly interested in the rise of queer theory as a postmodern critique of normative ideas about human sexuality.

Queer Theory

Queer theory developed in response to the lesbian, gay, bisexual, transgender (LGBT) identity movement. For most of the twentieth century, any sexual relationship that fell outside of a heterosexual mold was largely considered queer, and thus deviant. But with the rise of the LGBT movement, socially and politically, LGBT people who were once on the margins are now, more and more, in the mainstream. But queer theorists, such as Michael Warner, have noted that this mainstreaming effort has represented nothing less than a desire to be "normal"; to simply "fit in," and to do so by accepting the conventional norms of heterosexuality (i.e., monogamy, marriage, family, children, etc.).[27] But Warner is not convinced that adopting norms is a good thing. Warner's stunning critique of sexual normativity is worth considering. He laments that

> [t]hen and now, homosexuals were and still are afraid to be seen as queer. Then and now, they knew and still know that nothing else could haunt their attempt to be "ethical," in the restricted sense that prevails in America, as much as sex. Then as now, they bargained and still bargain for a debased pseudo-dignity, the kind that is awarded as a bribe for disavowing the indignity of sex and the double indignity of a politics around sex. The result has always been a set of hierarchies. Those whose sex is least threatening, along with those whose gender profiles seem least queer, are put forward as the good and acceptable face of the movement. These, inevitably, are the ones who are staying home, making dinner for their boyfriends, for whom being gay means reading *Newsweek*. The others, the queers who have sex in public toilets, who don't "come out" as happily gay, the sex workers, the lesbians who are too vocal about a taste for dildos or S/M, the boys who flaunt it as pansies or as leathermen, the androgynes, the trannies or transgendered whose gender deviance makes them unassimilable to the menu of sexual orientations, the clones in the so-called gay ghetto, the fist-fuckers and popper-snorters, the ones who actually like pornography—all these flaming creatures are told, in an earnestness that betrays no glimmer of its own grotesque comedy, that their great moment of liberation and acceptance will come later, when we "no longer see our lives solely in terms of struggle," when we get to be about "more than sexuality"—when, say, gay marriage is given the force of law. Free at last![28]

Thus, for Warner (and others), queer life is not a matter of assimilating to existing heterosexual/cultural norms. Rather, Warner identifies queer characters among those who eschew mainstream constructions of sexuality, fixed identities, and moral conventions.

Warner's critique of sexual normativity is emblematic of queer theory. In particular, queer theory seeks to reclaim the social/sexual margins, as well as to spotlight the artificiality of mainstream norms.

As David Halperin has said it, queer theory is a perspective of "positionality vis-à-vis the normative."[29] As such, queer theorists have suggested
that at the heart of queer theory is the exercise of transgression—that
is, the transgression of conventional boundaries in order to reveal "their
fragility and instability."[30] Queer theory serves, then, as a disruptive foil
to any normative statement about sexuality. It emphasizes the "hybrid,
provisional, [and] composite" nature of human sexuality, and it resists
concepts of sexuality that are grounded in "essential" or "fixed" ideals.[31]

As such, queer theory undoes conventional establishments—including religious ones. As the queer theologian Patrick Cheng describes it,
queer theory "in the words of the *Magnificat*, brings down the powerful and
lifts up the lowly. In particular, [it] seeks to unearth silenced voices or hidden perspectives."[32] Without question, then, queer theory is illuminating
insofar as it moves us to the margins to think anew (and critically) about a
proposed norm or conventionality. Doing so is helpful because ethicists and
theologians can be wrong when they confuse cultural norms for sustainable
moral and/or religious principles. Queer theory rightly challenges those
who assume orthodoxy and authority, and impose it harshly on others.

Sexual Justice

One approach to sexual ethics, via critical realism, is to emphasize the
aforementioned virtue of justice. The philosopher Aristotle defined justice
as a virtue that guides our relations with others as equals, such that "what
we call just is whatever produces and maintains happiness and its parts
for a [human] community."[33] To practice justice, the philosopher said, is
to pursue what is fair or fitting as it relates to the interactions between
people.[34] The pursuit of sexual justice, then, can be broadly conceived as
an effort to review matters of sexual morality in terms of equal treatment
of human persons.

As a matter of Christian sexual ethics, justice is a central concern. While the churches debate about who should be having sex, and
what people should be aiming at in sexual activity, these issues matter
very little if justice is altogether absent from the sexual relationship.
For example, sexual activity could be marital and open to procreation
(the hallmark of traditional sexual morality), however, if a spouse was
raping the other, the existing marriage and the reproductive probability
of intercourse would hardly secure the morality of the act. Conversely,
if two men were having sex, not married, nor having the possibility of
procreation, but they did satisfy basic criteria for justice, it would be

difficult to utterly condemn the sexual act, insofar as it manifested a recognizable human good (the just treatment of a human being).

It is important to consider, then, what count as the criteria for sexual justice. Given that this book is considering sexual ethics in a Christian context, we must glean how justice might be informed by Christian sources of moral authority. However, defining sexual justice through Christian source material is quite difficult. For example, the Bible does not *explicitly* define sexual justice in any way that resonates with ideals of gender or sexual equality. Recall that when we turn to the Book of Deuteronomy, raped women are either killed or married to their rapist (depending on the status of their virginity and/or betrothal).[35] Indeed, throughout the Hebrew Bible women are often assumed to be the sexual property of men. Neither does the New Testament answer questions about the criteria of sexual justice with any kind of clear detail. In fact, even when we turn to church teachings, a firm definition of sexual justice is also elusive. Different churches offer different definitions. For example, according to official Catholic teaching sexual justice includes fidelity to one's spouse in sacramental marriage. And yet, according to Protestants, sexual justice can vary from marital norms of faithful monogamy, to general principles of trust and respect between sexual partners. In fact, a handful of mainline Protestant denominations now acknowledge that licit sexual relationships need not conform to heterosexual or marital norms.[36] However, even though we can find a variety of Protestant and Catholic definitions of sexual justice, these church definitions tend to be relatively brief, conflating what is "just" with the dictates or principles of their religious teachings.

It is only when we turn to academic studies in Christian sexual ethics that we find more nuanced definitions of sexual justice for Christian ethics. For example, the Christian sexual ethicist Margaret Farley has said that in order to meet the requirements of justice, sexual partners should: make commitments to do "no unjust harm," procure "free consent," promote "mutuality," require "equality," enforce "social justice," and to do so within the context of long-term committed relationships that generate love (that is, a relational love that inspires love for others).[37] In contrast with Farley's view, the Christian feminist ethicist Carter Heyward teaches that sexual justice requires *mutuality, accountability,* and *boundaries,* but she does not think that commitments to long-term relationships are necessary for sexual justice to be realized.[38] We will explore Farley's and Heyward's ideas about sexual justice in more detail in chapter 10. The point here is only to demonstrate that we are in need of theorists like Farley and Heyward in order to talk about sexual justice in ways that respond to our modern moral concerns—which often the Bible and sacred tradition do not thoroughly address.

Of course, Christian communities will agree and disagree with various proposals about the requirements for sexual justice. Christians might choose to elaborate on, or whittle away at, any number of descriptions about the criteria of sexual justice (whether those are proposed by scholars, theologians, or church teachings). But some of the criteria are so unmistakably necessary that without them we would only be left with violence or exploitation. Thus, it seems reasonable to conclude that there are some self-evident criteria of sexual justice. For example: mutuality, boundaries, and accountability, not to mention, equality, free consent, and no unjust harm. Where these are present, I think we have to admit that many sexual relationships do satisfy these necessary criteria of sexual justice—even if such sexual relationships do not satisfy a particular church's view on sexual morality, as that is derived from interpretations of the Bible or articles of church teaching.

The Utility of Sexual Pleasure

One of the central, historic, problems recurring in Christian sexual ethics concerns the moral status of sexual pleasure. As we saw in the last chapter, it took until the twentieth and twenty-first centuries for mainline Christian communities to begin the process of undoing certain suspicions about sex and sexuality that first developed within the opening centuries of Christianity's institutional formation.[39] At issue was (and is) whether or not sexual pleasure is a good that should be sought for its own sake.

And yet, for many people, wrangling over the moral status of sexual pleasure seems rather unnecessary. If for no other reason, people want sexual experiences to be pleasurable. We usually do not seek out "painful sex" (notwithstanding the complexities of BDSM practices, which include pleasures of bondage, submission, and dominance—matters not always understood by those unfamiliar with such erotic intricacies). Thus, when we are told that enjoying sex is problematic when seeking pleasure for itself, such a warning often feels puritanical, not prudent.

So what's the problem?

Of its own, pleasure is not the problem. As the Christian sexual ethicist Christine Gudorf has correctly noted, "Like a hot tub for aching muscles, cool water on a hot day, a shot of morphine after waking up from surgery, and the taste of ice cream on the tongue, sexual pleasure makes us feel good. We like it. Pleasure itself is good."[40]

Indeed, any number of activities can result in the experience of pleasure. I agree with Gudorf that there is nothing wrong with pleasure so long as we are seeking it in a way that contributes to our genuine happiness, as well as the happiness of others. But consider again Gudorf's example of "ice cream on the tongue." That indeed is pleasurable. But if all we sought in our eating was the pleasure of ice cream, it wouldn't be too long before our happiness was compromised in some health-injuring way.

But that's ice cream. Sex offers different opportunities for plea-sures. And while there might not be such a thing as "too much sexual pleasure" while engaged in sexual activity itself, *how* we go about seek-ing it certainly qualifies whether we should. Figuring this out, however, requires us to have nuanced discussions about the moral status of sexual pleasure, and how sexual pleasure can contribute to our flourishing as human beings. The aforementioned ethicist Christine Gudorf offers a moral analysis of sexual pleasure that suggests why Christians should regard it as something good. I highlight her argument, insofar as she provides important ethical insights to contemporary Christian sexual ethics on this issue.

In particular, Gudorf suggests that if Christians treat sexual pleasure as a "premoral good" it can be properly enjoyed according to a utilitar-ian calculus.[41] Gudorf notes that "a premoral good does not mean that it leads to moral good [necessarily] but that it is ordinarily good, and should be understood as one aspect of the general social good."[42] As utility has to do with the promotion of the greatest good for the greatest number of people, corresponding with the enjoyment of pleasure and the avoidance (where possible) of pain, Gudorf is convinced that we only need to discern when it is best to pursue sexual pleasure, in order to pursue it for its own sake.

That suggestion is rather new to Christian sexual ethics, even if it is basic to postmodernists or sexual libertarians. What is more, Gudorf goes so far as naming sexual pleasure "as natural" an end for sex as procreation. She goes even farther and argues that "it should be the primary ethical criterion for evaluating sexual activity."[43] She explains:

> The reasons for choosing sexual pleasure as the primary ethi-cal criterion for evaluating sexual activity have nothing to do with the fact that the Christian tradition has largely identified

it with sin rather than virtue, but rather have to do with the
nature of sexuality and its effects. First, except for procreation,
all positive functions of sex depend upon sex being pleasurable.
Second, pleasure is more easily and immediately recognized than
intimacy and bonding, which develop over time and do not
necessarily, intrude themselves on human consciousness in the
same immediate, forceful way that sexual pleasure does. Third,
our society is beginning to recognize the many ways in which
we have been trained to avoid pleasure, and how destructive
and unhealthy such behavior is. Finally, if most of us in this
society are honest, the primary purpose for which we turn to sex
is pleasure, whether it is the pleasure of passion or the pleasure
of emotional intimacy.[44]

While much of historic Christianity has not been able to recognize these
claims, Gudorf believes her argument is consistent with larger themes in
Christian theology and ethics.

Specifically, Gudorf suggests that the premoral good of sexual pleasure is consistent with biblical teachings about the goodness of creation—especially as described in the Book of Genesis. In the opening
chapter of that text, all of creation is pronounced (by God) to be good,
indeed very good. However, this does not mean that everything in action
is itself good, especially in light of the human capacity for "sin" and
error.[45] Instead, it is the recognition that all things can participate well
in the created order. Gudorf suggests that Christians should evaluate
sexual pleasure as one of the goods of creation to be rightfully enjoyed.
What is more, she believes that Christians can do this especially well
when considering the qualities of the reign of God, as described in the
canonical gospels. For Gudorf this means emphasizing "inclusivity." She
explains:

According to New Testament sources, Jesus never directly
addressed sexual behavior. But Jesus taught about the reign
of God which was breaking into the world through Jesus in
parables, stories of everyday human activities, as well as through
his own actions and activities. In the parables, Jesus made clear
that the reign of God is both paradigmatically inclusive, and
that it is a thing of joy and celebration. . . . We do not have
sexual examples of the reign of God from the Gospels. But
for many in our society, sexual examples would be more than

merely acceptable ways of describing such experiences of God's reign on earth. For many persons, their primary experience of inclusive love, of openness to another, of being accepted and enhanced, of being empowered by love to reach out in love to others, is sexual. . . . [Thus] for many, the primary experience of divinity itself, as well as of God's intention for the reign of God, is sexual. There is in sex, as in Eucharist, the potential for participating in divinity.[46]

Gudorf admits that this claim will be startling to some. But when Christians consider the qualities of the reign of God, as described in the New Testament, Gudorf thinks it will be difficult for Christians to deny that sexual activity—sought for the sake of sexual pleasure—can also (in the right contexts) manifest principles of the gospel texts, especially inclusivity, joy, or love.

In light of the many centuries of Christian suspicions about sexual pleasure, Gudorf's argument is an important one to consider when thinking about Christian sexual morality. It is, indeed, difficult to imagine a "good" sexual scenario in which the enjoyment of mutual pleasure is entirely absent. And yet, even Gudorf notes that the good of sexual pleasure is not an unqualified good. Pursuing it requires careful discernment, which she negotiates through an ethic of utility. That said, Christians are in complete disagreement about how pleasure is "rightly" enjoyed. For example, a Roman Catholic heterosexual married couple may not think it is appropriate to pursue the good of sexual pleasure through the use of contraceptives. And yet, many Protestant married couples faithful to their church's teachings find nothing morally wrong with enjoying sexual pleasure, even while drawing on contraception to avoid pregnancy. What is more, gay and lesbian people can (and do) pursue sexual pleasure in ways that are essentially about inclusivity, joy, or love (gospel principles all), and yet these sexual unions have been a point of condemnation or controversy in both Protestant and Catholic churches.

Therefore, while we might get people to agree that sexual pleasure is a good thing (generally speaking), assigning "pleasure" as the criterion for sexual morality does not seem to satisfy moral questions about when it is actually best to pursue it (or how). Namely, accepting pleasure as a general good to pursue requires us to circle back again and justify why we are pursuing it. This suggests that sexual pleasure is not necessarily all there is to consider (or seek) when we engage in sexual activity. These comments, however, are not a critique of Gudorf's argument. Her approach to sexual ethics frees Christian thinkers to embrace sexual pleasure as a good. However, the pleasure argument seems to require an additional ethic—an ethic that can help, more specifically, to name the "ends" of sexual activity, which better justify why our enjoyment of sexual pleasure is indeed a good thing (in a given time, place, and with various persons). My suggestion is that an ethic of virtue does just that.

Conclusion

The four approaches to sexual ethics that we have just explored are important perspectives on sex and sexuality for contemporary audiences. Each challenges us—as the field of ethics does—to "give reasons for holding the moral positions that we do." I selected these four approaches because they provide important insights for my own argument about sexual virtue.

To begin with, critical realism is the ethical perspective from which I will be defining sexual virtue. The proposal that we can discern "fine goods" through critical discourses is one that I believe in. When Cahill says that we can (and do) sit down to talk with people across the world about hunger, justice, and women's rights, she is indeed correct that we are able to understand one another, as well as to generally conceive common goods that promote demonstrable human flourishing. However, that is not to say that we always agree about goods or definitions of human happiness. We most certainly do not.

We especially disagree when it comes to sexual morality.

But approaching sexual morality through the perspective of critical realism can intercede in some of our disagreements. Namely, critical realism demands that we acknowledge those real human goods that can demonstrably contribute to human happiness and diminish our suffering. In fact, it is the perspective of critical realism that allows us to admit that if any proposals about morality and human flourishing are unsupported by rational insights—or stubbornly ignore what is generally good for human beings—then we can say that such proposals may only represent circumscribed or partisan views, which of themselves may not be helpful for the promotion of genuine human happiness.

However, this is not to say that critical realism is a purely secular endeavor. Religious perspectives can also benefit from critical realism. For example, in light of philosophical conceptions of human rights, few Christians (today) read biblical passages about slavery as prescriptive statements about "God's will" for proper social order. The critical realist thus appreciates that religious texts and traditions can be illuminated through rational reflection, which can provide new insights into religious belief and practice.

Virtue ethics is one manifestation of critical realism. As we will see in the next two chapters, virtue ethics investigates what contributes to human happiness through critical reflection on the quality of our thoughts, actions, and feelings. Namely, virtue ethics seeks to uncover not only what is "meaningful" to us subjectively, but to give reasons why what we value actually contributes to genuine human happiness, as well as to the content of our character. Historically, virtue ethics has promoted prudence, temperance, justice, and fortitude as cardinal virtues for the human community to consider.

To that end, virtue ethics does take seriously that justice is necessary for human flourishing. Thus, reflecting on sexual justice (and injustice) is also an important matter of critical realism. Indeed, I am convinced that sexual justice is a key concept to wrestle with in contemporary sexual ethics. If justice is not one of our concerns, we cannot say (in any meaningful way) that we think of our sexual partners as equal to us—or that they really deserve fair treatment as equals. Described this way, the pursuit of sexual justice informs my argument concerning the cultivation of sexual virtue through the virtues of prudence and temperance. That is to say, whatever prudence identifies as proper ends to pursue in sexual relationships, those ends must not promote injustice.[47]

However, I believe we need to delineate between virtues in order to better understand their coordination. This is especially important when it comes to articulating a definition of sexual virtue. Namely, when we pursue sexual virtue through prudence and temperance, we of course need to be mindful of justice. But the overlapping of these virtues does not constitute the same definitions for each. In particular, even as justice is about the promotion of human happiness through fair treatment among equals, prudence and temperance will have us consider, primarily, what it means to enjoy (well) sexual pleasure, alone or with other persons, toward the right ends, and for the right reason.

My appreciation for critical realism, however, does not mean that I find postmodern arguments utterly lacking. As I suggested in my comments about queer theory, I do think that postmodernism helps to illuminate the unforeseen weaknesses of any argument that assumes a degree of normativity. Without question, there is much insight to be gleaned from the "queer positionality" of the margins. There, we find many of our moral assumptions challenged, and we can better see the artificiality of (certain) social/moral conventions. In my view, then, there is much wisdom to be acquired from queer positions and perspectives.

And yet, queer positionality has limited sight. At times it does not seem to apprehend, well enough, practical and reliable notions about certain common goods and the (practical) enjoyment of human happiness. Privileging queer theory (over other theoretical perspectives, especially critical realism) runs the risk of mistaking real goods with social constructions to dismantle. For example, in his book, *The Trouble with Normal*, the aforementioned queer theorist Michael Warner challenges why a gay man would ever want to "assimilate" to the performance of marriage and family when he could enjoy public sex and multiple sexual partners. Warner's queer positionality does not allow him to appreciate how some humans (whether LGBT or straight identified) might demonstrably benefit from long-term stable relationships. He seems to want us to repudiate marriage and family (instead of, perhaps, reforming these). What he offers instead is his nostalgia for gay sex (a narrowly urban view of it, anyway) when it was illegal, punishable, and thus pursued wherever it could be had. He offers us no reason to believe that living life in the "margins" will offer any kind of genuine happiness (but to be fair, a promise of "happiness" is not something he actually makes). Of course, this is just one example of queer theory articulated. While I find these particular comments of Warner's argument far too circumscribed (socially and morally), I appreciate his critique of marriage and I believe his work is helpful for contemporary discourse on sexual ethics. Thus, the only real critique of queer theory that I wish to highlight is that privileging the social "margins" is itself a kind of norm. However, this is not to say that we should fail to appreciate why some people might choose to navigate life resisting social conventions. But to suggest that this *is* the path of liberation, for everyone, is not very convincing—unless we belong to a consensus of queer theorists who agree with one another about what it means to be queer: theoretically, epistemologically, politically, or in practice.

But moral theories based in the consensus of relativists leaves us perpetually wandering. Some of us have commitments to promote human flourishing, with humble yet normative intent. Queer theory, at least in many expressions of it, resists the hope of the critical realist to uncover, as Cahill says, "goods whose possession truly constitutes happiness." And yet, queer theory is very helpful insofar as it promotes critical and careful thinking. But of its own merits, I do not think queer theory will help us to cultivate the kind of practical ethic that some of us seek.

Most human beings are not afforded the privilege to continuously perform "transgressions" as an ongoing critique of normativity. If I might draw on a religious metaphor, perhaps the queer theorist fulfills the call of the prophetic office, with all of its liminal insights and rewards. There is a special kind of respect for those who bear the prophetic mantle. But to extend the metaphor, the office of prophet is only one calling. There are also other callings, whether to the life of the laity, or to pastoral care, both of which have to do with the here and now. These kinds of people see the world more through the eyes of critical realism and seek to advance outlines of morality to guide the moral community, so as to promote as much happiness as possible—even while recognizing the limitations of human understanding. But we can only seek out real human goods when we glean insights from critical theories, such as the illuminating ones we discover in works of queer theory.

Exploring sex and sexuality outside of conventional norms is precisely what allowed Christine Gudorf to offer her argument about the utility, or good, of sexual pleasure. As Gudorf admits, the history of Christian ethics has often treated the desire for sexual pleasure as something to chastise, not praise. However, in spite of my appreciation for her argument, I think there are also good reasons to shift the moral conversation about sexual pleasure from her utilitarian view to the perspective of virtue.

An ethic of virtue accepts the natural place of pleasure in people's lives, but frames pleasure as something that accompanies an activity.[48] For example, being with our friends is pleasurable, but when we seek out our friends to unwind and simply enjoy life, pleasure is not all we seek. While enjoying the pleasure of our friends' company, we are about the business of sociality and building friendship. In a similar way, we enjoy sexual pleasure, but we enjoy it in light of other human goods that we pursue in our sexual activities and relationships. Certainly, sexual pleasure may be "immediate, and forceful" on our consciousness, as Gudorf says. But when we take the time to reflect on whether sexual pleasure is right to pursue at a given time, or with a given person, we start to realize that pleasure is not all we seek. It is part of what we seek, and we do so for all the reasons Gudorf names. But at the same time, we seek sexual relations with others for reasons having to do, for example, with fantasy fulfillment, play, intimacy, and so forth, not just the physical/

psychological pleasures of sex itself. Thus, in my view, the central moral question is not so much if we want to experience sexual pleasure. Of course we do! As Gudorf says, it's good, generally speaking. The experience of it is enjoyable and it emboldens our pursuit of a wide variety of sexual relationships. But is it *the* central criterion for morality as a matter of sexual ethics? I propose that it is not.

When we care about the contribution of sex and sexuality to human flourishing, pleasure is only one aspect of our enjoyment of sex, whether that involves the symbolic expression of love, the cultivation of relational closeness, or even the want to take a break from a stressful world and play with someone who seeks the same. Pleasure is a significant part of that, but more is happening in sex than stimulation and release. Embracing an ethic of virtue will allow us to truly appreciate pleasure as something that accompanies an activity, naturally and ethically. But as we will see, virtue ethics also encourages moral agents to think about what reasonable "ends" to pursue. We do this in order that sexual partners might intentionally live and do well in their enjoyment of sexual pleasure (whether with long or short-term partners, solo or in group—there's no need to assume any conventional scripts, just because we're employing the language of "virtue").

My sense, then, is that we should respect Gudorf's claims about the "premoral good" of sexual pleasure. But instead of naming "pleasure" as *the* end of sexual relating, I believe we do better to recognize pleasure as something that accompanies the sexual act. Pleasure is good to enjoy (morally), but only when we realize valid, rational "ends" of sexual activities that speak to the whole sex act, and not just its pleasure. Indeed, without having the confidence of knowing what is good to pursue, people often look back on sexual encounters with guilt or anxiety (even if those acts were pleasurable at the time). Of course, much of that guilt may well be unnecessary. But in other cases, especially when people pursue sexual pleasure without much consideration for wider social and moral issues, such encounters may not yield the best results, for oneself, or one's sexual partners.

However, with respect to specifically Christian concerns about sexual morality, I do think that Gudorf's insight about sexual pleasure "as a good of creation" is a reasonable theological perspective to hold when reflecting on Christian sources of moral authority, including scripture, nature, or church teaching (we'll examine these issues in later chapters). However, I still believe that approaching sexual pleasure from the perspective of virtue will allow us to move beyond the threshold of "pleasure," and to embrace "ends" of sexual virtue that open up moral dimensions of sexual pleasures, activities, and relationships that are sometimes unexplored by Christian communities.

∾

Admittedly, the "library of speeches" from which I speak about sexual ethics is selective. But that is the reality all moral agents face (traditionalists, progressives, and radicals alike). In the next two chapters I turn to offer a definition of sexual virtue that is shaped by my commitments to critical realism and sexual justice, as well as my sense that sexual pleasure should be respected as a general good. I do so naming recreation, relational intimacy, and selective acts of procreation as "ends" of sexual virtue. What the reader will find is that virtue ethics allows us to name (and defend) real moral goods of human sexuality, without at the same time insisting on hierarchies of those goods, or moral hierarchies of sexual identities, or hierarchies according to the sexual practices we engage.

Part II

A Moral Framework of Virtue

Three

Virtue Ethics and Sexual Virtue

[G]oodness of action in which human perfection consists cannot be understood in purely formal terms. It requires that the person acts and sustains activities in accordance with a (roughly) correct understanding of what it means to be a good human being.

—Jean Porter

What Are You Calling Virtue?

The language of *virtue* dances on the lips of many of our public figures. Politicians and preachers commend us to be virtuous. Warnings against *vice* are still heard in the public square and in political debate. Defined properly, there are good reasons to say that virtue ought to be praised and vice scorned. But careful and ongoing conversations about virtue and vice are rare outside of mandatory ethics classes, and these largely happen within the confines of colleges, universities, and graduate schools. That is not to say that the general public is disinterested in a life of virtue, or incapable of meaningful moral discourse. Life itself is a school of morality and the wise insights we glean from our experiences ought not to be devalued. And yet, the activity of ethics compels us to take one step further, and to engage one another on the basis of the strengths and merits of our thoughts about rights and wrongs, virtue and vice.

To revisit and reclaim an ethic of virtue, as I am inviting us to do, it is helpful to consider its best-known architect, Aristotle. The philosopher articulated a theory of virtue so compelling and complete that it is still taught in classrooms around the globe as part of classic moral theory. Not limited to the ancient Greek alone, virtue ethics has been adopted into the religious frameworks of Jewish, Christian, and Buddhist thinkers.[1] It was preserved by Islamic civilization during the Christian dark ages, and in that period received commentary by Muslim scholars.[2]

Virtue ethics continues to be influential to the activity of religious and theological ethics, especially among Christians. In the last millennia, official teachers in the Catholic Church—as well as many of the theologians, scholars, interpreters, and critics in the Catholic Intellectual Tradition—have offered highly nuanced and intellectually sophisticated statements on virtue.[3] Protestants too have relied on concepts of virtue to articulate what it means to live and do well as a follower of Christ in a world complicated by moral agency.[4] Whether Catholic or Protestant, serious Christian thinkers have drawn on virtue ethics as a matter of Christian ethics, and in doing so have often reformulated how virtue is best defined.[5]

Given that virtue ethics has such an impressive array of interpreters, an appeal to "virtue" in Christian and cultural moral debates really should not be a generic code for "morality." While we may end up disagreeing about what counts as virtue and vice, we at least have to say *how* we arrive at such claims. That does not mean that all who are interested in virtue must become dedicated scholars of Aristotle (or defend everything he said about it). But we must at least have a workable theory, outline, or sketch of virtue in order to be sensible and compelling.

In this chapter, I will offer an account of virtue that draws on the work of Aristotle. It is not my intention to give a full description of Aristotle's teaching on virtue, or to suggest that I am representing all of his thinking or his individual conclusions. Instead, I wish to draw on Aristotle's virtue ethics like a painter's palette, offering a sketch of virtue for contemporary use, from which I will offer some initial comments on sexual virtue. By offering a definition of virtue, I hope to show the reader not only a moral framework that is helpful for ethical reflection, but also the points at which we can legitimately disagree with one another on concepts of morality and human flourishing. Although I am concerned with definitions of sexual virtue within a Christian context, this chapter seeks to offer an overview of virtue philosophically, and not any distinctively Christian attributes. After providing a working sketch of virtue in this chapter, in the following chapter I will then invite the reader to consider how an ethic of virtue can be situated within a Christian framework. It is important to build the argument this way so that our judgments about particular virtues (and vice) are not simply reiterations of our moral intuitions, or prejudices.

Virtue Ethics: A Strategy for Happiness

Happiness: Living and Doing Well

Virtue ethics is distinguished from a number of other moral theories because it embraces a teleological view of morality. That is to say, it is an ethic concerned with proper ends or goals. While Aristotle recognized a number of specific goods that we might pursue in life (health, wealth, education, friendship, and so forth), there was only one "end" that appeared to the philosopher as complete in and of itself. Aristotle named this complete end human happiness.[6] For Aristotle, whatever other particular ends we pursue, we do so in light of enjoying happiness.

But in our time, happiness is a concept that exists without a singular definition. For some, it is the presence of joy. For others, it is a sense of satisfaction. Interpreters of Aristotle tend to agree that the happiness that he described is not simply momentary pleasure, or an unqualified pleasing psychological state, but is best characterized as the enjoyment of living and doing well.[7] The Greek term Aristotle used was *eudemonia*.[8] Because "living and doing well" is a qualitative concern, the kind of human happiness (or flourishing) considered here is not only a matter of physical, social, and psychological flourishing (which by human necessity it must anticipate), but it is something that involves our moral condition.[9]

The enjoyment of this kind of happiness (*eudemonia*) requires discerning what it means to live life well. But to do this, we need not swear obedience to conventional goods, or traditional scripts for morality. While some conventional teachings may help us to live life well, we really cannot pursue happiness without critical reflection on life and the choices we make. This is a heuristic matter. Virtue ethics admits that even as human happiness is the end toward which all human activity is directed, *how* people realize that happiness is often unique to their own personhood and context. On the one hand, then, virtue ethics is definitely a form of critical realism, insofar as it seeks to discern "fine goods" that contribute to true human happiness. But on the other hand, virtue ethics can only do so well by testing the strength of proposed norms and conventional codes of morality. We otherwise slip into parochial or partisan repertoires of moral rhetoric.[10] Thus, if we are going to set "living and doing well" as the definition of happiness (or flourishing), we must be vigilant not to ignore multiple insights, whether from people in the mainstream or from those on the margins.[11] This view of happiness invites thoughtful exploration of life and lifestyles, as well as spacious reflection on our experiences—

learning from the best of our choices, as well as from our mistakes. It is to appreciate that happiness is not a destination point after a life of following narrowly specified rules. It is the enjoyment of life in the here and now, made possible when our life is coordinated and cultivated in ways that "actualize our potential" for living and doing well as human beings.[12]

Virtue ethics offers a particular method for making decisions about what does (and what does not) contribute to human happiness. This method includes respecting the insights of right reason, imitating the habits of the wise, and learning to distinguish what sets virtue apart from vice. We will discuss these matters in more detail below. However, before we get to a description of virtue ethics, I want to acknowledge that there are a number of critics who will wonder if the definition of happiness as living and doing well is defendable philosophically. I believe that it is, and furthermore, I suggest that we only need to look to our day-to-day lives to understand why happiness (i.e., living and doing well) is not a hollow or arbitrary concept. Consider, for example, the natural goods that generally accompany reports of happiness, such as: health (of both mind and body); well-being (i.e., satisfaction, wellness, and/or wholeness); sociality (in particular, the fulfillment of our social needs); and bodily integrity (the basic freedoms of autonomy and mobility). When choices are made that harm these basic/natural goods, our moral intuitions alert us that such choices (and their results), are "worse" (qualitatively) than what otherwise could have been chosen and enjoyed. Generally speaking, we seek to maintain, or improve upon, these basic/natural goods, and when people tell us that various choices helped or hurt them in these regards, we understand what they mean when they say that such led to happiness or suffering. Those who would object, then, that defining human happiness is an impossible task would be wrong. We do it inductively every day. Because we do, we enlarge our storehouses of wisdom, out of which we are better able to discern "living and doing well" from its counterfeits.

Right Reason

Ultimately, virtue ethics declares that happiness depends on the light of reason. For whatever innate inclination we have to do this or that; or whatever appetite draws us toward something as desirable, we don't do anything consciously unless reason consents. That is one of the distinguishing characteristics of being human. Therefore, in order for human beings to experience happiness—to live and do well—we must pay attention to the exercise of our rational capacity: *what* we are thinking, *how* we consciously respond to others; and *how* we consciously act when motivated by our feelings and appetites.

Aristotle noted that while there is much about humans that we share in common with plants and animals, what distinguishes us from all of them is our capacity to reason well and to make intentional choices that result in genuine happiness.[13] This does not mean that every thought we think is right, or that the power to reason guarantees infallible answers. Nor does it deny that some things are revealed to us through our natural inclinations and sensual experiences. For example, it is not rational speculation about a cool swimming pool on a hot day that reveals its pleasantness; it is our actual experience of it. But reason is what allows us to reflect on various pleasures and pains, and to evaluate the choices and activities that lead to them. Reason allows us to consider the qualitative dimensions of life. It opens our moral imagination to the possibility of living and doing well. But because of our fallibility, Aristotle taught that reason contributes to our living and doing well only insofar as we are exercising *right reason*.

Of course, someone will likely ask the question: Who gets to decide what counts as right reason? A person might well suppose that there is no such thing as right reasoning, only different points of view. I am sensitive to this claim, and I think that a wide variety of perspectives are necessary to entertain in order to become wise. But I am not wholly convinced by such an assertion if its implication is that there really is no such thing as right reasoning.

For example, we would not grant that a person is possessed with right reason if they were to say that rape or sexual assault were "good," simply because these brought physical or psychological pleasure to the rapist or the assailant. We seem to recognize in many moral matters that there are common goods and obvious extremes that, if not recognized, can signal real moral delinquency, or even rational failure. So let's ask the question again: What counts as right reason? Surely it is not the intellectual insight that we stumble onto now and then. The claim to right reason carries with it an authority of sensibility, not random insight—although perhaps such stumbling is part of the process. What is more, it is also not likely the ideas of an individual alone, apart from the insights of the wider community—even if some individuals do prove themselves to "get it right," as lone voices during particular points of history.

If not a matter of stumbling onto right concepts, or the domain of an individual's monopoly on truth, "right reason" might best be conceived as a disposition to think carefully, and to do so by drawing on the accumulated wisdom of the human community. We do this well when we turn to the insights of those who are also committed to a life of careful reflection, have openness to new insights, and have the humility to admit that inasmuch as we can discern certain goods, we can also be wrong about that. We do well, then, to keep as wise counsel those whose humility and conviction are mutually informing.

Aristotle's answer to this question (in part) was that we should look to the wise among us in order to guide our sense of right reasoning. He taught that we should see the "wise" as role models and learn to reason like them and to choose as they would choose.[14] By this, however, Aristotle did not mean mindlessly copying those people we call wise, but that we might learn to think like wise people, benefiting from their teaching and cultivating that kind of wisdom in our own lives. But we do this in light of our individual context and situation. For example, I may find my grandmothers to be very wise, but I need to live and make choices in light of the contexts and particularities of my life—which at times, are very different from theirs. Thus, I think Aristotle offers us good advice to look to the wise, but not without some qualification.

In our time (and throughout all of history) we have been divided over who counts as the wise among us. This is especially true when it comes to sexual morality. Shall one look to the example and teachings of venerated clergy who practice celibacy and advocate heterosexual marriage for those who are not celibate? Shall a person look to the example and experiences of those who are married? Should we look to those who are polyamorous or in open relationships? What about to those who choose singleness? Should we look to the insights gleaned from gay and lesbian people who, when denied public and religious legitimacy, partner together in unique and creative ways? A wide variety of political, philosophical, and religious "wise" people compete for our allegiance. Their power is consolidated according to the number of people who accept that they are, in fact, wise.

If we are going to take Aristotle's advice to look to the wise among us (in order to gauge in us a sense of right reasoning, and to see what good choices look like), we need to take time to consider whom we have been listening to, and what "wisdom" we have internalized from them. We sometimes find that the practice and cultivation of right reason may come in part when we learn to depart from those who are not the sources of wisdom that we once thought that they were. When we realize in those awful (but insightful) moments that some of the "wise" among us have been imparting more partisan rhetoric than wisdom, we feel betrayed.[15] But when that happens, we need to remember that where our role models have failed us according to measures of integrity and honesty, they are nevertheless valuable as guideposts, pointing us (ironically) to the path of right reason and the enjoyment of genuine human happiness.

Happiness and Moral Excellence

Notice, however, that I am qualifying happiness with the words *true, real,* and *genuine.* This is an intentional word choice that some thinkers may interpret as an authoritarian posture on matters of morality. Objections will be made that no one has the right to impose definitions of what constitutes "right reason" or "true happiness" for any given person. I understand the motivation of that concern, especially if it is grounded in a commitment to inclusivity as well as moral flexibility. I too agree, and will argue, that spaciousness is necessary in moral reasoning. But if the objection comes from the dogma of radical moral relativism (the belief that there are no such things as demonstrable "goods"), then I fundamentally disagree. In my view, such relativism fails to recognize that there are certain life conditions that are so unmistakably obvious as "better" than others, that views to the contrary appear intentionally (and sometimes aggressively) dismissive of practical reason.[16]

There are better and worse states of being in relation to others; and the "better" states have much to do with realizing basic human goods that contribute to our living and doing well.[17] For example, in 2010 the American columnist Dan Savage launched the "it gets better" campaign to encourage lesbian, gay, bisexual, and transgender teens to hope for a happier life outside of the closet and outside of the cruel halls of their schools (not to mention some homes and churches too).[18] Around the world, people supported the "it gets better" initiative and declared that there are "better" states of being to hope for—"better" in relation to the trials of the closet and the pain of prejudice. These kinds of distinctions between "better" and "worse" states of being were offered as reasonable (if not well-tested) insights into life about what does, and does not, contribute to genuine human happiness.[19]

Promoting a happy life may be an activity fraught with contested views, but at its core it is an appreciation of the demonstrable good in our lives and in the lives of others. As the Pulitzer Prize winner Marilynne

Robinson has rightly noted, "There is no snobbery in saying things differ by the measure of their courage and their honesty and their largeness of spirit, and that the difference is profoundly one of value."[20] To recognize this is not a symptom of moral vanity. It signals a commitment to pursue the good in life (whatever that turns out to be), recognizing that the way we coordinate our thoughts, actions, feelings, and social interactions really does contribute to human flourishing or suffering—and thus, the qualitative/moral distinctions we make can be of great value when they help us to live "better" lives.

Many human beings have learned through as much trial as error that some things do in fact yield our happiness, and others do not. Indeed, we can only begin an investigation into what constitutes happiness (*eudaimonia*) within the context of our present experience of happiness or its absence. As I have said, to define "living and doing well" is a heuristic and inductive matter. It requires mindfulness, and it requires a kind of compassion for the human community that wants what is best for each and every person. To promote happiness as "living and doing well" requires us to care about the quality of our lives, as well as the quality of other peoples' lives too—not in an effort to rigidly imprison ourselves (or others) with new moral hierarchies, but to encourage moral discourse between a wide variety of people and communities about the value of our lives. This concerns the value of our lives in relation to one another, and ultimately, the hope of enjoying life by being the best we can be. This happiness is not, as Robinson says, a kind of moral "snobbery." Quite to the contrary, pursuing happiness as "living and doing well" is a rather simple recognition that what we value in life is what we pursue—and what we pursue contributes to the quality of our lives, and to the quality of all lives as our actions ripple out from us.

Let us return, then, to the claim that right reason is important for us to cultivate if we are going to live and do well. It is precisely right reason that allows us to consider what contributes to genuine happiness. That is, right reason allows us to think carefully about how certain material goods, relationships, projects, emotions, and pleasures contribute to true human happiness. We are poised, then, to ask another question: How do we learn to live life, such that we come to enjoy true happiness in all of our various human capacities and relationships? Aristotle said that it is in the practice of virtue that the happy life is made possible.

Virtue

Virtues are enduring character dispositions (or traits) to do the right thing, at the right time, and for the right reason.[21] To say that virtues are enduring character dispositions means that virtues have the quality of being good habits. In order to live and do well in the details of life, Aristotle taught that it is necessary to cultivate good habits that dispose us to seek out that which is truly fine and excellent.[22] The ethicist Robert Fitterer said it well when he wrote:

> For the key to complete virtue is not simply to know that courage, temperance, magnanimity, even temperedness, and justice are all excellences of the human soul, but to know that they are such because they really are good and noble in their own right, because they are genuinely choice-worthy for their own sakes, because they really are pleasant to embody as well as to behold, and because they really do make up vital aspects of a whole life well-lived.[23]

Of course, there will be some among us who will *still* question if such a normative description of virtue is philosophically defensible. But I also take it that a number of people will agree that "genuinely choice-worthy" character traits are sometimes clear to us, not always obfuscated by moral complexity.

We can expect, however, that one critique of this perspective will come from the simple observation that humans have possessed skewed concepts of what is "genuinely choice-worthy." The critic might point to histories of slavery, segregation, or any number of other oppressions that humans have manifested. The critic will go on to tell us that if we have previously (and frequently) been wrong about concepts of the "good," there are no guarantees that virtue can in any way be pursued with confidence. In the end, the critic will repeat a concern that we frequently encounter: that virtue is an exercise of moral imposition, dressed in arbitrary and unverifiable definitions of what is "good." And yet the very recognition that the human community has sometimes been *wrong* about what is genuinely choice-worthy suggests that we do indeed have the capacity to recognize what is more or less right. If that were not true, the critique would fail to hold any meaning.[24] That is to say, when the critic points to examples of humans getting it "wrong," the critic's identification of the "wrong" is necessarily in relation to something otherwise regarded as right or good. The critic may rely on a subjective defense, but we can say something stronger: that practical reason, well cultivated, has the capacity to discern *actual* goods. Recall the insight from Lisa Sowle Cahill:

> Although contentious relativists like to overestimate disagreement, we can and do sit down to discuss hunger or justice or the quality of women's lives with people from other parts of the world and we still find it "possible to proceed as if we are talking about the same human problem." Human experience can disclose goods which constitute a full human life, and practical reason can guide action toward them.[25]

Virtue ethics helps us to realize "goods," not only by intellectually identifying them, but by encouraging moral agents to make habits of pursuing "the good," and to enjoy it, as part of a life well lived.

Of course, proponents of virtue should admit that we can be wrong about our concepts of the good. We can also admit that there are many moments of moral complexity (more than what our need for moral certainty would otherwise want). Yet we can also maintain that there are, in some cases, justifiable reasons for naming something as morally good, and that we do so with a moral weight meant to be respected.[26] To pursue virtue, then, is to hold to the ideal that we might come to know what is genuinely praiseworthy and to make habits of such—not with intellectual or moral arrogance, but with a centered conviction that human flourishing is worth our effort, in thought and deed.

Except for the radical postmodernist, then, many of us find good reason to hold that certain things can be reasonably described as either contributing to or detracting from our experience of happiness. Aristotle agreed and taught that in order to know virtue from vice (in part), we must examine the ends of specific human activities and their contribution toward human happiness.[27] For example, the philosopher said that the end of house building would be a livable house; the end of medicine, the reduction of pain, and hopefully, the improvement of health.[28]

The concept of "ends" might be further illuminated by some contemporary examples. Consider athletics. In American football a "good" offensive play is one in which yards are gained, a first down reached, or a field goal scored. These are particular "ends" that contribute toward overall success. Without them, victory could not be enjoyed. The same could be said about the arts. In dance, a "good" routine or performance is one in which individual and coordinated moves contribute to a piece well performed. Morally speaking, "ends" of human activity function in a similar way. As Aristotle wrote, "There is some *end* of everything achievable in action, [and] the good achievable in action will be this *end*; [and] if there are more ends than one, the good achievable in action will be these *ends*."[29] But we must remember that an ethic of virtue concerns itself with "ends" not only as a matter of discerning what is best in a given situation, but also, how that contributes (or not) to our most complete end, human happiness (*eudaimonia*).

Sorting Out Virtue and Vice

When it comes to the enjoyment of living and doing well through the practice of virtue, Aristotle taught that we not only need to know what proper end to pursue, but also what we ought to avoid. Aristotle said that in order to be virtuous at all we must avoid the extremes of any situation: at one end of the extreme, excess, at the other end, deficiency.[30] Avoiding the extremes requires that the practice of virtue take on the character of realizing the "mean" in the choices we make.[31] Some have summarized Aristotle on this aspect of virtue as promoting a general rule of "moderation in everything." This is not wholly wrong, but it does not grasp the nuance of virtue ethics either. In order to avoid excess and deficiency (vice), Aristotle recognized that the moral agent must be attentive to individual context. An example may prove helpful.

Many Americans were shocked to learn that during the 2008 Summer Olympics Michael Phelps needed to consume 12,000 calories a day in order to perform well—and perform well he did![32] But consider that many of us are told by health and nutritional specialists that we need somewhere between 2,000–2,500 calories a day in order to be in good working order (more or less depending on person, body type, and so forth). Imagine if both Michael Phelps and the average American decided to cultivate virtue with respect to eating. In order to do so, Phelps and the average American would need to engage in careful reasoning about what to eat and how it contributes to their bodily needs—and then to eat with proper measure.

Virtue ethics does not provide Phelps and our average American a fixed definition of this virtue chiseled in stone. It requires them both to realize virtue according to their individual contexts. For Phelps to simply copy the eating habits of the average American, he would suffer deficiency. For the average American to simply copy the eating habits of Phelps at the Olympic Games, that person would suffer excess. Virtue, then, is not simply "moderation in everything," as some people say. We learn from this example that virtue, and thus real good, is something that is realized in context and with respect to oneself as a unique individual. Both Phelps and the average American realize the "mean" between excess and deficiency, but they do so in different ways according to the outward appearance of things.

There is an important lesson to be learned in this example that will likely challenge some people's concept of morality. Namely, even though people might possess a common sketch of virtue (one that describes happiness, right reason, "ends," avoiding the extremes, and so forth), we should *not* expect the practice of virtue to be the same in detail for every person. But what we can expect is that virtue will promote a human life well lived.

Virtue and Moral Agency

Since the life of virtue is characterized by making habits of doing the right thing, at the right time, and for the right reason, virtue ethics admits that we are born neither a saint nor a sinner. From this perspective, we are all born (or at least many of us) with the capacity to live and do well, or its opposite.[33] The character we cultivate according to the habits we practice is truly *our* responsibility as moral agents. Aristotle taught that it is simply not possible to stumble upon virtue. We must be intentional in our pursuit of it through careful deliberation, decision, and voluntary effort.[34]

At the same time, Aristotle placed no small emphasis on our ability to cultivate virtue on such things as a good education, living in a just society, and having good examples in our friends and mentors. Thus, in his view, our social environment matters to the cultivation of virtue and the enjoyment of human happiness. In my view, there is no reason to disagree with this insight, generally speaking. But here, again, we cannot read into such descriptions any sense of conventional morality or narrowly defined character types. To draw on Aristotle's insights (well) requires us to avoid reifying old dualisms of who is "in" and "out," "dirty" or "pure." It requires us to think well about the companions and communities we are involved with, and to consider how they contribute to our overall flourishing. To that end, virtue ethics is not an "individualistic" ethic. Virtue ethics considers the whole community to which people belong, and it encourages us to carefully consider the relationship between the individual and the larger social whole. In particular, virtue ethics encourages us to think beyond ourselves and to consider that what we value and how we live creates an interconnected web of social and moral relations that we otherwise call "community." Therefore, to be mindful of virtue is not simply a matter of being "good" oneself (and defining that in absence of wider social relations). Rather, it is to work toward creating a "good" community through our own practice of virtue—and by doing so, to transform the character and norms of the community itself.

Categories of Virtue

Aristotle distinguished between two categories of virtues: those having to do with the intellect (the intellectual virtues), and those having to do with our actions and feelings (the character virtues). In order to enjoy human happiness, Aristotle taught that it is necessary to cultivate and coordinate the intellectual and character virtues. Of course, very few of us would dare to say we have arrived at perfect virtue. But we may find that the *practice* of the virtues contributes to greater levels of happiness. If this is so, then it is worth our time to consider what might count as a particular virtue (in theory), in order to better lean toward the practice of virtue in the choices we make.

The Virtue of Prudence

Chief among the intellectual virtues is the *virtue of prudence*. Prudence is the virtue of reasoning well about the truth of things, and in particular, about what counts as a good end in a given situation.[35] The virtue of prudence is the habit of "right reason" necessary for happiness to be enjoyed at all.[36] As the religious ethicist Diana Cates notes, prudence is cultivated by learning to reason as one who is wise, and to choose as a wise person would choose.[37]

In theory, the virtue of prudence habituates us to reason well so that we more easily apprehend that which is good to pursue in any number of possible situations. Admittedly, sorting out what counts as a particular good "end" to pursue is where disagreements abound. But virtue ethics helps us to think about the pursuit of good "ends" by demanding that what we choose can be shown to contribute to our overall happiness or flourishing. As we have already seen, this includes prudential reflection on avoiding the extremes of excess and deficiency in any given situation. It also requires prudential reflection according to our given personal contexts. Therefore, the very process of discerning what counts as excess, and what contributes to flourishing, requires careful reflection.

In my view, discerning good "ends" of human activity is something that is now more verifiable than ever. But it requires us to bridge ethics and scientific inquiry. Namely, I do not think that we can afford to ignore the correlation (at least generally) between what is healthy for human beings—mentally, socially, and physically—and what is usually good, morally. To "live and do well" cannot, as I have said, ignore our creaturely nature. Christian ethicists Patricia Jung and Aana Marie Vigen have made this point well. Jung and Vigen say (and I agree) that well-tested and reasonable descriptions of human well-being should be resources that we consult when constructing our accounts of living and doing well (morally).[38] Thus, as we defer to prudence in order to think well about what a happy life, we will do ourselves a favor by consulting all of those disciplines of knowledge that reveal critical insights about human health and well-being (mindful that issues of health and well-being are often unique to individual contexts).

I believe this approach is a key that will unlock at least some of our moral disputes. To genuinely emphasize prudence is to think carefully about what *actually* contributes to human happiness. In order to do this we must have accurate descriptions of what is possible for the human being, not only generically for the species, but more specifically, for the person. Scientific insight is therefore relevant because it provides increasingly accurate descriptions of the natural functions of human beings, whether as a species or of a given person when individually studied. As science yields more accurate descriptions of human "nature," we can prudentially reflect on that information in order to consider what might help us to live and do well according to the ends that are "good" for us to pursue. Of course, even when armed with scientific data, not everyone will recognize our claims to prudential reasoning. What is more, we have to be careful not to conflate what is "given" or "natural" with what is "good" morally (even if such end up correlating from time to time). This view on prudence and science has strong implications for any discussion on sexual morality.

Namely, in order to talk about sexual virtue, it will be necessary for us to practice the virtue of prudence and to think well about what counts as right ends to pursue, in order to flourish as sexual/human beings. The kind of data we need to think about the actualization of our sexual flourishing are available to us, in part, from the social and natural sciences. While we must ethically interpret the data of the sciences, we cannot ignore this information either.

Turning a blind eye to well-tested scientific insight on sexuality artificially narrows what prudence can apprehend about the contribution of sexuality to human happiness. Of course, science has not always yielded accurate descriptions of human sexuality. When we examine the scientific libraries of the eighteenth, nineteenth, and early twentieth centuries, we can find disturbing diagnoses and practices. Psychologist and psychiatrist Christopher Ryan and Cacilda Jethá give some harrowing examples. They note that when masturbation was commonly regarded as a moral offense—and a threat to physical health—one notorious doctor would suture the foreskin of adolescent boys' penises (with silver wire, no less) in order to prevent erections and masturbation.[39] By the hand of the same physician, women too would have their clitorises burned away with certain acids to avoid the pleasures of clitoral orgasm.[40] In addition to these disturbing examples, we know that homosexuality was once generally diagnosed as a disorder, something to be cured through any number of reparative therapies—therapies now regarded by most specialists as unproductive at best, damaging at worst. But in spite of these errors, we can also say that the nature of science is to refute its findings until reliable theories are sustainable, and facts verifiable. Therefore, while the sciences have not been perfect, they've sought out accuracy, and we have benefited from the long arc of the scientific method. Generations after us will benefit from even more accurate descriptions.

But allow me to repeat: these comments are not made from the perspective that science—of itself—will necessarily tell us what is morally good. But science does help to reveal what is possible for human beings, and from this information we can consider what it means for us to live and do well as the kind of creatures that we are. The moral evaluation of our creaturely nature belongs to the virtue of prudence. Thus, in my view, as prudence is informed by the sciences, it will allow us to boldly seek out sexual ends that help us to actualize our potentiality for living and doing well as sexual beings. It will also empower us to question definitions of sexual virtue that stretch rational credibility. But reflexively, an emphasis on prudence requires that our sexual ethic be one that is open to ongoing reflection on what "ends" of sexuality demonstrably contribute to the overall happiness (*eudemonia*) of human beings. The virtue of prudence will keep us permeable to insights borne from new data about the human/sexual condition. It will allow us to pursue whatever turns out to be truly good for our flourishing, instead of simply enfolding ourselves in tradition or dogma, which tend to be impermeable and closed to newly discovered or proposed truths.

Character Virtues

In coordination with the virtue of prudence (and the other intellectual virtues) are the *character virtues*. These virtues have to do with our actions and feelings. Aristotle taught that we should cultivate these virtues so that we might learn to act according to reason, and not simply to "act out" from basic inclination, appetite, or emotional response. This category of virtue is important insofar as we are not just rational creatures, but also embodied sensory beings that are drawn toward certain objects on a sensory level (for example, by appetite) and repulsed by others. Appetites and other feelings do not have built-in moral governors, and so it is necessary for us to learn to respond well to our appetites and inclinations—insofar as that is possible.

Therefore, while the virtue of prudence may illuminate for us what count as good ends to pursue, we need to *practice* virtue. It is not enough that prudence helps us to see (intellectually) what we ought to do. In addition to this intellectual sight, we must (where we can) make good habits of responding to our desires, according to the light of reason. Because prudence is the virtue that assigns "ends" for the character virtues, Aristotle actually included prudence as a character virtue, as well as bravery, temperance, generosity, magnificence, magnanimity, mildness, friendliness, wit, and justice.[41]

The Moral Dimensions of our Appetites and Emotions

Cultivating the character virtues requires careful attention. As humans we have a range of feelings, some we call appetites, others we call passions. In coordination with what we value consciously, we experience these appetites and passions as a broad range of emotions. While I am sensitive that some of our appetitive and emotional experiences are complex and deeply personal (for which mental health care specialists are better suited to give advice), many of us can work on our more manageable appetites, as well as our impulses to respond from certain emotional states.[42] We might sympathize with one another, then, that we sometimes indulge particular appetites, or act out from certain emotions, without reflecting on them mindfully. For example, the anger one might feel when cut off in traffic might not be the best emotional reaction when considering what is actually happening. The driver who just cut you off might be on the way to the hospital because her partner is in labor prematurely. Or, in another case, the driver's son is severely wounded and in need of medical attention. Given new information about a situation might change some of our emotional responses—at least the kind that are permeable by new insights.[43]

And yet, when we do act more from appetite, or from emotional impulse, reason is still present. So we face an important question: Why do we engage in activity that we otherwise know is toward the wrong "end," ill-timed, simply responsive, or even inordinate?

An answer from the perspective of virtue ethics is that human beings sometimes consent to certain appetites or passions where the character virtues are not fully present.[44] In these moments we do so under the impression that satisfying our desires will result in a momentary experience of happiness—without much thought for what other consequences may follow. In these instances we abdicate the authority of right reason to an appetite or passion, which in themselves have no foresight. Acting directly from feelings of hunger, sexual attraction, anger, and thirst (among others) *does not* necessarily promote the kind of behavior that represents our human best. But admitting this does not mean that the emotions (or sensory appetites) are problems to cure.

Instead, we can say that our appetites are natural to us as human beings, and our emotions hold a central place in human life. For example, our appetites can (though not always) signal those things we need to meet our basic creaturely needs. What is more, our feelings sometimes disclose, more accurately than our words, *what* and *who* we value. Without question, then, our appetites and feelings are very important to the coordination of a human life, well lived. But because of the indiscriminate nature of appetites, not to mention the strength of our passions, we can also say that the light of reason helps us to respond to our inclinations and emotions—at least, as that is possible. We do this so that we are not tossed to and fro by emotional states, which often result in activities that have less than consistent (or desirable) consequences. Just as an excellent athlete or artist must train, so too the character virtues help us to respond well to many of our emotional states. The character virtues help us to better reflect on certain situations, so that our actions and feelings benefit from the light of reason. Indeed, the character virtues actually help us to better enjoy the practice of virtue, insofar as the character virtues help us to take pleasure in the right thing, at the right time, and for the right reason. Namely, as we come to genuinely take pleasure in the practice of virtue, we will likely find that our enjoyment of it will help us to choose the "good," especially when other options are best avoided.

This is an insight that I believe is important to contemporary reflection on sexual morality. All too often we have settled for the lowest common denominator of sexual ethics, according to the mantra of "do no harm." That is, of course, the right place to begin when seeking out sexual relationships. But the standard of "do no harm" may not help us to think carefully about more complex matters related to human sexuality. For example, as it often happens in our culture, people may find it possible to "hook up" with relative ease, according to the want (or appetite) for sexual pleasure. What is more, people may be able to do so with mutual intentions to "do no harm." Clearing that moral hurdle is indeed good. But if that is the only moral concern we hold, then we might fail to consider whether "hooking up" in that situation, or in others, is actually beneficial to our pursuit of human happiness. Surely (or hopefully), a "hookup" is pleasurable. But what about other important matters involved with sex, like affection, fantasy, play, self-worth, health, human relations, social justice, and prudence (to name a few)? I am not convinced that "do no harm" helps us to navigate the morality of sex beyond the requirement of mutuality. What is more, I'm not convinced that navigating the morality of sex is something we should do on our own (i.e., make up on our own), under the guise of "privacy." Surely, we can have public conversations about sexual morality in the spirit of prudential reflection and care for human flourishing—and surely, at least some of these conversations will help us to better discern when sexual activity does (and does not) contribute to our living and doing well. My suggestion, then, is that we turn from moral minimalism and embrace the concept of sexual virtue, in order that we might mindfully (and graciously) discern "ends" of human sexuality, which will help us to enjoy sexual pleasures as one part of our overall goal of enjoying human happiness (i.e., living and doing well).

Temperance and Sexual Virtue

Aristotle taught that it is through the cultivation of the character virtue of temperance (in coordination with the virtue of prudence) that moral agents are able to practice sexual virtue. According to Aristotle, temperance is the virtue concerned with desires for the pleasures of touch. Because our sensory desires for the pleasures of touch are indiscriminate on their own, cultivating a virtue (temperance) that helps us to act well from our desires for pleasure (toward the right thing, at the right time, and for the right reason) is something that many people will agree is important in the pursuit of happiness. Aristotle said that the virtue of temperance specifically has to do with the desires for pleasures of touch in eating, drinking, and sexual activity. When we fail to practice the virtue of temperance in matters related to these, Aristotle said that we become like beasts when we are excessive and we are insensible when we are deficient.[45]

To recognize that our sensory desires for the pleasures of touch are "indiscriminate" is not to also suggest that there is something wrong with desires for pleasure, or pleasures themselves. Such pleasures naturally occur with much of our eating, drinking, and sexual activity. What is more, it should only be expected that the experience of sensory pleasure will lead us to desire more of it. As I noted in the last chapter, I agree with the sexual ethicist Christine Gudorf, that pleasure is a premoral good. Recall, then, the insight from Gudorf that "a premoral good does not mean that it leads to moral good [necessarily] but that it is ordinarily good, and should be understood as one aspect of the general social good."[46] Because pleasure is a premoral good, our desire for pleasure requires that we choose *well* in our pursuit of it, insofar as the desire for pleasure itself doesn't help us to know (specifically) what is best to choose in a given situation. Gudorf agreed with this insight, but asked us to navigate the pursuit of pleasure according to a utilitarian calculus of pleasures and pains, in light of other human responsibilities and duties.[47] But from the perspective of virtue, pleasure is approached somewhat differently.

Aristotle noted that feelings of pleasure are natural to us as the kind of creatures that we are. But he also noted that pleasures (and pains) *accompany* activities.[48] The problem, said the philosopher, is that humans sometimes get into the habit of simply repeating what has felt good to us, without thought for what leads to our actual happiness. If for no other reason, we tend to associate the experience of pleasure with happiness itself. Therefore, in order to enjoy pleasure in ways that contribute to our living and doing well, the virtue of temperance is assigned in order to illuminate why we pursue the pleasures of food, drink, and sex, and how the experience of these pleasures can contribute to our genuine happiness (or flourishing) as human beings.

Recall, however, that we want to experience pleasure is not the problem. As the philosopher noted, "The base person is [only considered] base because he pursues the excess, but not because he pursues the necessary pleasures; for all enjoy delicacies and wines and sexual relations in some way, though not all in the right way."[49] Thus, the question from the perspective of virtue ethics is not whether we should enjoy pleasure; the question is whether we should pursue a pleasurable activity in a given situation, and then toward what end.[50] Notice, then, that this view does not allow us to assign pleasure as *the* criterion of sexual morality.

Yes, we pursue pleasurable sexual activities. But as human beings with complex desires and needs, we pursue such pleasurable activities in coordination with other ends. For example, when we pursue a pleasurable sexual experience, we are likely doing more than just "seeking pleasure." We are likely pursuing pleasurable sexual activity for certain reasons, perhaps intimacy, play, fantasy fulfillment, and so forth. Thus, the pursuit of temperance—as the practice of sexual virtue—requires us to identify and realize certain "ends" that contribute to our happiness as sexual/human beings.

Aristotle had high praise for people who practice the virtue of temperance. The philosopher taught that such virtuous people are known because they do not take pleasure in that which is excessive, nor do these people refrain from enjoying natural pleasures when these are ordered toward good ends. Indeed, Aristotle argued (generally) that people who practice the virtue of temperance will rightly desire anything that is "pleasant and conducive to health or fitness" or "anything else that is pleasant," so long as these contribute to living and doing well.[51]

If we focus our thinking about temperance with respect to the cultivation of sexual virtue, Aristotle's insights are helpful for *innovative* moral reflection. Drawing loosely on Aristotle's definition of temperance, I propose that our understanding of sexual virtue should start with the recognition that sexual activity is pursued well when we are not driven only by our desires for sexual pleasure. We can admit to the premoral good of sexual pleasure, but we need more than that to determine if pleasurable sexual activity is being pursued in the right places, at the right time, with the right people, and for the right reasons. So, for example, sexual virtue would not be practiced by those who engage in activities that maliciously detract from one's life or health, or the life and health of another. Likewise, sexual virtue would not be practiced by those who fail to see their sexual partners as full human persons deserving complete respect, dignity, and autonomy. On the other hand, sexual virtue *would* be practiced by those individuals who desire and enjoy the pleasures of sexual activity, and then in ways that realize recognizable human goods.

Of course, such a statement demands an answer to the question: Toward what justifiable end or ends should we act when motivated by the desire for sexual pleasure? A compelling answer will be one in which the end or ends we name can be shown to contribute to genuine human happiness (i.e., living and doing well). And yet, according to a number of scholars, Aristotle's answer (in part) was that sexual pleasures were of a lower sort, and sexual intercourse itself was closer to animal behavior than something distinctively human (i.e., rational).[52] However, Aristotle did recognize procreation as a good end of sexual activity, and he tended to favor it as an expression of sexual virtue between men and women. His other views on sexual activity are either lost to history or his comments (ranging from rather neutral statements to negative judgments) are specific to particular examples.[53]

We need not, however, seek to piece together Aristotle's own conclusions about sexual morality. Our goal is to define sexual virtue in light of what we now understand about human sexuality. While the scholar of Aristotle may wish to debate the philosopher on the merits of his moral conclusions, we are pursuing a contemporary definition of sexual virtue. Indeed, we do well to turn from Aristotle's particular conclusions, as twenty-first-century educated people tend to know more about human sexuality than the philosopher did. To limit ourselves to his moral understanding of human sexuality would be a peculiar choice. If for no other reason, most modern thinkers do not sustain his circumscribed views on any number of social issues (e.g., we do not accept his view that women are inferior to men). Thus, as we must do with many historical figures, it is important to glean what is valuable from the philosopher's moral theory, and then reapply those principles within our own context.

Reapproaching Sexual Virtue

As a matter of thinking about sexuality in our time, I suggest we should review what we know about human sexuality that the philosopher did not. For example, we might start with our modern understanding(s) of sexual diversity. Peer-reviewed scientific studies in psychology, genetics, and the social sciences have all indicated that there is a spectrum of innate sexual inclinations, basic to the human condition. These motivate the desire for sexual relating between human beings.[54] What is more, the inclinations have been categorized (generally speaking) according to heterosexual, homosexual, and bisexual orientations. According to these categories, many of us have constructed social identities as "straight, gay, lesbian, or bisexual" people. Of course, there are people who do not identify with any of these orientation groups, but for many of us, these social-sexual identities reflect deep and central truths about our sexual and relational lives.

Although there are diverse sexual orientations and identities, there seem to be shared sexual realities between people, as a matter of being human. That is to say, even though the directionality of our individual sexuality (homo-, hetero-, or bi-) may be different from one another, "how" the basic components of human sexuality work—and what value we assign to sexual acts—can be quite similar. This includes the experience of having sexual inclination, or attraction, generally speaking. Sexual attraction is a powerful emotion, and it can be empowering. We experience this on intellectual and sensory levels, the coordination of which defies simple explanation. But we can say that sexual attraction (whether for the same sex, different, or both) arouses distinctive aspects of our body and mind. It motivates and inspires certain curiosities and fantasies. It also motivates us to pursue a wide variety of sexual activities that realize some of our deepest (and most natural) human longings, both biologically and psychologically speaking.[55] Indeed, our sexual desires often move us to seek other people not only as those who appear suitable to us on a sensory level, but who we also regard as valuable sexual partners, in various and meaningful sexual acts or relationships.

The meanings of our sexual acts are multivalent:

Sexual activity can be *communicative*.[56] It can be a symbol through which we express meaningful feelings toward other people.

Human sexual activity can be *recreational*.[57] It can be a mode of play in which we delight in one another as human/

sexual beings; enjoying one another through bodily contact, without reducing ourselves or a sexual partner to a
simple instrument for self-gratification.

Human sexual activity can be a form of *disclosure*. It can be
a way of knowing and being known.[58]

It can be energetically *generative*. It can be engaged in such a
way as to renew our sense of vitality, life, and joy.[59]

Human sexuality can also be generative in a *procreative* sense.
That is, we can choose to exercise the reproductive powers
of sexuality.

The above statements are largely gleaned from the social and
natural sciences, and therefore they do not tell us, specifically, what is
in fact morally good to pursue in a given situation. But as I have said,
we cannot reflect accurately on "living and doing well" in the *moral*
sense without also reflecting on what the sciences teach. If for no other
reason, the sciences better reveal to us how we function as human/
sexual beings: psychologically, socially, and biologically. Denying that
the sciences help us to know more about human sexuality and sexual
flourishing is, in my view, arbitrarily dismissive of volumes of literature
and scientific study.

The sciences *do* help us to understand ourselves as sexual beings.
They give us handles for better grasping the complexities of our sexuality. This in turn allows us to think about how we might best order our
sexual lives according to what is in fact possible in light of a person's
given sexual "nature." Thus, I agree with the religious ethicist John
McNeill, who once concluded that what is good for us in a therapeutic
sense sexually, will *likely* be part of what contributes to our moral excellence as well.[60]

Thinking in these terms, I suggest that there at least three possible
"ends" of sexual virtue: *recreation, relational intimacy,* and *selective acts
of procreation.* While there may be other ends that could be proposed,
these three appear to be reasonable candidates to aim at, especially in
light of our modern understandings about the multifaceted nature of
human sexuality. Namely, they are ends which are not only "possible"
for us to pursue, according to our creaturely nature as human beings,
but "ends" that can also be good for us in the moral sense—whether
we pursue them one at a time or in coordination, and then, in various
kinds of sexual relationships (long or short term). To do so will require
prudential reflection.

However, I am not suggesting that these "ends" should be pursued by everyone. Rather, I am claiming that these ends appear to be "goods" that we can pursue in sexual activity, and that with more analysis (in later chapters), we can make the case that they help us to realize sexual virtue. However, if we name sexual "ends" to pursue, the corollary suggests that there may be good reasons, in some cases, *not* to pursue sexual activities, even if they might yield us some immediate sensory or psychological pleasure. But we need good reasons for holding back from otherwise pleasant sexual experiences. Virtue ethics helps us in this regard. Namely, an ethic of virtue invites us to think about sexual pleasures and relationships beyond the immediate gratification of sexual pleasure, and to think about how our sexual lives contribute to our happiness. Virtue ethics invites us, then, to imagine that our sexual activities and relationships can be emblematic of the "good." That said, I am not suggesting that sexual virtue should be imagined through a narrow lens. I want to lift up the possibility that many of the sexual activities and relationships that have been condemned as "unnatural" or "immoral" (according to traditional norms) could actually be expressions of sexual virtue in light of my proposed "ends." If we dare to give prudence the whole landscape of human sexuality, we must consider a wide variety of possibilities, and then recognize "the good" wherever it appears.

Conclusion

Admittedly, my sense of what might count as "ends" of sexual virtue will be contested. To be sure, we will do more analysis on recreation, relational intimacy, and selective acts of procreation in later chapters. But before we do this, I need to address a primary reason why many people will initially disagree with this list of "ends." Insofar as right reason is necessary in order to name legitimate ends of sexual virtue, a number of people will tell us that reason is incomplete without insights from sources of religious authority. As many religious people will argue, reason only reveals so much about morality. God, they will say, has not only assigned the "ends" that we ought to pursue in life, but also those things that we ought to avoid. Many of these religious people will also tell us that it is only when we accept our God-given limitations and imperatives that we will at last be able to live and do well as human beings.

As one might expect, this includes matters of human sexuality.

Because my goal is to articulate an ethic of sexual virtue within a Christian framework, I am interested to know how religious insights from Christianity can shape concepts of virtue. There is perhaps no better example of Christian virtue ethics than the one articulated by the systematic theologian Thomas Aquinas. In the next chapter, we will turn to insights from Aquinas, who will help us to see what it is that we will have to attend to if an ethic of virtue is going to be meaningful to Christians at all. At minimum, it will require that we move beyond claims about the insights and demands of right reason alone, and to put these in conversation with the theological authorities of a religious worldview (specifically a Christian worldview), which can—and do—reshape a definition of virtue and its practice.

Four

Christian Virtue Ethics

Many of us have left the faith communities of our childhood because of the abusive ways in which these doctrines have been used against us.

—Patrick Cheng

A Brief Reflection on Christian Ethics

The activity of ethics takes place within a variety of contexts, including religious ones. This is true in any number of our world's religious traditions, and it certainly has been important to the institutional life of Christianity. Much like philosophical ethics, Christian ethics seeks to define the meaning and value of human life through critical reflection on the moral realm, but as uniquely informed by Christian principles. But asking Christians to agree on what those principles are, or how they should be applied, is another matter altogether.

Approaches to Christian ethics are as diverse as there are different kinds of Christians—and yet, there are some distinguishing features. Scripture, church teaching, reason, and experience are commonly acknowledged as the sources of religious authority in Christian ethics, whether among Catholics or Protestants.[1] In light of these sources, moral norms in Christian communities are argued, settled, and revisited. Of course, these sources of authority are interpreted, respected, and weighted differently, and this often reflects matters of denominational and theological distinction.[2] Indeed, the particular sources people draw upon in Christian ethics (and how they do so) will have substantial effect on *what* in human life is said to resonate with—or fall short—of the reign of God.

Christian ethics, however, is not merely interpreting scripture or church teaching to one's own moral satisfaction on particular issues. It also attends to how one thinks about morality more broadly. This includes reflecting on what should count as strengths of character, whether or not humans have any rights or obligations, as well as a wide variety of other moral matters not always explained in Christianity's authoritative sources. We ought not be surprised to learn, then, that in the history of Christian ethics theoretical approaches to morality have also varied. For some, this has meant enfolding Christian ethics around a rubric of law or duty.[3] It has also included an approach to Christian morality through an ethic of virtue.

There is perhaps no better example of Christian virtue ethics than the one provided by the medieval theologian Thomas Aquinas. While many significant church figures (both Catholic and Protestant) have leaned on concepts of virtue, it was Aquinas who (arguably) provided the most detailed explanation of virtue ethics within a Christian framework. It is in his consummate work, *The Summa Theologica*, that Aquinas demonstrates how many of the concepts of Aristotle's virtue ethics make sense in light of Christian faith.

In this chapter, I will draw on the teachings of Aquinas in the same spirit I drew upon Aristotle. Namely, I do not seek to represent all of Aquinas's teachings, nor advocate all of his conclusions—nor even to engage his many interpreters. But I do wish to draw on Aquinas to show the reader how an ethic of virtue might be qualified by a Christian world-view. Because Aquinas drew on Aristotle's teachings about virtue, I will streamline the theoretical description of virtue ethics, especially where the ideas are similar to what we have already interpreted from Aristotle. But where theological differences emerge, I will invite the reader to consider these more carefully, and then in light of contemporary issues. I do this to show the reader how certain Christian perspectives must be considered if an ethic of virtue—especially sexual virtue—is going to be compelling to Christians at all.

As the reader will soon see, Aquinas's approach to morality sets the stage for us to think new thoughts about sexual virtue in light of Christian faith. Of course, there are always limitations to any moral framework, and I do recognize that even the best of Aquinas's insights may not speak to the concerns (or questions) of other disciplines. But I believe there are principles to be wrestled with in his moral theology that can help mediate at least some of our debates about sexual morality, especially from the Christian perspectives that dominate so much of contemporary discourse on the subject.

Christianity and Virtue Ethics:
Living and Doing Well in the Reign of God

Natural and Supernatural Happiness

The insight from Aristotelian virtue ethics that human happiness is best defined as "living and doing well" is something that most Christians can affirm. Living and doing well appeals to cultivating the best of ourselves and to being excellent in all that we can be. Even so, the Christian narrative does not end with living and doing well on a natural level. It declares that there is a higher end, God, to whom all things should tend. Framed this way, the highest form of happiness that a person could imagine—according to a Christian worldview—is happiness with God. That is, living and doing well in relation to God. This is the view of Thomas Aquinas, who taught that if a person is going to live by an ethic of virtue and enjoy the highest form of happiness, it cannot be according to the rule of reason alone (although on the natural level that is part of it), but it is also and more deeply a way of functioning morally in relationship to God, who makes it possible for one to exist at all.

According to Aquinas, there are two kinds of happiness. The first is natural happiness. It is achievable by right reason when we cultivate the natural virtues (such as the ones outlined by Aristotle). The second kind is supernatural happiness. According to Aquinas, this happiness is experienced when a person enjoys friendship with God.[4] But the problem, he taught, is that human beings do not experience God perfectly in this life, and this is due to sin. Because of the disturbing effects of sin, Aquinas did not expect complete friendship with God until the life to come.[5] And yet, Aquinas still believed that a measure of supernatural happiness could be had in this life. According to Aquinas, God makes such friendship possible by infusing humans with faith, hope, and love. These are qualities of the Christian life that were first articulated by the apostle Paul in the New Testament (1 Corinthians 13:13), but which Aquinas designated as the theological virtues.[6]

Just as the natural virtues are good habits that order us toward human flourishing, Aquinas taught that the theological virtues are good habits that allow us to enjoy happiness insofar as we are ordered toward God. For that to be possible, Aquinas taught that the virtue of faith is given to humans, by God, so that we can understand what God has revealed. Since God is supernatural, some of the "revealed" truths about

God exceed reason's natural powers of apprehension (for example: incar-
nation, grace, atonement, etc.). Reason does not "see" all the truths
about God. Faith does, and so it is by faith and through faith that
humans are able to contemplate the things of God. For Aquinas, then,
faith is the infused habit of assenting to the truth of what has been
divinely revealed. For example: assenting to the truth of some scripture
or an official church teaching. In addition to faith, Aquinas said that
hope is also a virtue given by God so that humans might continue to
tend toward God. This virtue is important, as Aquinas acknowledged
that there are many difficult situations in life that might persuade people
to tend away from God (who at times seems far away, or unreal). In
Aquinas's imagination, then, hope is the infused habit that keeps people
anchored in their faith, and thus ordered toward God—even when that
is difficult. Finally, Aquinas taught that God infuses the virtue of love,
which itself is characterized as unconditional loving friendship. This
infused love disposes humans to love God, oneself, as well as other
human beings.

A Qualification: The Possibility of Virtue without Faith

This religious view has interesting implications for how a person lives
life, morally speaking. How we apprehend God by faith (if we do), what
we believe it means to tend toward God (hope), as well as what we say
it means to live according to the reign of God, and in friendship with
God (love), will qualify what it is we count as living and doing well.
In particular, if we accept Aquinas's reassessment of human happiness as
twofold, some Christians may find that the idea of friendship with God
demands things that natural happiness does not. Reflect, for example, on
seasons of religious fasting, such as the Muslim observance of Ramadan
or the Christian penitentiary weeks of Lent—neither of which would
be practiced except for faith in God, for reasons of spiritual discipline.
Likewise, we might consider vows of poverty, monastic community, or
celibacy, which (for some) are vows motivated by a sense of who God
is and what God demands of a "religious" life.

Not one of these examples is essentially grounded in a concern
for human happiness, or flourishing, by reason alone. These, and other
examples of human activity (or inactivity), are shaped uniquely by one's
sense of what it means to be happy with God. As a result, the distinction between supernatural and natural happiness opens a special query

to Christian reflection on human morality. Namely, if one were to agree with Aquinas that faith, hope, and love are given by God so that human beings can live and do well, as creatures of God, what about those who do not believe, or who do not believe in the same way? As we shall soon see, considering this question will be fundamental to establishing how, and in what way, Christians can dialogue about sexual morality. I invite us, then, to explore a nagging theological question in Christianity—whether one needs to be a Christian in order to be good.

In our own day, especially in the context of American public discourse, we find some Christians making the outrageous claim that a person cannot cultivate morality, or serve as a good political leader, apart from identification as a Christian—or for that matter, a particular kind of Christian.[7] This has been a problem for American Christians struggling with ethics and social order for as long as the country has existed. For instance, we know—in one long and very embarrassing example—that nineteenth-century American Catholics often suffered prejudice at the hands of their Protestant neighbors. This prejudice was not merely a matter of theological difference. There was, at the time, a real *social* fear among many Protestants that American Catholics would advance an ethos and lifestyle more in line with the dictates of the pope (a foreign leader) rather than support the emerging American identity and culture, ordered toward democratic liberties.

To make matters worse, such American Protestants advanced a slippery slope argument that the religious and moral teachings of the Roman Catholic Church would uproot and destroy the decency and democracy of the new American nation.[8] In one instance, President Ulysses Grant gave a speech in which he derided Catholic teaching and Catholic schools as centers of superstition, which did nothing to edify the nation.[9] In another case, James Garfield (before his presidency) presented Catholic immigrants as a threat to "modern civilization."[10] Indeed, throughout the nineteenth century, the generalized fear was that the foreign hierarchy of the Roman Catholic Church (and their teachings) represented one of the greatest challenges to the American pursuit of individual liberty and the common moral good. This fear continued into the twentieth century, perhaps most notably directed against John F. Kennedy, who as a presidential candidate (and later president) would have to assure voters that his non-Protestant Christian identification in no way disqualified him as a person of good character or a reliable civil servant.

To this day, particular expressions of Christian privilege continue to play out in American moral and political discourse. For example, even the two-time conservative presidential candidate Mitt Romney had to face serious questions about his viability for the presidency, simply because of his Mormon faith. Knowing that both his moral character and his political integrity were under question, Romney said in 2007, "It is important to recognize that while differences in theology exist between the churches in America, we share a common creed of moral convictions. And where the affairs of our nation are concerned, it's usually a sound rule to focus on the latter—on the great moral principles that urge us all on a common course."[11] Romney's comments are well said, except that he too would go on to use his own moral and faith perspectives to define some of the social policies of his political campaign, but without also engaging in constructive dialogue with those who held opposite views.

For example, in 2012, Romney would go on to support the idea of a federal constitutional amendment that would ban civil/legal marriage equality for same-sex couples.[12] He did so as a matter of moral, political, and religious conviction. And yet, in the same year, more than half of Americans supported marriage equality: morally, politically, and/or religiously.[13] But wherever support for equality was advanced, certain religious and political groups (usually aligned with Romney) claimed that the equality view was nothing less than a war on "traditional" marriage and family. On one side, then, mainline to progressive Christians called for inclusivity, as well as equality under the law. On the other side, conservative to fundamentalist Christians insisted that their "traditional" definition of marriage and family was not only better, but necessary for the American nation to survive. To my knowledge, no significant effort was made to address these differences through bipartisan summits, religiously or politically.

These disagreements demonstrate to us that moral issues can (and do) become partisan wedges when religious people believe that their *faith* gives them access to a better view of morality and social order. As a result, many people have used their faith as a platform to discredit other views instead of drawing on their faith as a perspective from which one might engage in meaningful moral discourse (and ethical critique). Fortunately, there are other options for people of faith to consider. Indeed, I suggest that Aquinas's moral framework might help Christians to understand why defensiveness and dismissive attitudes need not be one's initial inclinations in the face of theological and moral disagreements.

First of all, Aquinas's moral framework dismantles the idea that accepting Christian perspectives is necessary for reliable moral insight.

According to the theologian, a person will *not* be lost to utter immorality if not a Christian him- or herself. Even though Aquinas was deeply convinced of his religious worldview, the theologian also taught that people who stand apart from Christianity are certainly capable of achieving natural virtue, and thus natural happiness, which is to live and do well according to the light of reason through the cultivation of the natural virtues.[14] For Aquinas, even though humans suffer from the marring effects of sin, he did not think that sin had so ruined the human creature that we are without some reliable use of our natural faculties.

I interpret Aquinas to mean that even though Christians need to take the category of "sin" seriously, it would be a mistake for Christians to say that God has utterly abandoned humans to sin (or total ruin), or that humans are incapable of discerning any moral goods, unless they accept the Christian faith. For Aquinas, it was rather obvious that the practice of natural virtue is not something closed off to those who do not identify as Christian. If for no other reason, those who are committed to an ethic of virtue can admit that whenever right reason (prudence) is exercised—regardless of a person's religious commitments—it can uncover real human goods and facilitate human happiness, naturally speaking.[15] But as we saw in the last chapter, prudence requires intellectual spaciousness. Recall, in fact, that prudence welcomes diverse perspectives to be considered before coming to moral conclusions. This is true not only for those enlightened by reason alone, but also for people of faith. However, the subject of sexual morality has often been denied such prudential spaciousness, especially in Christian ethics. Oftentimes Christians find themselves deeply divided over standards of sexual morality because they are ideologically welded to their own interpretations of religious texts or traditions, which in turn can prompt a dismissive attitude toward other points of view. But Aquinas's moral theory actually invites Christians to put contrasting perspectives in dialogue first, before assuming that those who disagree with us are lost to immorality.

In fact, Aquinas's very style of arguing was to articulate a number of positions that were not his own, respond with what he took to be the right answer, and then consider replies to possible objections.[16] In my view, Christians would do well to resurrect that kind of ethical discourse, and to grant many voices seats at the table of ethics, instead of perpetuating the authoritarian monologue of supposed orthodoxy. Of course, there will always be some people who will refuse the intellectually rich method of prudential thinking. For example, there are some Christians who insist that apart from faith in God through Christ, people are trapped in sin and therefore have a fatally flawed view of all things, whether about truth, moral goods, or human happiness. For Christians such as these, reason is remarkably untrustworthy, especially the reasoning of non-Christians—or even the reasoning of people who have contrasting religious views. But such a position is not very realistic, nor defensible.

It would be very difficult to show evidence, for example, that secular humanists, Muslims, Hindus, or Buddhists *all* utterly fail at rationality, or morality, when compared to Christians. As a matter of fact, the majority of people on earth do not profess Christianity—and many of these, if not most, are more than just minimally decent members of the global community. Indeed, it is no secret that a great number of non-Christians outshine the morality of those who claim to be followers of Christ. What is more, there is such a wide variety of Christian denominations that it is more accurate to say there are *Christianities*, and thus there are multiple Christian ethics to consider (some surely better than others, in terms of theological and philosophical consistency, cogency, etc.).

Our day-to-day experience tells us rather plainly that a lack of faith in Christ (or an absence of allegiance to a particular church) does not render a person morally evil, nor without the capacity to cultivate real and recognizable virtue. All we should expect, then, is that there may be times when a person who operates by reason alone (or by any other religious view) will come into conflict with how certain Christian perspectives shape or define the practice of virtue. When that happens, we might simply have to admit that one's theological understanding of Christian source material (which shapes definitions of faith, hope, and love) may so qualify one's definition of virtue that agreement (or convincing another) may sometimes prove difficult.

Even though there are situations like these, there will be other times when the person of reason and the person of faith will find significant rational agreement on what is right to pursue in a given situation—and therefore, what counts as virtuous and good. And so, even as theological commitments will uniquely shape one's sense of virtue, the Christian community should *not* expect that the virtues acquired by reason alone will be unrecognizable to people of faith. Described this way, Christian ethics need not be conceived as a discipline that is opposed to rational reflection, nor do we need to assume that engaging ethics through Christian perspectives must exclude other religious and philosophical points of view.

The Theological Virtues: Additional Comments

However, even if Christian ethics can admit to the need for dialogue and spaciousness, the claim that Christians have special insight due to faith, hope, and love is one that we need to qualify. Namely, there is a specter of arrogance in the suggestion that Christians are uniquely infused with virtues from God. Such a teaching might prompt—in some—a sense of moral superiority according to religious identity. We should resist thinking about the infusion of the theological virtues so literally. When Christians awake to the theological virtues, it is usually not a mystical event, but a process mediated through religious formation, and then within particular curriculums of Christian education. These rely very heavily on inherited interpretations of sacred texts and theological traditions. Thus, any curriculum of Christian education represents only one of many views. We also ought to restate the obvious: Christians most certainly do not have a perfect understanding of what it means to live and do well according to the virtues of faith, hope, and love. While faith, hope, and love ultimately shape the Christian's worldview and practice, these virtues are always defined and mediated through human interpretation and personal agency.

A Brief Summary of Aquinas on Virtue, in a Christian Framework

According to Aquinas, then, a Christian worldview can admit to three categories of virtue. In his categorization of the virtues, Aquinas acknowledged the previously mentioned theological virtues, consisting of faith, hope, and love. But he also included Aristotle's categories of the intellectual and moral virtues.

Prudence and the Intellectual Virtues

Chief among the intellectual virtues, Aquinas (like Aristotle) cited the importance of the *virtue of prudence*: the habit of knowing "the right reason of things to be done."[17] Apart from this virtue, Aquinas understood that it would be impossible to live and do well as a human being. Aquinas acknowledged that people need "right reason" not only to apprehend what we ought to pursue (and avoid), but also to think carefully about all of the contingencies and complexities that human life encounters. This emphasis on prudence is not a departure from religious thinking. Aquinas recognized that reason is a gift from God, and not a power to be downplayed or underdeveloped.

Moral Virtues

Even as Aquinas recognized the importance of prudence, he also acknowledged that we are embodied sensory creatures and experience life as such. What we see, smell, touch, hear, or taste can arouse in us sensory desires, whether to eat, drink, fight, flee, or pursue sexual activity (to name a basic few). But because we are rational beings, how we respond to our inclinations can, in many cases, be enlightened by rational reflection on our sensory experiences. Recognizing this, Aquinas (like Aristotle) defined the category of *moral virtues*.[18] In concert with the virtue of prudence, the moral virtues habituate us to act well in light of our inclinations, and then toward ends that contribute to our living and doing well.

Infused Virtues

In addition to these three categories of virtues, Aquinas also taught that there is a distinction between virtues that are infused in humans by God, and those that are acquired by reason and human practice.[19] In Aquinas's view, God not only infuses people with the theological virtues, but also, and in some cases, God infuses humans with moral and intellectual virtues that help humans relate well to God.[20] As religious ethicist Diana Cates has noted, these other infused virtues "dispose us to be ordered in a supernaturally elevated way, but specifically with regard to everyday matters."[21] Admittedly, this is a perspective that can only be appreciated by respecting Aquinas's theological commitments. Namely, recognizing the "infused virtues" requires belief in one who could do such infusing (i.e., God). However, even though Aquinas recognized that some of the intellectual and moral virtues might come to us by grace, he did not think that God was the puppeteer behind our moral agency. In spite of whatever graces might come to human beings, Aquinas continued to affirm that humans ought to intentionally cultivate the intellectual and moral virtues where we can, by reason, discipline, and voluntary effort. In other words, believing oneself to be a Christian is no guarantee that how one thinks, or what one chooses, is in fact good, or divinely approved.

Reviewing the Framework

If we pause here and reflect on the moral framework that Aquinas has given us, the theologian's categorization of virtue uniquely gives the Christian community a roadmap for functioning morally in light of natural *and* supernatural happiness. Whereas prudence is the necessary, and thus, ruling virtue according to a natural ethic of virtue, the Christian religious framework adds the theological virtues, and approaches the natural virtues (anew) in light of these. People who are interested in how Aquinas specifically coordinated the theological, intellectual, and moral virtues would benefit from a study of his consummate work, *The Summa Theologica,* as well as the analytical work of his interpreters. My goal here is not to provide that kind of detailed analysis. I want to keep our use of Aquinas's teachings in abstract in order to see how virtue ethics, generally speaking, has worked and can work in a Christian framework. More specifically, I wish to show how it shapes concepts of sexual morality. We see such religious thinking very clearly in Aquinas's treatment of sexual virtue.

Aquinas on Sexual Virtue

Temperance and Sexual Virtue

Aquinas (like Aristotle) named the virtue of temperance as the virtue that perfects human desire for the pleasures of touch in food, drink, and sex.[22] According to the theologian, we learn to practice temperance by observing a well-reasoned rule, which he called "the need of human life."[23] This rule acknowledges that our desires for the pleasures of touch in food, drink, and sex are good, because when we respond well to these appetites they prompt us to seek activities that keep us alive, whether as individuals or as a species. In light of this rule, Aquinas said that the virtue of temperance is defined, minimally, by crafting our desires for food, drink, and sex in such a way that we do not bring an end to life.

Even so, the virtue of temperance is not simply a virtue to keep individuals or the species alive. Aquinas taught that the virtue of temperance can be practiced beyond its "necessary sense."[24] However, the theologian qualified his views on the objects of temperance: categorizing our desire for the pleasures of food and drink as distinct from our experience of desire for sexual pleasure. Some important ethical insights can be gleaned from his varied treatments of these desires, and so we will look first (albeit briefly) at the theologian's teachings concerning desires for the pleasures of food and drink.

Like Aristotle, Aquinas accepted that temperance can be exercised when our enjoyment of food and drink are "becoming," even if they are not used for their "necessary" purposes. Aquinas acknowledged that so long as our desires for the pleasures of food and drink are not "a hindrance to health and a sound condition of the body" the virtue of temperance helps us to enjoy pleasant objects "moderately, according to the demands of place and time, and in keeping with those among whom one dwells."[25] I understand Aquinas to mean by this that there are situations in life (such as celebrations or other social functions) in which the virtuous person will exercise prudential flexibility in making choices concerning nonnecessary matters that our natural senses desire. So yes, many of us can enjoy that martini or a piece of chocolate cake and still exercise the virtue of temperance—unless such would represent a hindrance to our health and the sound condition of our body. To discern this well, a person would require the virtue of prudence to apprehend how much food and drink is celebratory (and how much is excessive), and in what ways the moral agent should engage in celebrating or socializing (respecting one's own physical limits and concerns for health and well-being). Indeed, as we learned in the last chapter, "moderation" will express itself differently according to context and person—and thus there is no "one" rule here, except the rule of right reason. And yet, this measure of flexibility narrows considerably in Aquinas's teaching when he treats the matter of sexual pleasure.

Chastity

With respect to the desire for sexual pleasure, Aquinas taught that *chastity* is the species of temperance that allows human beings to cultivate sexual virtue.[26] Aquinas said that sexual virtue is best called "chastity," believing that the desire for sexual pleasure was of a most difficult sort to order, and had "greater need of chastisement and restraint" than any of the other desires for the pleasures of touch (such as for food, or drink).[27] Such a statement might seem to echo with the inherent suspicions about sexual desire that many of Aquinas's theological predecessors held. But I do not think we can say that Aquinas completely agreed with them. The theologian actually respected that the inclination to engage in sexual relations was natural, and thus not wrong, but only insofar as humans were inclined toward the proper sexual "end." The problem, in his view, is that most humans experience *inordinate* sexual desire. Such desire is inordinate, Aquinas taught, because humans are wrongly inclined to seek sexual pleasure for its own sake.

It wasn't that Aquinas rejected the place of pleasure in human life. Quite the opposite, he respected that natural functions are accompanied by pleasures that we should enjoy. However, there was something about the desire for sexual pleasure for its own sake that the theologian found to be less than our human best. Scholars have suggested that Aquinas held this view because he found no moral or theological value in enjoying sexual pleasure for itself. As John Giles Milhaven has noted, Aquinas found too little about sexual pleasure that contributed to our rational nature, and so he did not regard sexual pleasure as a choice-worthy object for its own sake[28] Thus, while Aquinas accepted that sexual desire was a natural human inclination (at least, when it is well ordered), and sexual activity a natural good too, he nevertheless thought that desire for the pleasure of *sexual touch* (for its own sake) was of such a "lower" sort that sexual pleasure could not possibly count as a worthy end for the rational creature. In fact, for Aquinas, the human mind (weakened by sin) is too easily convinced to indulge the want of sexual pleasure, and then, by any means imaginable—including "sinful" sexual activities. To that end, Aquinas believed that sexual desire needed proper channeling to a good and virtuous "end."

Aquinas and the End of Sexual Virtue

As one must do in the pursuit of any virtue, we must deliberate on what ends of human activity contributes to our living and doing well. So when considering sexual morality from the perspective of virtue ethics, we must identify reasonable "ends" of sexual relating in order to realize *sexual* virtue. In the last chapter I noted that this requires the light of prudence. Aquinas agreed. However, for Aquinas, the definition of sexual virtue (or any virtue for that matter) is specifically informed by religious sources of moral authority.[29] For Aquinas, this included official church teaching, interpretations of scripture, and theological reflections on human nature.

Marital and Procreative Norm

Aquinas's judgment was that a wide variety of the religious sources in Christianity agree that procreation, within the context of monogamous marriage, is the single proper end of human sexuality. It is important to read two interrelated goods within the one end of "marital procreation" that Aquinas affirmed. The first is obvious, in that Aquinas demanded that any sexual act we call licit must be within the context of heterosexual marriage, and that it always remain open to biological reproduction. The second good, however, actually concerns the relationship between the spouses. And yet, the reader of Aquinas will not find this second good explained in the theologian's writings on sexual virtue. Instead, one must read the *Supplement* to the *Summa Theologica*, where Aquinas explains the goods of marriage.[30] There, Aquinas admits that so long as spouses keep their sexual activities open to procreation, marital sexual activity is also an expression of fidelity and love.[31] Therefore, it is important to recognize that Aquinas did, in fact, care about qualitative relational concerns between spouses. Even so, the procreative demand is so primary in Aquinas's moral reflection that these other marital/ relational goods fail to count as expressions of sexual virtue should procreation be contravened.

Indeed, Aquinas could not imagine a legitimate use of our sexual faculties that in any way closed off the possibility of biological reproduction. Anything else, in his view, violated God's revealed law found in scripture and church teaching. However, even as Aquinas most certainly came to a narrow conclusion about the "end" of sexual virtue, it is important to stress that the theologian exhibited real concern about the meaning, value, and consequences of sexual relationships. For example, Aquinas was concerned that apart from marriage, genuine love could not be secured between sexual partners. This was an important concern to the theologian, because in his view sexual intercourse was *the* physical symbol of marriage, and marriage—in his view—could only be practiced in love.[32] Aquinas also feared that any children brought about through nonmarital intercourse might be denied proper parenting, which he counted as an injustice to the child. If we could only imagine love and sexuality the way he did (not that we should), and if these concerns were our only concerns (though some of them, like care for children, are quite important), then we might see why Aquinas regarded his sexual ethic as humane for sexual relationships.

What is more, according to his form of natural law thinking, Aquinas perceived "procreation of the species" as a self-evident good, not only in the general sense (that it is good to keep the human race going), but also that procreation should function as the norm for sexual morality (when engaged in sexual activity).[33] In short, as Aquinas contemplated the human creature, he interpreted procreation as the primary/natural purpose of sexual activity, intended by God. Aquinas then fixed this precept of the natural law as the "end" that sexual activity must seek, in order for sexual virtue to be realized whatsoever.[34] Admittedly, though, natural law thinking can be a bit slippery. On the one hand, natural law thinking—in a Christian context—is a matter of reflecting theologically and morally on "nature" through the lens of biblical interpretations and church teachings. On the other hand, natural law thinking predates the Christian religion and suggests that practical reason is capable of discerning certain moral norms from nature—that is, we can discern certain things are "good" for us (morally), according to reflection on the kind of creatures that we are. To that end, when Aquinas draws on natural law to substantiate his views on sexual morality, it is very much a Christian reading of the natural law. And yet, it would seem that Aquinas drew on the natural law expecting that thoughtful non-Christians should come to his same conclusion. Namely, insofar as Aquinas trusted that practical reason (when exercised well) can cultivate natural virtue apart from Christian faith, so too he seems to presume that the precepts of the natural law are self-evident to all who think carefully about the order of "nature." (We will return to natural law thinking in chapter 8.)

Apart from realizing sexual virtue in marriage—and then by engaging in acts that are always open to procreation—Aquinas was concerned that human beings would not only commit individual instances of sin, but perhaps even worse, cultivate habits of sexual immorality. To steer people away from immorality, Aquinas taught two categories of sexual sins (or vices) to be avoided: sexual vices against nature and sexual vices contrary to right reason. According to Aquinas, sexual vices against nature include any sexual activities that do not result in procreation.[35] Present in this list of sexual vices, Aquinas named masturbation, bestiality, and same-sex intercourse.[36] (If we were to agree with Aquinas, we would also have to include the use of contraception in heterosexual intercourse, marital or otherwise). Aquinas then defined sexual vices against reason as those sexual acts that could result in biological generation, but did so with the wrong person or in a harmful way. This list includes: fornication (which Aquinas defined as any sex between an unmarried man and woman), incest, adultery, seduction (which Aquinas defined as sexual intercourse with a woman who was still under the authority of her father), and rape.[37] Aquinas further noted that abstaining from sexual activities—for the wrong reasons—was also a vice. For example, it would count as a vice to be repulsed by sexual activity altogether. He named this the vice of insensibility, but considered its existence very rare. Aquinas is likely right about that. However, the reader should be careful not to confuse this vice with celibacy. For Aquinas, celibacy was an expression of virtue, whether by those not married, or as a prerequisite for those serving as clergy.

In summary, then, Aquinas taught that sexual virtue (chastity) is practiced by right reason, and in light of God, when human beings chan-nel sexual desire toward monogamous sexual activity, between loving married partners, and then only sexual activity that can result in pro-creation (vaginal intercourse). Aquinas did not wholly demonize sexual desire or activity when "well ordered," but he did treat sexual desire as an especially important passion to constrain because of the human proclivity to inordinately seek after pleasure for its own sake. That, for Aquinas, disordered God's intent for human sexuality. Because of this proclivity to seek pleasure for its own sake, Aquinas was concerned that consistently indulging sexual pleasure could (and likely would) ruin reason's ability to discern between what "feels" good, and what "is" good—not only in matters of sexual relations, but also in an overall "darkening" of the mind, and an eventual eradication of prudence.

Readdressing Sex, Virtue, and Happiness in the Reign of God

The reader will note that Aquinas's conclusion on sexual morality is very similar to many contemporary "traditionalists'" arguments, especially the kinds that seclude sexual activity to heterosexual marriage, and then with a strong emphasis on procreation. In fact, I suspect that those who might be critical of bringing Aristotelian theory into Christian ethics, but who nevertheless agree with Aquinas's conclusion on sexual moral-ity, may (now) better appreciate that virtue ethics can, in fact, provide a helpful framework for thinking about Christian ethics.

Still, the very framework that allowed Aquinas to name sexual virtue the way he did can also be used to critique that view. Consider: Aquinas's definition of sexual virtue shows us that within a Christian framework we must put several perspectives into conversation. First, we must have an accurate understanding of human sexuality (or the "nature" of human sexuality). Second, we must exercise the virtue of prudence, and then in light of interpretations of religious sources of moral authority. It is only by attending to these matters *well* that we can say anything persuasive about what count as legitimate "ends" of human sexuality, as a matter of Christian virtue ethics. Thus, the interpretive door is hardly shut on the subject of sexual morality. Far from being a settled issue, the definition of sexual virtue in a Christian framework is open to competing definitions according to how we understand the nature of human sexuality, how we employ prudence, and how we interpret scripture and church teaching.

As I concluded at the end of the last chapter, I believe that it is possible to show that the heterosexual, marital, and procreative norm is not the only definition of sexual virtue that one can articulate. I hope to convince people that there are several justifiable "ends" of human sexuality. In the last chapter, I suggested that recreation, relational intimacy, and selective acts of procreation (all properly defined) are three legitimate ends of sexual virtue. What is more (and as we will see in later chapters), I believe it can be demonstrated that these ends are valid in a Christian worldview. But let me be clear. Such a statement does not mean that heterosexual, married people who seek procreation are under attack. By no means! I fully expect that heterosexual married couples may indeed practice sexual virtue within their relational context, according to the light of prudence, and with respect to their religious commitments. I encourage that. I am merely suggesting that there are other ways in which sexual virtue can be realized—and that we might recognize these other ways as prudent and good.

So how do we get there?

In order to unlock the grip of the heterosexual, marital, and procreative norm, we first have to confess that this "traditional" view represents an evolution of moral doctrine, which was derived from centuries of human interpretations of the Christian source materials (see chapter 1). By virtue of what human interpretation is—that is, insights into texts or traditions that are both illuminated and limited by the finitude of the interpreter—interpretation always invites critique and reformulation. If for no other reason, people are morally responsible for how they (and we) interpret and advance moral norms, whether about sexuality or anything else. Namely, any time we interpret and advance moral norms, those can either contribute to the happiness of others, or unfortunately, to real suffering (see chapter 9). Given that incredible responsibility—and recognizing that none of us have a monopoly on the truth—members of the moral community (including Christian ones) would do well to admit that some of our views about sexual morality might be wrong (in part, or in whole).

To that end, I believe Aquinas's theoretical approach is a generally good one, and I believe it can intervene where many of our debates about sexual morality have collapsed into partisan and religious rhetoric. In particular, Aquinas's ethical framework invites us to think carefully about our desires for sexual pleasures—and our attainment of these—in light of what possible "ends" will contribute to our flourishing (i.e., living and doing well). From the perspective of Christian ethics, this requires us to think about the ends one seeks in light of faith in God—especially as that faith is shaped by interpretations of Christian source material (e.g., the Bible, church teachings, and so forth). Thus, Aquinas's moral theory brings us back to the table of ethics not to repeat our given views (i.e., our talking points or monologues), but to test our thoughts about the ends of sexual virtue, both philosophically and religiously, through meaningful ethical discourse.

And yet, for as much as Aquinas's ethical framework allows us to reapproach sexual morality through discourse about virtue, his explicit definition of sexual virtue is itself disputable. On the one hand, this is a matter of how we might better interpret Christian source materials in light of critical insights into Christian scriptures and church teachings that Aquinas did not possess. We will approach these source materials in later chapters. However, Aquinas's definition of sexual virtue is also disputable because of what I take to be an arbitrary shift in his moral theory. Namely, whereas Aquinas has a remarkably flexible view of the virtue of temperance in matters of eating and drinking, he shifts to a narrow expression of it in chastity. I invite the reader to briefly consider why this is problematic.

Aquinas allowed that we may enjoy the pleasures of food or drink beyond their necessary use (i.e., to keep us alive), so long as that was in a becoming and moderate way. For example, certain celebrations rightfully call for enjoying some rich food and perhaps some strong drink. For Aquinas, the virtuous person knows how to enjoy these in the right way, at the right time, and for the right reason. Aquinas found nothing oppressive about the desire to enjoy the physical pleasures of food and drink, even when recreating with friends.

It is inconsistent, then, (at least, in my view) that the theologian treated sexual activity so differently. Aquinas shifted from a rather flexible view about the enjoyment of "nonnecessary" pleasures regarding food and drink, to a rigid implementation of sexual virtue, defined by "chastity" (i.e., marital/procreative sex), or celibacy. To justify this view he had to lean heavily on a narrow reading of the natural law, as well as upon the church's medieval judgments about sexuality—judgments that we know were steeped in suspicions about the relationship between sin and sex itself. From those church judgments, Aquinas even categorized offenses to chastity, so that Christians might know all the ways in which sexual activity can be pursued toward an unbecoming (i.e., sinful) "end."

I do not dispute that some people have pursued sexual pleasure to "unbecoming ends." But it is not necessarily true that the enjoyment of sexual pleasure apart from marital love and procreation is always immoral. That, in itself, is the moral assertion I am challenging.

To suggest, as Aquinas did, that sexual activity must be open to procreation in every instance denies the modern insight that sexual activity is multivalent and can be enjoyed for different reasons and toward different ends—ends that are complete in themselves and have nothing to do with procreation. As I noted in the last chapter, I do not think we can continue to deny the multivalent nature of human sexuality, especially in light of what we know from contemporary scientific studies in sexuality. Aquinas's perspective simply lacks insight into such complexities, and his argument (as well as those like his) rises or falls on whether his religious interpretations are sustainable.

Aquinas is long gone, however, and so our argument cannot really be with him. Our argument is presently with those who perpetuate conclusions such as his, and who do so by justifying a narrow definition of sexual virtue by citing religious authorities. But this, as we will see, does not turn out to be an impenetrable defense. In the next several chapters we will examine how it is that scripture, nature (and natural law), as well as church teaching can be reinterpreted on matters of sexual morality. As we do this, I ask the reader to entertain the possibility that the sexual norms of heterosexuality, marriage, and procreation are ideals that emerged from particular social, historical, and theological worldviews, and not necessarily the most complete statement on sexual morality that one can articulate from a Christian perspective today. Indeed, I believe we will find that even as religious sources of authority have been interpreted to advance a narrow view of sexual morality, new insights into these texts and teachings will allow us to articulate more generous definitions of sexual virtue

Part III

Religious Sources of Moral Authority

Five

Understanding Scripture

Jesus said to them, "Is this not the reason you are in error? You do not know the scriptures or the power of God . . ."

—Mark 12:24

Christian Ethics and Scripture

A Brief Review

In the last chapter I noted that if a definition of sexual virtue is going to be compelling to most Christians, it will have to be informed by recognized sources of religious authority. The Bible is a preeminent source of authority for Catholic and Protestant Christians. It has been called the "word of God" as well as "the rule" for matters of faith and life. As one New Testament verse puts it, "All scripture is inspired of God and is useful for teaching, for reprimanding, correcting, and training in justice, so that the people of God may be fully competent and equipped for every good work."[1] And yet, the ancient Jewish sage Sirach wisely warned Bible readers: "Now, those who read the scriptures must not only themselves understand them, but must also as lovers of learning be able through spoken and written word to help the outsiders [to understand]. . . . You are invited therefore to read it with goodwill and attention. . . . For what was originally expressed . . . does not have exactly the same sense when translated into another language."[2]

Sirach's call for interpretive mindfulness is still relevant today.

In the following chapters I will offer reflections on the Bible with respect to selected issues of sexual morality. This is a challenging task. Bookshelves have been filled with texts written on the Jewish and Christian scriptures, often elucidating the many ways these scriptures can be interpreted. What I offer here is by no means comprehensive. However, what I do hope to show the reader is that the Bible—well interpreted— does *not* clearly demand that our definition of sexual virtue limit sexual expression to heterosexual activity, or to marriage and procreation. I do this by first offering a brief introduction to scripture and its general use by Christians. That is the focus of this chapter. In the next two chapters I will explore the issues of marriage and homosexuality. In these chapters I will analyze commonly cited texts that are used to perpetuate the argument that heterosexuality and marriage are *the* norms of Christian sexual morality. As a note, what I offer in these chapters is indebted to the work of many biblical scholars. But how I organize these insights on scripture and sexuality (and how I interpret them) is something I hope might yield a small contribution to those who spend time thinking about the Bible and sexuality.

A Comment on Proof-Texting

When it comes to constructing a theological belief, or a moral argu-ment, one biblical verse here or there does not settle an issue in any indisputable way. A wide variety of Christians (both conservative and liberal, Protestant and Catholic) seem to agree that using a single verse to ground a matter of doctrine, or ethics, is problematic. For example, most Protestants tend to disagree with their Catholic friends that Jesus's command to "eat my body," and "drink my blood" should be taken liter-ally when it comes to sacramental theology. Likewise, most Catholics are unconvinced by their Protestant friends when verses about grace and faith are cited to advance the Protestant ideal of "salvation by faith alone." Drawing on single-verse "evidence" to champion a moral or theological cause is what we normally call *proof-texting*. Such biblical minimalism is problematic, as it usually exposes interpretive inconsisten-cies. For example, the apostle Paul's comments about appropriate head coverings for women and hair length for men, in 1 Corinthians 11, do not seem to be a major concern for many Christians today. But for some reason, many of the same Christians who will ignore the need for women to veil their heads (at least, according to 1 Corinthians 11:2–15) nevertheless cling to "proof-texting" on issues of sexual morality, as if passages in the Bible are suddenly clear to anyone literate enough to read it, or hear it spoken.

Proof-texting does not help us to know what a text of scripture might be about or how it is best interpreted. Careful readers of the Bible know this and intentionally steer *away* from oversimplifying the biblical texts. This is an important reminder as we approach the Bible to shape our sense of sexual morality. Namely, as we go about defining sexual virtue in a Christian framework, we *do* need to attend to scripture, but I submit that we can only do so well by treating scripture seriously— equipping ourselves with a critical eye for detail.

The Bible: Parts and Compilation

Consulting the Bible is more like approaching a bookshelf than it is a book. Each text was written in a particular time, in a given language, with idioms and cultural references not always accessible to the modern reader. What is more, the steps by which these texts became bound in one "book" cover centuries of editorial choices and many theological disputes.

The Hebrew Bible—or "Old Testament," as some Christians call it—is made up of three parts: The Torah (the law); the Nevi'im (the prophets), and the Kethuvi'im (the writings). The Hebrew Bible was written by Jewish authors who, in various ways, conceived the relationship between the biblical God, the Jewish people, and the rest of the cosmos. The majority of the Hebrew Bible was written in Hebrew, and thus the texts draw upon idioms, worldviews, and geopolitics that were familiar to Semitic people living in the ancient Near East. In its compilation, Jewish theologians debated about which texts to include as sacred text. The current form of the Hebrew Bible was established sometime between 200 BCE and 200 CE.[3] During this time, texts were either accepted or rejected as belonging to the corpus of scripture.

The New Testament also came together through a process of compilation. While the gospel narratives and individual letters were penned between 50–150 CE (and in the Greek language), the New Testament was not collected into its current form until the fourth century.[4] Before that time, Christian communities were using a wide variety of texts *as* scripture—sometimes using texts that modern Christians no longer use; sometimes not having particular books or letters that contemporary Christians venerate today.[5]

When it comes to studying the Hebrew Bible and the New Testament, we no longer have original manuscripts of the texts. Manuscript copies were made, and yet even a basic study of the copies show that the editors did not always keep its content entirely the same.[6] This is evident when we compare earlier copies of the texts with later copies, in which we find a number of changes—sometimes due to a scribal error, sometime an intentional (if not significant) addition. For example, in the Gospel of John, the well-known story of the woman caught in adultery, whom Jesus spared from stoning, is missing in the earliest manuscript copies we have of that gospel.[7] In other New Testament texts, there are variant word choices—sometimes depending on the theological preferences of the transcriber and/or editor.[8] Thus, the biblical texts were not only written and compiled; they also evolved through the process of copying and editing.

Christian Approaches to the Bible

Making things all the more complex, Christians approach the Bible with their own unique understanding of it. My fundamentalist friends describe the Bible (in particular, the words written in the Bible) as literally the words of God. They tend to believe that we need only commonsense levels of interpretation in order for scripture to be made sensible. Usually this entails trusting that the surface reading of a text renders its meaning. Other Christians teach that the Bible does contain inspired teachings from God, but that this is communicated through finite human language, such that any divine truth is impossible to know apart from very careful linguistic, historical, and contextual study of the various texts. Still other Christian thinkers have suggested that there are no straightforward meanings to the biblical texts whatsoever, except what a person or community assigns to the texts through interpretation.[9] What is more, we know that in some Christian institutions (such as the Catholic Church) scripture is understood to be interpreted accurately *only* by the official teachers of the church.

With such a wide variety of approaches to the Bible, it is simply a matter of fact that there is no one Christian approach to, or understanding of, the Bible. Descriptively speaking, self-identified Christians do not agree on what the Bible is as sacred text, nor do Christians agree with the interpretation and application of the biblical texts. These disagreements on the Bible fall along denominational lines, but also individual lines as well. I am wary, therefore, of anyone who claims with a narrow rigidity that the Bible is "very clear" on issues of sexual morality—or anything else for that matter. Such a statement does not mean that I think the Bible is irrelevant to moral reflection. Quite the opposite! I respect that scripture (and its use) is part of what often qualifies a distinctively Christian worldview. However, scripture is only understood and applied through interpretation. In my view, dialogue, careful study, and interpretive options offer a greater hope for biblical illumination than the pontifications of those who present themselves as the final authority on the meaning of scripture.

Thus, when drawing upon Christian scripture to inform a sexual ethic, it is important (as I suggested above) to understand much about this collection of text: its original languages, its many translations, its multiple genres, its historical contexts, the authors who were responsible for the composition and compilation of its parts, the audiences to which its components were first delivered, and so on. It is good, therefore, to consult the work of biblical scholars who engage in this sort of critical study within the context of scholarly peer review. Serious readers of the Bible do this so as to get many intelligent perspectives on how one might engage well in the activity of biblical interpretation. Without engaging in biblical scholarship, or relying on the work of biblical scholars, interpretation of the biblical texts quickly becomes an activity in which we assume that our contemporary understanding of certain words or passages somehow accurately captures the real or intended meaning of the text.

Christians and Critical Study

Many Christians have come to agree that the best of biblical scholarship illuminates possible interpretations of the Bible that one cannot possibly know by simply reading the text itself.[10] The study of the sources, the languages, and contexts of the biblical texts is what we otherwise call critical study. Critical study of the Bible does not sacrifice the veneration of the Bible as sacred, a belief that many Christians hold dear. Critical study of the Bible often results in keen insights and potential meanings of the text itself, which can benefit interpretive choices. With those biblical scholars (and theologians) who search out meaning in the biblical text, I agree that critical study can aid us in apprehending what a portion or the whole of scripture might be about, such that we are in a position to consider the moral implications of scriptural teaching for contemporary Christian life. Simultaneously, I agree with those biblical scholars who say that interpretations of the Bible reflect powerfully the activities of its interpreters. That is to say, interpretations do not in any straightforward way uncover the meanings that are simply "there in the text," as if the Bible speaks for itself and its best interpreters simply listen.[11]

While the interpreter does bring something to the text, I do not think that we should abandon the effort to find meanings that are, to some extent, contained in and controlled by the text itself. I leave open the possibility that thoughtful investigations of scripture can provide people with insights into principles that are, to some extent, "held" in the Bible, from which religious and ethical implications can responsibly be drawn. I can agree that we may not know the meaning of a text with certainty (and, indeed, there might be multiple meanings to be known), but I also remain hopeful that there might still be good reasons, in particular cases, to prefer one interpretation over another partly because it reflects certain meanings that are, to some degree, contained in the text.[12]

License and Malpractice

Without question, then, the use of the Bible as a moral authority must be treated very carefully and with deference to the complexity of its antiquity. As the biblical scholar Thomas Sheehan once commented in his public lectures on the historical Jesus, Christian clergy who fail to study the Bible with respect to its sociohistorical and linguistic intricacies do so as a result of either ignorance or apathy. If in ignorance, Sheehan says that such ministers teach about the Bible without a valid license. If ministers ignore the insights of history and context, Sheehan charges that their use of the Bible is an act of malpractice.[13] This insight is a critique that I think is well worth pondering. If Christians do not heed this criticism, they leave the impression that for them the Bible is really a salad bar or buffet: a spread from which they can take what they want for themselves (or to force on others), leaving the rest behind out of arbitrary preference.

I believe it is fair to say, then, that thoughtful (and faithful) students of the Bible will recognize how problematic it is to simply try and read the Bible as if its meaning is somehow always clear. And yet these simple appeals to what "the Bible says" litter many of our conversations about sexual morality. Of course, I do understand that a number of well-meaning Christians read the Bible (without consulting biblical scholarship) and believe that they are being rightly taught by "God's Spirit." This is a deeply personal belief and one that I do not wish to offend. At the same time, we know that there are many examples of people who have done strange (if not heinous) things because of their interpretation of the Bible, or because they felt led by "the Spirit of God." Too often we hear of brutal child murders and bizarre public disruptions done in the name of the Bible, and hence, in the name of God. The Reverend Dr. Mel White has captured an example of this well. In his examination of homophobia in America, White followed the story of a gay man's murder at the hands of two brothers. Both brothers identified as Christian. One brother explained the murder this way:

> I had to obey God's law rather than man's law. I didn't want to do this. I felt I was supposed to. . . . I have followed a higher law. . . . I see a lot of parallels between this and a lot of other incidents in the [Bible]. . . . They threw our Savior in jail . . . our forefathers have been in prison a lot. Prophets . . . Christ . . . My brother and I are incarcerated for our work in cleansing a sick society. . . . I just plan to defend myself from the Scriptures.[14]

Sadly, this tragic case is not the only instance in which crimes have been committed in the name of Christian scripture.

While proof-texting is a charge often aimed at fundamentalists, the Christian theologian Brian McLaren notes that moderate to progressive Christians have also been accused of reading the Bible selectively. He writes:

> I was surprised to see that one of the world's leading atheists agreed with the "No picking and choosing" rule, albeit for a different reason. By picking the Bible's love verses and soft-pedaling its hate verses, he suggested, moderate believers give cover to extremists. They help maintain respect for the book their less moderate counterparts will use to inspire and defend violence. In order to deprive extremists of this cover, he said, we must decisively throw out the whole book as a bronze age collection of dangerous myths and destructive superstitions.[15]

McLaren's atheist does indeed have a point—Christians do select which scriptures they primarily cite, and which of these they use to interpret other texts.

But such an admission does not mean that interpretation is itself *always* an exercise of arbitrary preference. McLaren turns to the Celtic theologian Richard Kearney who responds:

[W]hen [critics] . . . accuse believers of "picking and choosing,"
they are actually accusing them of being responsible believers.
This is what faith is about: making a choice, venturing a wager,
discriminating between rival interpretations in order to make
the best decision regarding love and hate, justice and injustice.[16]

Agreeing with Kearney, McLaren adds:

Siding with some voices and against others isn't simply picking
and choosing according to one's own tastes, then. Nor can it
be reduced to a simple matter of objective scholarship or logic.
Interpretation is also and always a matter of ethics, a matter of
the heart and the conscience. So we can expect hostile people
to side with hostile voices in the text; fearful people with fearful voices, and peace-loving people with peace-loving voices.
Interpretation will always to some degree manifest the character
of the interpreter along with the meaning of the text.[17]

If this is true, then the study of biblical interpretation is not only an
in-house endeavor for Christians, but perhaps even more importantly, it
is a critical matter for people who are interested in *how* and *why* Christians use the Bible in matters both moral and theological.

Concluding Words on the Bible and Interpretation

Without question, people of Christian faith will interpret the Bible as
they will. But if the Bible is going to be utilized as a religious source of
moral authority in the activity of ethics (the very activity in which we
give and demand reasons for holding the positions of morality that we
do), then we cannot merely accept the *given* reality that people interpret
the Bible as they will. Rather, we must demand of each other compelling
reasons for interpreting the Bible the way that we do. What is more, we
must also be careful to register our own attachments to particular biblical interpretations. If in our dialogues we find ourselves recognizing that
there is no real support for the interpretation we hold, but we hold to
it anyway, such suggests that we might be more interested in preserving
a certain status quo, or agenda, than a commitment to a careful study
of scripture and the responsible interpretations that can be drawn from
that study.

In the next two chapters, I invite the reader to consider biblical interpretation with respect to a number of issues pertaining to sexual morality. I ask the reader to hold in mind how we might integrate these interpretations with a definition of sexual virtue. These issues include two primary concerns: whether or not the Bible demands that we should limit sexual activity to marriage arrangements, and whether or not the Bible condemns homosexuality. As I hope to convince a wide number of people, when we access the biblical texts with rigorous biblical scholarship there are no compelling reasons to believe that the Bible is best interpreted to confine sexual activity to its practice in marriage or heterosexuality.

Six

Sex and Marriage

Must We Wait?

As to marriage or celibacy, let people take which course they will, they will be sure to repent.

—Adapted from the sayings of Socrates

A Peculiar Biblical Interpretation

Covered Vice

And when a man, having prayed to God and cast himself upon [God], sees that he cannot refrain [from sex], let him take a wife in order not to lead an immoral life, or behave like a dog, or a bull, or some wild beast. Thus when he marries, as ordained by God, that is how vice is covered, and hidden, and not brought into judgment. And herein we see the inestimable goodness of our God, that although he leaves this vice in us, which indeed ought to make us feel ashamed, he nevertheless ordains a helpful means by which it may be overcome.[1]

Thus says the great Protestant reformer John Calvin: Sexual desire is a "vice" left in us by God for which we should feel ashamed.

And marriage? It is the receptacle of our vice by which a man might direct his shameful sexual urges into something respectable—which for Calvin, was largely controlled by the ideal of marital procreation.[2]

The sexual role of a woman? Even if she is a man's loving companion, she is also the object of base sexual desire, which, when "covered" in marriage, allows her to yield sexual modesty and chastity.[3] That is, she is to be a mother.

Of course, Calvin is not the only Christian theologian who treated sexual desire as shameful, and marriage as its only remedy. To this day a number of Christians (both Protestant and Catholic) teach that people ought to wait to engage in sexual activity until marriage has been secured. Until wedding rings are exchanged, many contemporary Christians teach that sexual desire is a burdensome inclination that tempts people to "sin." Those who advocate this view usually turn to the Bible (as one source) to justify their claim.

When we turn to the Bible, however, it is not at all clear that marriage is a necessary prerequisite for the practice of sexual virtue. When we examine the historical and cultural settings of the biblical literature, especially with respect to the New Testament, there are good reasons to suggest that no easy (or obvious) connection can be made between first-century understandings of marriage and sexuality and our understandings of these today. Like a master archeologist, we must dig carefully through strata of history and context so as to reconstruct (if that is even possible) what marriage and sexuality meant to the early Christian communities. This we must do if we are to interpret any enduring principle about sexuality and marriage from the New Testament that might be useful for contemporary Christian discourse on sexual morality.

Marriage in the New Testament

Make No Assumptions

Quite a bit of scholarship has been done to describe the models of marriage and family that were customary during the time of Jesus and the first-century churches.[4] These studies show that preexisting Jewish and Roman concepts of marriage and family dominate much of the New Testament literature. In the few instances that the New Testament addresses sex or marriage, it is largely in response to these two cultural models. The reader of the Bible who is unaware of this may think New Testament references to sex or marriage have the same meanings that they do today. We must not make that assumption. As the theologian Raymond Lawrence notes, Christian reflection on sexual morality is doomed to failure unless we grasp the "alien nature of the context" that shaped first-century Christian comments on sex and marriage.[5] Without understanding how sex and marriage functioned in the first century, our interpretation of these texts will always skew toward our assumptions or our prejudices. But as the reader will soon see, much about ancient views on sexuality and marriage are not very recognizable to us. Indeed, we would call little of it even praiseworthy.

We do well, then, not to forget that marriage is very much a social institution, defined and practiced distinctively by different people, in different times, and in different ways. The reader of the Bible has to be careful not to assume that what is written in the Bible about marriage always reflects timeless judgments with respect to what marriage should be like in Christian practice. For example, no Christian to my knowledge endorses the biblical teaching that a virgin who has been raped should be bound to her rapist in marriage without recourse to divorce (Deuteronomy 22:28–29). I also know of very few Christians who advocate for men or women to abandon their spouses and children to work an itinerant ministry, as many of Jesus's disciples did (Mark 10:28–31). In my view, these examples illuminate the need to treat our views on marriage and sexuality very carefully when reaching moral conclusions from the Bible.

It is good, therefore, to investigate how marriage was defined and practiced in the time of Jesus and the early churches. Since it was out of Judaism that Christianity grew, we can start with a description of the Jewish understanding and practice of marriage that would have been recognizable to Jesus and his disciples. We will examine Roman norms and practices when considering, more specifically, the teachings of the apostle Paul.

A Brief Overview on Jewish Marriage Customs

Scholars of Jewish law (both the Written Torah and the Oral Law) tend to agree that marriage in ancient Judaism functioned as a law or duty for Jewish men to fulfill.[6] For these ancient Jewish men, this included the right to take more than one wife, as evidenced by the biblical polygamy laws.[7] By the first century, polygamy was by no means an antiquated practice. It was *the* definition of "traditional Jewish marriage." If a first-century Jewish man did choose monogamy, it was likely for practical reasons. However, whether men were monogamous or polygamous, rabbinical Judaism named a number of other religious duties for Jewish men to fulfill. We find these duties explained in the Talmud— which admittedly came later than the first century, but is believed (by traditional Jews) to capture both the sacred oral law (*halachah*), as well as the teachings and rulings of the rabbis from antiquity. Talmud thus claims to preserve a portrait of traditional Jewish teachings that reach back into history, even into biblical eras. When we consult Talmud, we find that traditional Judaism not only expected a Jewish man to get married, but also to meet his wife's, or wives', *marital* dues, including food, shelter, clothing, and satisfying his wife's/wives' need for sexual pleasure.[8] In addition to providing for these, Talmud states that Jewish husbands were also to produce at least two children with a given wife, in order to fulfill the law of procreation.[9]

But even as these marriage laws were placed on Jewish men, these men were also given the freedom to exercise divorce. According to scholars, Jewish men used to have a unilateral right to divorce their wives, which could be exercised without much provocation or warning.[10] Jewish women, on the other hand, had few rights to divorce, apart from being able to prove that their husbands had committed a "hard fault" against them.[11] Unlike men, who could simply procure the certificate of divorce, women were expected to show extensive evidence in order to nullify the marriage contract. One reason for this, as William Countryman notes, is that women were regarded as the property of men.[12] As such, a woman could be dismissed as "damaged" or "unwanted" property, while the man remained a free agent with relatively little stigma for practicing divorce. Of course, we who look back on such inequalities see a grievous injustice. And yet it has also been suggested that the marriage arrangements of ancient Judaism offered at least some kind of social justice for Jewish women and children.

One notable example of spousal justice was in the negotiation of the *ketubah*, or marriage contract. This document not only negotiated dowry rights, but also what a woman would be owed if divorced by her husband.[13] Readers would not be wrong to think of this as an ancient religious form of prenuptial agreement. Thus, while women may have been denied divorce rights, in theory they were guaranteed means of survival outside of the marriage. Along with the rights of the *ketubah*, it has also been suggested that ancient Jewish views guaranteed other rights for women that might not be known by readers of the Bible today. Raymond Lawrence explains:

> In first-century Palestinian Judaism, there were no bastards, except in certain rare cases of incest. Every child was the full responsibility of the natural father. Any sexual union with an unattached woman was tantamount to marriage, in terms of

obligation and responsibility. Even sex with a prostitute carried such moral obligations. Jewish polygamy, rather than abusing women, arguably provided better for the welfare of women and children than did the monogamy of Rome.[14]

Although Lawrence's comments are made in the aggregate, and therefore do not capture certain nuances and complexities, they *do* demonstrate significant differences between first-century Jewish assumptions about sexuality and marriage, when compared to any number of Christian views on marriage and sexuality today.

Jesus, Sex, and Marriage

Polygamy, marital Torah duties, as well as male-unilateral divorce rights framed the Jewish context in which Jesus's teachings on marriage were likely situated. Therefore, if there is any insistence on Jesus's part that sexual activity should be limited within marriage, or that marriage must take a certain form, we should expect to find it in his teachings about these issues. And yet every time Jesus taught on sexuality and marriage he did so in a confounding way. The Gospel of Luke captures one interesting case.

In Luke 20:34–35 Jesus is asked who a woman would belong to in the resurrection of the dead, if she had been married to seven different brothers (having been a widow to each one on earth). The question was posed by a branch of Jewish religious scholars who did not believe in the resurrection of the dead. But Jesus responded, "Those who belong to this age marry and are given in marriage; but *those who are considered worthy of a place in that age and in the resurrection of the dead neither marry nor are given in marriage.*"[15] This statement has been interpreted by some Christians to support celibacy as the ideal Christian lifestyle. However, the aforementioned theologian Raymond Lawrence notes, "Had Jesus been a proponent of either monogamy or celibacy, this would have been the place to make his case. He does not. The text shows that he levels an implicit critique against marriage—that there is no marriage in the resurrection—but beyond that he leaves us in the dark."

However, whereas Jesus's teaching in the above passage unsettles the place of marriage in the Christian life, he offers other teachings that speak to its content. Perhaps his most notable teaching on marriage is found in Matthew 19:3–9. In this passage Jesus is confronted by teachers of the law who ask him about the permissibility of divorce and remarriage. The text captures this response from Jesus:

> Have you not read that the one who made them at the beginning "made them male and female," and said, "for this reason a man shall leave his father and mother and be joined to his wife, and the two shall become one flesh"? So they are no longer two, but one flesh. Therefore what God has joined together, let no one separate. . . . It was because you were so hard-hearted that Moses allowed you to divorce your wives, but at the beginning it was not so. And I say to you, whoever divorces his wife, except for unchastity, and marries another commits adultery.[17]

A number of Christians have interpreted this passage to mean a variety of peculiar things. For example, the often-venerated theologian St. Augustine drew on this passage to forbid remarriage for those who had been divorced. Others have said that Jesus was defining marriage as something between one man and one woman *only*; and demanding that sexual activity be limited to this union.[18] I suggest that such interpretations miss the point.

Given the reality of Jewish marriage and divorce laws (the context in which Jesus offered these statements), it seems more reasonable to propose that Jesus was addressing the custom of unilateral divorce rights that some Jewish men used against their wives. Notice that Jesus did not give a systematic definition of marriage as an institution, nor did he give a detailed sexual ethic. Compared to the meticulous rules in the Torah, he is very brief.[19]

Consider again his response to the question on divorce and remarriage. The gospel narrative remembers Jesus teaching that any man who divorced his wife (except, perhaps, for sexual immorality) would commit adultery by remarrying.[20] Biblical scholar William Countryman notes that Jesus's teaching actually grants women greater religious and social standing than what the Torah had permitted. By casting men as guilty of adultery when remarrying after divorce, Jesus repositioned men as the property of women.[21] Indeed, according to most biblical scholars, biblical references to "adultery" were not generic citations of infidelity. These referred, instead, to the "stealing" of sexual property (or the giving away of that which was not one's to give). Typically, this was a matter of men engaging in sexual activity with women who belonged to another man. Thus, for Jesus to teach that men would be guilty of "adultery" by divorcing and remarrying meant that the man's first wife still "owned" him. By remarrying, he was giving away sexual property (himself) that still belonged to his original wife. Because Jesus made the man his wife's property, the man ceased to have the right to leave his wife by breaking the legal/marriage contract with her. Without question, this teaching would have been startling to many people in the first century, who were more accustomed to patriarchal privilege. Denying men unilateral divorce rights spoke to larger issues of gender equality.

Of course, Jesus was not the only rabbi in the first century to address the divorce and remarriage laws in the Hebrew Bible. There were many different positions that the rabbis took, and Jesus was likely aware of those rulings. His teachings could be situated as more or less radical in comparison to his Jewish contemporaries. And yet, an issue remains. For as much as Jesus's teaching on divorce and remarriage elevated the role of women, his teaching is also incredibly *alienating* if left to a surface reading. In particular, the surface reading of Jesus's teaching seems to indicate that remarriage (after divorce) is utterly forbidden. Many Christians will likely hope that the historical Jesus was a person who surely knew that divorce and remarriage are often the results of complicated and painful realties.

It is with good reason, then, that some readers will bristle at this blanket treatment of divorce and remarriage. In the face of our own experiences, or the experiences of friends and family, Jesus's teaching in the Gospel of Matthew seems downright cruel. It certainly lacks sensitivity to the complexities of human relationships.

And yet, it could very well be that the historical Jesus—or the gospel writer—lacked the kind of relational sensitivities that many of us regard as basic requirements of human compassion. Jesus *could* have had a narrow view on this matter. If for no other reason, he was not the most ardent champion of marriage and family as social institutions. This is evidenced by his many "anti-family" teachings.[22] But casting an image of Jesus as insensitive to relational complexities is not the only reading of this passage. In my view, the severity of Christ's teaching is best interpreted in light of Jesus's prophetic identity.

In the Jewish tradition, especially among the writings of the biblical prophets, there is a practice known as the prophetic exaggeration.[23] The prophetic exaggeration is a rhetorical tool in the service of some larger argument. The formula was fairly standard. Certain prophets would exaggerate a particular claim in order to command the attention of an audience. Severe proclamations served this rhetoric quite well. For example, in the Hebrew Bible we find a number of instances where the prophets would announce the wrath of God and God's condemning judgment against *all* of the earth. But where such severe proclamations are made in the text, they are usually followed—only a few chapters later—with an assertion of God's universal love and mercy.

In many of these passages the enunciation of judgment and con-demnation functions to "grab hold" of the hearer or reader and to shake things up (usually self-righteousness, hardheartedness, or idola-trous thought). To that end, in the fire of God's wrath the reader does not find annihilation, but discipline and purification. Indeed, what we find in these passages are not doctrines of everlasting condemnation, but movements toward reconciliation and promises of steadfast love.[24]

The great Jewish theologian Abraham Heschel noted that it is only in the genre of prophetic exaggeration that the prophet is capable of expressing (in finite human language) both God's pathos against injus-tice, but also God's everlasting love. Readers of the Bible who assume a surface-level meaning to any of the prophetic exaggerations fail to understand that the likely point of these statements was not to cast dualistic categories of the damned and saved, nor to find final statements on doctrine, but instead, to reset the hearts and minds of people to live in ways that resonate with proposed ideas about the reign of God. This was not the only way biblical authors sought to accomplish such goals, but it was one existing biblical genre.

It would seem that Jesus knew of this genre and drew on it in a number of his teachings. For example, in Matthew 5:30, Jesus is remem-bered as saying, "And if your right hand causes you to sin, cut it off and throw it away. For it is better that you lose one of your members than that your whole body go into hell." In Matthew 19:21 Jesus is quoted as telling a person, "[I]f you want to be perfect, go and sell all your possessions and give the money to the poor, and you will have treasure in heaven." These are but two examples where the teachings of Jesus are quite stark or severe, and yet few Christians would claim that Jesus *really* intended for people to sever body parts as a matter of religious practice, or to demand that everyone sell everything that they have. There are good reasons for not taking these passages literally. We seem to agree, as conservatives and liberals, that there are principles to learn from these passages of prophetic exaggeration, and not simply dictations from Christ to be followed literally.

Jesus's teaching on marriage and divorce strikes me as very much in the vein of prophetic exaggeration. We have to remember that the

Jesus who offered this stark teaching on divorce and remarriage is the same Jesus who is remembered as saying that his life was to fulfill the old Hebrew call "to preach good news to the poor," to "proclaim freedom for the prisoners and recovery of sight for the blind, to release the oppressed," and "to proclaim the year of the Lord's favor."[25] When we consider the many teachings of Jesus it is difficult to imagine that the one who had concern for the brokenhearted and oppressed would somehow be callous and unconcerned about the complexities of human relationships, including those that take place within the social constructs of marriage. Therefore, if Jesus was employing the prophetic exaggeration (as he seemed to do in other cases) then Jesus's statement on divorce and remarriage functioned to "grab hold" and "shake up" those who would abuse divorce rights and denigrate women. His teachings on marriage did not speak to painful and complicated situations of divorce, nor did his teaching offer a detailed sexual ethic.

We are left, then, with a portrait of Jesus's teaching that simultaneously critiques the necessity of institutional marriage (Luke 20) and yet humanizes the institution by demanding equality between partners (Matthew 19). Thus, it would seem that for Jesus, the relationship between human partners is not something limited or controlled by legal document or religious ritual. To make this point Jesus appealed to one of the human origin stories in the Torah, in particular the legend of Eden and its inhabitants: Adam and Eve (Genesis 2:4b-3). The story describes human communion out of loneliness and an example of human relationship not governed by contracts or rituals. Drawing on this narrative in the abstract as he did, Jesus pointed to the heart of human relationships to challenge those who would define marriage solely as a contract (to be entered or abandoned upon simple will). This challenge, I suggest, is one part of the level critique Jesus consistently made against the presumed necessity of marriage (and their arrangements) in his time.

At the same time, Christ's critique of institutional marriage does not appear to be a denigration of intimate sexual or domestic relationships, for those who desire as much. Rather than dismissing special relationships altogether, Christ's critique of institutional marriage appears to be grounded in a concern that human beings care about how people relate to one another. Many human beings have a need to belong, to love, and to be loved. For a variety of reasons usually having to do with property, procreation, and social ordering, most civilizations have constructed relational institutions that do this, but also mediate (if not prescribe) the way we love one another—and this we have called "marriage." Jesus was relatively uninterested in preserving an institution of marriage so much as he seemed to care deeply that those who give themselves to such an institution do not confuse the marriage contract (and all the various other laws) with the subject of the relationship itself. If the outward social/legal/ritual definitions of marriage, divorce, and remarriage were important to participation in the reign of God, we would likely find that kind of careful delineation from the teachings of Christ. What we discover instead is a challenge to take our relationships seriously, in mutuality, and to recognize the significance of our relationships.

The ramification of Jesus's teachings on marriage leaves us with a certain dilemma. Having decentered institutional marriage from its expected place in life (Luke 20:34–35), Jesus also unlocked what would have been expected sexual norms associated with marriage. He left these matters largely to individual practice. Jesus did not give any rules or guidelines for sexual activity, except that people be true to the promises that they had made. Most specifically, this meant avoiding adultery when married. Whereas Jewish law had defined adultery in terms of patriarchal property ("taking another man's wife"), Jesus reformed adultery laws to make partners mutual property—and thus, equals. He did not explicitly comment on mutual sexual relationships between people who were not married. Indeed, his only other teaching on sexuality was a brief statement on "lust." In it, he taught a group of men that if they "lusted" after a woman who was not their wife, they had committed a kind of adultery with her.[26] The teaching did not denigrate sexual desire (which is natural to the human condition), but demanded that men consider the quality of their sexual thoughts and desires. Since Jesus is remembered as using the language of "adultery" in association with "lust," his concern was more or less a critique of those who imagine others as sexual objects simply to be "had."

Thus, when it comes to marriage and sexuality, all we can really say is that Jesus responded *only* to the social institution presented to him and then invited people to consider the essence of those relationships, not their outward forms or conventional rules. This is consistent with some of his other teachings, especially those in which Jesus found ways to point to the interior qualities of a relationship (or an issue) rather than defining its outward form. For example, Jesus taught by parable that a good tree (much like a human) is known by its fruit, not by the outward appearance of the tree.[27] In another place, Jesus taught by parable that if one is concerned with "purity," one should not worry about what's on the outside, but rather, on what is within.[28] Christ's emphasis on the interior qualities of human relationships (sexual or otherwise) is a comprehensive critique against any religious person (past or present) who would make judgments on morality (or righteousness) on the basis of rules that concern themselves with outward form at the expense of quality. If Jesus did not endorse inhumane interpretations of religious law and social custom, it is difficult to imagine why those who follow his teachings ever approve of rigid sexual laws that are steeped in simple convention. I turn once again to Raymond Lawrence, who creatively concluded about Jesus's teachings on marriage and sexuality this way:

> Anyone who attempts to portray Jesus either as a monogamist, polygamist, or celibate will be left at the altar by the canonical texts. On the basis of the texts, it is far easier to make a case for Jesus as a libertine. But it would have to be a case of a qualified libertine, who was at the same time very respectful of the Torah, and in no respects frivolous in his approach to human behavior. Jesus seems clearly to have been a situational ethicist with a bias. His bias was that any human behavior was permitted if it did not harm anyone and contributed to human well-being in body, mind, and soul. [For Jesus] behavior must proceed from love for others.[29]

If such is an accurate (albeit general) description of Jesus's ethic, then contemporary Christians would do well to interpret principles of the gospel to apply contextually—*not rules to follow rigidly*—as a matter of engaging in Christian sexual ethics. At minimum, I agree with the aforementioned biblical scholar William Countryman, who has said that sexual relationships in accord with the gospel should be "free of falsehood and violence toward [one's partner] and in some way be compatible with the Christian person's relationship with Christ."[30]

Paul, Sex, and Marriage

The ordering of human relationships is a matter addressed throughout the New Testament. What we find in these texts, especially in the epistles (or letters), are examples of first-century Christian communities wrestling with the principles of the gospel in light of their social and historical contexts. Marriage was one of the social institutions with which early Christians wrestled.

Even as many of the first-century Christian communities had pre-existing concepts of marriage and family from the Jewish tradition, they were also exposed to different ideas about it through the Roman Empire. As many scholars tell it, Rome supported the social institution of *pater familia* (the father family). The *pater familia* was one ruled completely by the husband/father, and as Rosemary Radford Ruether has said, it is best described as a unit of production and not just a kinship of blood relatives.[31] The blood relative line (traced through the father/husband) was called the *domus*.[32] The "family," however, consisted of a man/husband/father, his wife, his sons, their wives, their children, the workers of the household, as well as the slaves. With respect to sexual morality, men often consorted a variety of sexual partners other than their wives; however, the Roman institution of marriage was monogamous for the purposes of procreation and preserving legitimate familial heirs.

Within the framework of *pater familia*, the father was literally the authority for the "household." To call one "father" was not simply to recognize one's male biological parent. It was to signal to whom it was that you belonged, and who it was that possessed you in authority. As Andrew Clarke has well noted, "All relationships within the family were defined with reference to him, and unlike many modern societies this authority existed over both minors and adults."[33] (One might wonder, then, if this is why Jesus drew on the language of "father" to symbolically describe God. Culturally, it was synonymous with "power" and "authority.") Solidifying his power all the more, the father was the social and political representative of the "family" in the larger structure of Roman society.[34]

Many discussions in the New Testament regarding marriage, as well as the roles of men and women, were situated within the Roman construction of *pater familia* (which itself was in a tenuous relationship with Jewish norms). Clarke notes, "The Roman *familia* was so integral to Graeco-Roman society that members of the early church were bound to have been influenced by this power institution."[35] But even if the early churches were influenced by the Roman model of *pater familia*, they do not appear to have rigidly accepted it. For example, the patriarchy supporting the hierarchy of *pater familia* seems to be challenged by a kind of early Christian egalitarianism, as when the author of Galatians proclaimed that "in Christ there is no male or female."[36] Sometimes the New Testament literature even depicts an antifamily position as far as familial fidelity is concerned.[37] Consider that even the Gospel of Luke captured Jesus teaching, "If anyone comes to me and cannot hate his own father and mother and wife and children and brothers and sisters, yes, even his own life, he cannot be my disciple."[38] Given the context, Jesus was not (likely) teaching to "hate" family members (as we would conceive that today), but rather, to grant Christian discipleship higher authority than the customary *pater familia* would have allowed. This was no small concern. For example, the second-century Christian martyr Perpetua (a Roman convert) found herself in the gladiator arena for obedience to her heavenly "father" over that of her earthly father and his presumed authority.[39] In fact, because the early Jesus movement critiqued obedience to the family, Jesus was considered something of a social insurrectionist. Rosemary Radford Ruether is thus correct to say that the New Testament "vision of the church as an alternative family was itself in profound tension with existing social constructions of the family in the Jewish and Greco-Roman worlds."[40]

And yet, in other places in the New Testament literature the Roman institution of *pater familia* appears to be tacitly accepted.[41] In one place, it is loosely drawn upon as an analogy to describe the relationship between God, Christ, and the Church.[42] In other instances, the leaders of the early churches seemed content to work within the social institution of *pater familia* (insofar as the civil ordering of marriage and family was concerned), so long as Christian principles were practiced within. For example, in the letter of Paul to the Ephesians it is said that for a man to be the head of the wife (and the family) he must serve sacrificially, like Christ.[43] The "father/husband" as servant-leader would have been quite the inversion of *pater familia* according to Roman practice. Indeed, it reveals to us that early Christians had little serious interest in simply keeping the social/civil status quo. It would seem that they were willing to work within the framework of first-century models of marriage (whether Jewish or Roman), but not with any enduring loyalty to the cultural models themselves.

Thus, where first-century Christian leaders tacitly accepted given cultural models of marriage, they did so believing (apparently) that the gospel could transform how those relationships were best lived out. Indeed, far from being social activists who sought to redefine marriage and family through governmental channels, early Christian leaders (such as Paul) had little problem with Christians living in the cultural models available to them, but only so long as they lived in those cultural models with the principles of the gospel.[44] Many of whom did so fully believing that their savior, Jesus, would soon return and usher in the renewal of the world. With a heightened eschatological worldview (that is, believing the end was near), efforts to change existing cultural models of marriage and family (or any other social structure) were less important than the task of being a disciple of Christ and preparing for his return. All that we can say, then, is that the diversity of ways in which *pater familia* was treated by early Christians suggests no moral demand to uphold such a patriarchal model of marriage and family. *Pater familia* was simply a reality to be contended with by first-century Christians. For contemporary Christians to try and recreate some form of *pater familia* because it is described in the New Testament would be a mistake.

But a New Testament text that addresses the relationship of sexual activity and marriage more specifically is found in the Pauline text, 1 Corinthians 7:1–9, 25–31:

> Now concerning the matters about which you wrote: "It is well for a man not to touch a woman." But because of cases of sexual immorality, each man should have his own wife and each woman her own husband. The husband should give to his wife her conjugal rights, and likewise the wife to her husband. For the wife does not have authority over her own body, but the husband does; likewise the husband does not have authority over his own body, but the wife does. Do not deprive one another except perhaps by agreement for a set time, to devote yourselves to prayer, and then come together again, so that Satan may not tempt you because of your lack of self-control. This I say by way of concession, not of command. I wish that all were as I myself am. But each has a particular gift from God, one having one kind and another a different kind.
>
> To the unmarried and the widow I say that it is well for them to remain unmarried as I am. But if they are not practicing self-control, they should marry. For it is better to marry than to be aflame with passion. . . .
>
> Now concerning virgins, I have no command of the Lord, but I give my opinion as one who by the Lord's mercy is trustworthy. I think that, in view of the impending crisis, it is well for you to remain as you are. Are you bound to a wife? Do not seek to be free. Are you free from a wife? Do not seek a wife. But if you marry, you do not sin, and if a virgin marries, she does not sin. Yet those who marry will experience distress in

this life, and I would spare you of that. I mean, brothers and sisters, the appointed time has grown short; from now on, let even those who have wives be as though they had none, and those who mourn as though they were not mourning, and those who rejoice as though they were not rejoicing, and those who buy as though they had no possessions, and those who deal with the world as though they had no dealings with it. For the present form of this world is passing away.[45]

For some Christians, this passage settles the question as to whether or not sexual activity can be had outside of a marriage arrangement. Some will understand that the surface meaning of the text is also its conclusion: that sexual activity should be limited to marriage. But this is not altogether so clear. One interpretive option is articulated by the biblical scholar Dale Martin. As Martin analyzes Paul's writing on sexual desire and the Christian life, Martin has noticed that Paul is rather negative with respect to matters of sex and sexual desire. Martin writes:

> [W]henever Paul broaches the subject of sex and the desire associated with it, he has nothing good to say about it. In 1 Corinthians 7, for example, Paul nowhere mentions a positive kind of desire as opposed to the "burning" that he hopes marriage will quench. He says that sex within marriage functions to guard weak Christians from the pollution of [sexual immorality] (7:2); it is a duty that Christian spouses owe to one another (7:3); and it protects Christians from satanic testing (7:5). The romanticism of modern Christian (especially Protestant) attitudes about marriage—that it functions as the "fulfillment" of divinely created and "healthy" human sexuality, or at least heterosexuality; that it is the "normal" outcome of love between a man and a woman; that human beings were practically created *for it*—is strikingly, though not surprisingly, absent [in Paul's writing].[46]

As Martin goes on to explain it, the problem for Paul was that sexual desire threatened to derail one's desire for God and thus "spiritually pollute" the Christian—in particular, by keeping the Christian distracted by the things of "this world," rather than focusing on the things of God.[47]

While Martin's interpretation clearly emphasizes a "sex-negative" reading of the Pauline text, James Brownson suggests a different interpretive angle. Namely, Brownson notes that this text is situated within a larger cultural debate about marriage and celibacy, between existing (and competing) Stoic and Cynic camps.[48] As Brownson explains, the Stoics allowed for marriage insofar as it was seen as the basic building block of society—with respect to social order and procreation. Meanwhile, the Cynics advocated for freedom from marriage (and thus freedom from its duties and responsibilities) in order to pursue the study of philosophy—without distraction—in celibacy. Brownson imagines that the Christians of Corinth were at odds with one another over which of these two lifestyles (marriage or celibacy) best reflected participation in the reign of God: marriage for the up-building of society (now with Christian families), or celibacy, in order to devote oneself to the ministries of Christ. For Brownson, Paul is attempting to communicate to the Corinthian Christians that both marriage and celibacy are permissible in the Christian life, and then according to "calling" or "gift." Thus, in Brownson's view, Paul's problem was not with sexual desire itself. Brownson imagines instead that Paul was addressing excessive sexual desire; the kind without "boundaries or limits," and thus, the kind of sexual desire that demotes people as objects simply to be taken.[49] Thus, Brownson interprets Paul as directing people toward marriage in order to learn how best to enjoy natural sexual desires—recognizing that for Paul, marriage was the known relational shelter for the practice of mutuality and love between sexual partners.

Both Martin and Brownson help to illuminate the difficulties of interpreting this text. I draw on both to construct a guiding moral principle for Christian ethics. Namely, if Brownson is right that Paul was concerned with sexual passion because it could become excessive—and thus dislocate one's love for God and neighbor—then neither the "problem" of sexual desire, nor the peculiar "solution" of marriage *necessarily* amount to a universal diagnosis or prescription for Christian sexual ethics. We could state it a different way, such that the real problem identified in the text is the dislocation of one's desire from God. It is not sexual desire in and of itself that derails one from God, but sexual desire that is perhaps excessive, similar to any other desire, thing, relationship, object, job, or idol, on which a human might focus to the exclusion of God.[50] To that end, Paul prescribed marriage as a solution for excessive sexual passion. At this point, however, we need to recall the important insight from Martin: that Paul's "marriage solution" is not offered with romantic love, or relational fulfillment in mind. Instead, marriage is prescribed so that sexual passion might be extinguished, in order to attend to particular religious matters (prayer, temptation, etc.;

revisit 1 Corinthians 7). This too is a peculiar teaching, and one that most Christian ministers (today) would not likely articulate as the primary reason to get married. So why does Paul? We cannot know that with certainty, but there is perhaps one clue in the text. Namely, these teachings on sex and marriage are contingent on the "impending crisis" and the near eschatological horizon that Paul refers to in the text.

Biblical scholars have debated the vague reference to the "impending crisis" that Paul references in the text. Whatever it was, it had a particular effect on how Paul thought the Christians of Corinth needed to navigate their lives. What we know more certainly is that Paul also had in mind an eschatological vision of the return of Christ and the Day of Judgment.[51] In light of this, Paul could have meant that natural things such as sexual desire (as well as marriage and family) might need sublimation or denial, whether to prepare oneself for meeting God or in order to go out and help prepare others. As scholars Luke Timothy Johnson and Mark Jordon put it, "Eschatology calls all human institutions into question."[52] Indeed, these scholars note that in the Pauline texts there is a tension between living life in the here and now, and living in light of the age to come. How Paul taught on issues of sexuality, marriage, and family, Johnson and Jordan say, was always caught in this tension—and more or less depending on developments in Paul's eschatology, which became less "expectant" as time wore on. For this reason, we sometimes find positive statements on marriage and family in the Pauline texts, and sometimes teaching to sublimate sexuality and intimate relationships in light of what Paul believed was going to be a near eschatological event (the end of time and Christ's return).[53]

So what do Christians do with this passage, given that Paul's concern for Judgment Day is at least two thousand years premature? With respect to sexual passion, we might simply acknowledge that without careful cultivation, how we act from our sexual desires can become excessive, and maybe even self-destructive. To acknowledge this is not to say that having sexual passion *is* excessive or destructive, but that we should be as attentive to how we act on it, as we are with any of our other passions or inclinations. To that end, Christians need not sublimate sexual desire, but instead, consider how one might act on it in ways that contribute to living and doing well, and then in light of God as the Christian's highest end.

Thinking in terms of sexuality this way, the context of a sexual relationship *is* important (i.e., who is having sex, and why), and yet, I think it can be argued that the context for sex—for Christians—need

not be a conventional one (i.e., heterosexual marriage). As it was noted
above, a significant aspect of living a Christian life (from many New
Testament perspectives) is not necessarily a matter of deferring to con-
ventional/cultural norms to evaluate "good behavior." To the contrary,
the "good" is identified in the New Testament as that which participates
in the reign of God. Christians seemingly do this by embodying and
practicing the principles of the gospel in all aspects of life (as the "gospel"
is interpreted by the Christian and/or faith community). The suggestion
I am making here, then, is that gospel principles (e.g., neighbor-love,
justice, and kindness, to name a few) can be practiced in any number of
sexual contexts. Indeed, the sexual relationships a person might engage
could be marital or nonmarital, LGBT or straight, in committed relationships, or perhaps even of a casual sort. Thus, as Christians think
about having sexual relationships, it would seem that the real religious
and moral concern (for Christians) is to be mindful of how their sexual
activities actualize principles of the gospel. Where those principles are
possible to embody in any number or variety of sexual relationships,
the Christian community should have ample reason to recognize these
as "holy" or "good."

And yet, there will be some Christians who will tell us that this
is hardly a substantiated reading of Paul's teaching. Such Christians can
show us that within certain English versions of the Bible (such as the
King James Version) several of Paul's letters condemn the sin of "fornication." Some modern Christians define fornication as sexual activity
outside of marriage, between two nonmarried people. Defining the terms
this way has led some Christians to conclude that sex outside of marriage
is forbidden (whatever the cultural ambiguities of the New Testament
passages on sex and marriage might be). But Paul did not spell out that
condemnation as clearly as some contemporary Christians would like
to believe. Where English versions of the Bible read "fornication," the
Greek term is *porneia*.

Porneia is a nebulous term and means "sexual immorality." Its gener-
ality is its sting. One can simply point to something and call it "*porneia*"
with considerable moral disdain. But as the biblical scholar Robert von
Thaden has argued so well, the New Testament enunciation "*porneia*"
does not straightaway tell us what sexual immorality is, or what counts
specifically as a matter of sexual vice (morally or religiously).[54] Thus,
while we might all agree that sexual immorality (left in the abstract)
should be avoided, the term itself, in the New Testament, does not tell

us what counts *as* sexual immorality. Christian communities are left to discern the nature of sexual immorality in light of their faith commitments and their insights born of human experience.

Concluding Thoughts on the New Testament, Sex, and Marriage

As we have seen, the oft-cited principles of the New Testament (neighbor love, justice, kindness, etc.) do not of themselves demand that "good" sex is only found in marriage. However, that is not to say that marriage is unimportant. It is simply to acknowledge that when we study the New Testament and turn to apply its principles within the context of our sexual varieties today, it seems altogether possible to embody these principles without marriage (or a heterosexual union). Indeed, I think many of us will agree that marital status does not guarantee the practice of sexual virtue. Husbands have raped their wives, and spouses have withheld sex as a form of punishment (whether to get their way, or as a passive-aggressive expression of dissatisfaction). Therefore, just as we might admit that marital status does not guarantee sexual virtue for the Christian, we might also say that marriage is not really required for sexual virtue to be realized. For those who are Christian, it would seem that the New Testament texts point to the possibility that when gospel principles are practiced, they can transform the quality of any human relationships. And if the gospel principles can reach into any human relationship, that must include the transformation of any sexual relationships. Thinking in terms of the Bible and sexual ethics this way, it seems to require the Christian community to embrace any relationships in which the gospel principles can be practiced, including in and through sex, marital or not.

Seven

The Bible and Homosexuality

The source of antigay feelings among Christians must be sought elsewhere.

—John Boswell

Queer Eye for the Bible

Commanding the attention of many Christian churches is a fierce debate on the ethics of homosexuality. Some institutions, such as the Catholic Church, insist that homosexual orientation—even if experienced innately—is a moral disorder, a defect resulting from the fall of humankind into sin.[1] While the church admits that it is not blameworthy to experience any innate disorder, including same-sex attraction, the church also says that Christians ought to resist every expression of that desire. Indeed, the church teaches that same-sex activity, even between loving partners, is always an instance of "intrinsic moral evil" and "grave immorality." In other words, it can be a matter of mortal sin.[2]

Yet other Christian churches, such as the United Church of Christ, the Metropolitan Community Church, the Episcopal Church, the Presbyterian Church (USA), and the Evangelical Lutheran Church in America (to name a few), have opened the doors more inclusively to the lesbian, gay, bisexual, and transgender (LGBT) community. Each of these denominations welcomes LGBT people into membership without diagnosing homosexuality as disordered or intrinsically evil. Some of these denominations even provide religious marriage rites for gay and lesbian couples, as well as ordination to the offices of ministry. Such a wide range of responses to homosexuality reveals disparate understandings of sexual ethics among the churches. This has to do, in large part, with how Christian communities draw on the Bible to settle the morality of LGBT issues.

If the Bible is going to help Christians settle moral questions about homosexuality, it will be necessary to read it with a "queer eye" for discernment. At minimum, this means reading the Bible with an informed understanding of what homosexuality is (as an orientation, especially as described by the sciences) and what contemporary LGBT relationships are like, generally conceived. This we hold in comparison to what the biblical texts have to say about same-sex activities, in light of *their* cultural frameworks, not ours. This means employing a critical study of the texts, recognizing that we cannot project our modern understanding(s) of LGBT relationships onto millennia-old documents, whose authors did not possess categories of sexual orientation, nor did they necessarily have concepts of egalitarian relationships between people of the same physical sex.

To limit the scope of our biblical study on this issue, I will ask the reader to consider the texts that are often used to condemn same-sex relationships. These have sometimes been called "the clobber passages," insofar as they have been used as "proof-texts" against same-sex relationships.[3] For LGBT people, and straight allies, reading these texts will likely be painful. LGBT readers know all too well how the Bible has been used to condemn and exile. At the same time, a careful study of these passages might also be a challenge for those who think the Bible is very clear on the ethics of homosexuality. Indeed, when we examine the clobber passages carefully, we come to find out that these passages sometimes reveal attitudes about gender and sexuality that most Christians would not accept today. Finding this out can be troubling to the person of faith. But this kind of critical and careful study is what we must do in order to adequately discern whether or not contemporary notions of homosexuality are really condemned in the Bible.

The Hebrew Bible and Homosexuality

Genesis: Sex, in the Beginning

Many of the debates about "the Bible and homosexuality" have much to do with a half dozen verses spaced out between the Hebrew Bible and the New Testament. The theologian Patrick Cheng notes that of the "more than 31,000 verses" in the Bible, "Christian communities have spent countless hours in recent decades arguing about the meaning of only six or so verses (that is, 0.02% of the Bible) that purportedly relate to LGBT people."[4] In addition to those "six or so verses" that are commonly cited to condemn homosexuality, some Christians also look to the creation stories in the book of Genesis in an attempt to construct a theology of heterosexuality as God's original intent for human sexual relating.

The creation narratives in Genesis 1 and 2 do not give the reader much detail. In the first chapter, God is depicted as creating the world in an orderly fashion, over the course of six days (and resting on the seventh). Before the seventh day, the text says that God created humankind, consisting of males and females, who are charged by God "to be fruitful and [to] multiply." In the second chapter, the creation narrative is reset and we read about a garden named "Eden," and in it, a man formed from the dust of the ground (Adam). The second chapter offers slightly more detail than the first about the relationship between human beings. Namely, the dirt-person/Adam was alone, and not one of the creatures of the earth was found to be a suitable helpmate. The text then says that God caused a sleep to come upon Adam, and from one of Adam's ribs a woman was formed. Upon waking, Adam says, "This at last is bone of my bones and flesh of my flesh; this one shall be called Woman, for out of Man this one was taken."[5] The author of the text then goes on to explain, "Therefore a man leaves his father and his mother and clings to his wife, and they become one flesh."[6]

The biblical scholar Richard Hays says that this text (among others) clearly affirms "that God has made man and woman for one another and that our sexual desires rightly find fulfillment within heterosexual marriage."[7] He goes on to say, "This picture of [heterosexual] marriage provides the positive backdrop against which the Bible's few emphatic negations of homosexuality must be read."[8]

The *Catechism of the Catholic Church* offers a similar interpretation, teaching that the Genesis texts point toward God's intent for human sexuality in terms of male/female complementarity. The *Catechism* teaches:

> Everyone, man and woman, should acknowledge and accept his sexual identity [sic]. Physical, moral, and spiritual difference and complementarity are oriented toward the goods of marriage and the flourishing of family life. The harmony of the couple and of society depends in part on the way in which the complementarity, need, and mutual support between the sexes are lived out.[9]

However, the problem with the complementarity argument is that it privileges physical complementarity at the expense of *interpersonal* complementarity.

As the moral theologians Todd Salzman and Michael Lawler have noted, human/sexual complementarity is multifaceted and includes (at least) five dimensions: physical, emotional, psychological, spiritual, and relational.[10] I would wager that Christians would agree that these components are integral to genuine complementarity in intimate relationships—and that sexual complementarity should not be reduced to a reproductive utility. Indeed, Salzman and Lawler note that physical/sexual complementarity need not be read as "reproductive" complementarity. They say:

> Reproduction is achieved via a human activity, but it is not itself a human activity. Though humans achieve reproduction through a sexual act, that act itself is not an act of reproduction. If reproduction were the purpose of the sexual act, then all reproductive-type sexual acts would have the possibility of realizing this purpose. Women who have had a hysterectomy, however, or infertile men continue to have and to use *sexual* organs, but they are without reproductive organs. All sexual human beings have sexual organs, but not all sexual human beings have *reproductive* organs.[11]

Noticeably, the creation narratives in Genesis 1–2 do not address these complex human/sexual realities. Nor do these stories address the diverse ways in which sexuality orients human beings toward particular sexes, or particular people. At best, these stories provide a general sketch of human longing and belonging.

At the same time, some Christians like to remind us that Genesis describes the creation of "Adam and Eve," not "Adam and Steve." Fair enough: the Bible does not explicitly explain the origins of sexual orientation, or the reason for heterosexual, bisexual, and homosexual differences. But notice, Genesis doesn't explain many other things either. For example, it doesn't explain to us the origins of racial differences. While that may not bother a number of Christians today, it may be helpful to remember that nineteenth and twentieth-century American racists used the Bible to suggest that Caucasians were God's original design and that people of color (especially those of African descent) were inferior to whites—whether by virtue of the fall of humankind into sin, or by God's designation.[12] As with racist uses of these texts, when we try to push the Genesis narratives to say more than they do about sexuality, we start to impose upon the text what is not actually there. As I interpret these stories, I understand that the Genesis narratives are *theological* sketches of life's beginnings. Genesis 1 imagines an intelligent creator behind the unfolding of life, while Genesis 2 acknowledges the human need for sociality and kinship—if not also a cautionary tale about the choices we make and their consequences. To suggest that the Genesis narratives speak in any specific way to matters of gender complementarity, or sexual orientation, or even same-sex relationships really pushes the texts beyond their original scope. As the biblical scholar James Brownson notes, the creation narratives of Genesis (especially chapter 2) points toward the need for human companionship out of loneliness. As Brownson says, these creation texts reveal "at bottom [the] longings for human community and fellowship," not a divine dictum that heterosexuality was God's only "plan" for human sexuality.[13]

That being said, it is good to pause here and remember how curiously these same texts have been used (morally and theologically) to speak to issues of sex and sexuality. Recall that some of the earliest Christian theologians did not think that sexuality was even part of the created order. For them, sexual desire (if not sex itself) resulted from the fall of humankind into sin (e.g., Gregory of Nyssa).[14] What is more, recall also that for ancient Judaism, interpretations of the Torah (of which Genesis is a part) accepted men in polygamous marriages.[15] In other words, Genesis 1 and 2 have been interpreted by many people to mean *many* things. To demand a narrow interpretation of Genesis 1 and 2 in order to justify a heterosexual, marital, monogamous, and/or reproductive sexual norm is, at best, simply "one more" interpretation by a religious community trying to make sense of these texts for contemporary use. At worst, it assumes a heterosexual norm and draws its antihomosexual conclusions on the basis of presumption.

However, such comments are not to deny that the Genesis narratives clearly value the capacity of sexual union to result in reproduction. Indeed, the texts say that humans were given this power and commanded by God to use it. But the texts do not tell us *when* we should reproduce with a mate, or the morality (or immorality) of not engaging reproduction at all. Consider: if we exercise a plain reading of the text, the command to "be fruitful and multiply" is extended over *all* living creatures. And yet, Christians tend not to read the reproduction mandate as a universal duty for each person to fulfill.[16] In fact, the largest

Christian denomination, the Roman Catholic Church, gives women and
men options out of reproduction by entering a celibate religious life.
Protestants too have failed to interpret a "mandate" to reproduce from
the Genesis narratives—going so far as to allow artificial birth control for
men and women who do not wish to produce offspring. That is quite a
bit of moral flexibility for celibates and heterosexuals, even though the
plain reading of the text says that reproduction is a divine command!

Of course, I'm not suggesting we adopt a plain reading of the texts.
But I do think that the contextual use of these passages by celibates
and contraceptive-using heterosexuals means that we need to be just
as contextually flexible about how we understand the Genesis texts in
light of gay and lesbian relationships. Any final "biblical" word on the
moral permissibility of homosexuality, then, will have to be derived from
other biblical texts that make reference to—in some way—same-sex acts.

The Sin of Sodom

There are two explicit texts in the Hebrew Bible that are often cited
to condemn homosexual orientation and same-sex relationships. The
first is the infamous story of Sodom and Gomorrah (in Genesis 19). In
the story of Sodom and Gomorrah, two male messengers (also called
"angels") arrive in the city of Sodom as strangers. They become the
guests of a man named Lot.[17] While Lot was providing the angels a
meal and a place to stay, the text says that the men of Sodom (both
young and old) arrived at Lot's door, en masse, and demanded that he
give them the visitors so that the men of Sodom might "know" them—a
euphemism for sexual intent. Lot tried to dissuade the men of Sodom
by offering up his two virgin daughters, so that no harm would come
to his male visitors.

The offering of the daughters is ethically reprehensible, and yet the
text is silent about the threat of their forced sacrifice. At the same time,
the text simply accepts it as a viable option that the men of Sodom
might actually take the women, rather than the men. But according to
the text, the men of Sodom refused that offer, and replied to Lot, "Now
we will deal worse with you than with [the visitors]."[18]

The interaction between Lot and the gang from Sodom reveals
much about the meaning of the story itself. To the point, inasmuch as the
men of Sodom were indeed there for a physical sexual event, the scene
was hardly romantic, or even seductive in a homoerotic sense. As many

scholars tell it (including conservative scholars, such as Richard Hays), the men of Sodom had come to *rape* the visitors.[19] The gang scene—let alone the forcible demands of the crowd—make it difficult to imagine that the intentions of the men of Sodom were for anything other than sexual violence. The men of Sodom were not gay in any recognizable sense, nor were their intents recreational or intimate.

It is not the only time such a scene occurs in the Hebrew Bible.

An equally disturbing story can be found in Judges 19:16–30. In this text, a Levite man and his female companion (his concubine) were traveling away from home and came to rest in the town of Gibeah. Extending them some unexpected shelter and other provisions was "an old man of Gibeah," whose name we never learn. The story then takes a violent turn. Just as it happened in Sodom, a gang of men from Gibeah came to the door of the old man's house and demanded that he let them have the Levite so that they might "know" him. Instead of giving the gang his male guest, the old man offered up his virgin daughter, as well as the Levite's concubine, saying to the crowd, "Violate them, do to them whatever is good in your eyes. But to this man don't do such a vile thing."[20]

As the mob became more incited, the panicked Levite pushed his concubine out to them. Had this been a gang of gay men, the following unspeakable tragedy would not have occurred. But as the text reports: "They took her away and raped her repeatedly all night long until morning, letting her go only when dawn was breaking."[21] The text goes on to report that she died from the injuries she suffered. To make matters worse, her body was cut up into many pieces and sent throughout the land as an indication of what evil had occurred in Gibeah. There was no justice for this nameless woman. She is only memorialized by those of us who think of her as one of many women (then and now) who suffer at the hands of predacious and vicious men.

Phyllis Trible was right to call a text such as this a "text of terror."[22]

While biblical texts like these are *infuriatingly* silent on the abuse and slaughter of women, they very obviously describe incidents of intended and actual rape. At issue, however, is not only a matter of sexual violence. When we examine the cultural setting of the story, we find good reasons to believe that the sexual violence was a vehicle for inflicting public *shame*.

What many Christian readers of the Bible might not realize is that same-sex rape was a patriarchal tool, often used in the ancient near east, to inflict social shame onto other men. Anal rape incurred "shame" because it forced a man to take the (lower) position "of a woman" through sexual penetration.[23] Public knowledge of male penetration was considered so shameful (in some cultures) that same-sex rape was occasionally used as a form of punishment.[24] Thus, when we compare the story of Sodom and Gomorrah with other rape narratives in the Bible (such as Judges 19), and when we put it in historical context, we can see why so many biblical scholars argue that the intention of the men of Sodom was rape, not recreational sex among self-identified gay people. It is my hope that no reader of this text will suggest that same-sex rape is somehow equivalent with mutual or loving same-sex relationships today.

Contemporary Same-Sex Rape and the Moral Status of Penetration

Same-sex rape still functions as a weapon of shame and denigration. This is especially prevalent in prisons, where anal rape is used to establish hierarchies of dominance. According to the *Human Rights Watch*, which cites data from the Bureau of Justice Statistics, as many as seventy thousand American prisoners are sexually assaulted or raped per year.[25] Where these are incidents of same-sex rape, such happens not because prisons are overrun with homosexuals, but because same-sex rape is used as a social tool in the hands of heterosexuals. Like in the ancient Near East, same-sex rape still functions to make another man "inferior." It does so by robbing him of his so-called masculinity, by forcing him to take the position of a "woman" (that is, to be penetrated). Clearly, such a practice is not grounded in same-sex desire, but a lust for power and domination—and this rooted in violent and misogynistic tendencies. Those who think that physical penetration makes one "womanly" (and thus shameful) perpetuate grossly skewed roles concerning sex and gender. In particular, the denigration of penetration serves to demean women (in general) because it frames a receptive sexual position as a demoralizing act.

We still participate in such systematic sexist thinking when any of us perpetuates the idea that those who are penetrated (whether male or female) are somehow inferior to those who do the penetrating. Such views run deep in our culture and are reaffirmed in much of our sexualized language. How else do we explain that a "pussy" is one who is weak? How else is "fuck" a curse? For what other reason do some people accept that it is better for a gay man to be a "butch top" than a "femmy bottom?" Overcoming this sexual dualism will take serious effort on our part. As Carter Heyward correctly noted, "We cannot comprehend the meaning of sexuality . . . without viewing its place in the context of power relations between genders. In particular, we must understand sexism, the oppression of women in which men are expected to play their manly roles—*on top of women*."[26] Or more simply: many men find their worth and sense of superiority in their ability to "top" others, and by doing so, making the penetrated "inferior." In Sodom, the agenda was nearly the same. Namely, the men of Sodom were attempting to inflict shame on the visitors through violent acts of sexual penetration—making "bottoms" out of any stranger, so that nobody would mistake who, in that town, was on "top."

Biblical Sodomy

However, there are still those in our society who associate Sodom and Gomorrah with homosexuality. This is an unjustifiable interpretation when we study this scripture carefully. The real point of this text is to condemn violence and gross inhospitality. Indeed, even other biblical texts indicate that the "sin" of Sodom was something other than homosexuality. The Book of Ezekiel puts it this way, "This was the guilt of your sister Sodom: she and her daughters had pride, excess of food, and prosperous ease, but did not aid the poor and needy. They were haughty, and did abominable things before me; therefore I removed them when I saw it."[27]

If there is a sin of "sodomy" that we can derive from the story of Sodom and Gomorrah, it is the sin of violence, especially to those who come to us for shelter and protection. It is curious that any informed reader of the Bible would absorb this passage and think that it has something to do with same-sex attraction or LGBT relationships. If we must reduce this passage to a sexual sin, it is the sin of rape. Of course, there are passages in the Bible that condemn heterosexual rape as well, but no one to my knowledge infers that condemnations of heterosexual rape should be projected as a condemnation of heterosexuality. Those who wish to make Sodom and Gomorrah about homosexual orientation or same-sex relationships do so by making a blanket association of anal rape with anal intercourse, which is often practiced by gay males. But that kind of blanket association is not only wrong, it is offensive: it suggests that somehow a gang-rape scene legitimately reveals what goes on in same-sex activities. What is more, the blanket association of Sodom and Gomorrah with anal intercourse between men discounts that heterosexuals also practice anal intercourse—and not infrequently.[28]

Sex and Leviticus

The only other section in the Hebrew Bible that Christians have commonly cited to condemn same-sex activity is in the Book of Leviticus, chapters 18 and 20. Leviticus 18:22 is probably the more familiar passage. It reads: "You shall not lie with a male as with a woman; it is an abomination." Leviticus 20:13 echoes that commandment, but adds, "If a man lies with a male as with a woman, both of them have committed an abomination; they shall be put to death; their blood is upon them." For those Christians who frequently turn to these passages, the surface-level reading of Leviticus is usually interpreted as a *universal* moral condemnation of same-sex activities, especially between men.

This interpretation is not supported by a contextual study of the texts.

There are a wide variety of things in the Hebrew Bible (especially the first five books of the Bible) that are labeled as "abominations." Shellfish, mixed fabrics, rabbits, pigs, hawks, and fields sown with different seeds are only but a *few* of the things labeled as "detestable" or "abominations" within the Hebrew (or Old Testament) texts.[29] One can find these abomination lists especially in the Book of Leviticus. However, serious readers of the Bible know that these are not prima facie moral condemnations, but part of the Jewish holiness and purity codes. As the biblical scholar William Countryman notes, these codes were used to define ritual purity (in a physical sense for religious activities) as well as a means of demarcating Jewish people from the rest of the nations (the Gentiles), and then in a cultural sense.[30] Jewish people had a number of these distinguishing practices and characteristics. They included (and still do for some Jewish communities) male circumcision, methods for cutting hair, types of dress, as well as more than six hundred other customs that are otherwise known as the commandments of the Torah.[31] And to complicate matters all the more, these written laws are often mediated by the sacred oral law (now written down in the Mishnah and Talmud).[32]

Leviticus 18:22 and 20:13, then, represent statements on sexual activity that must be read in the context of the Jewish holiness and purity codes. As Rachel Biale has noted, one central concern of these codes had to do with the "mixing" of certain kinds of things.[33] This was not only a concern when it came to sexual relationships, but to the mixing of all things. When reading the Torah, sometimes the laws concerning the "mixing-of-kinds" seem rational and practical (for example, a hygienic concern not to mix with people who had open sores). Other times (such as not eating bacon) the laws appear without a rational or natural explanation. All we can say is that to touch or mix certain kinds of things that were "forbidden" by the Torah was to commit an "abomination," or something "detestable." But we must remember that these laws were particular (and peculiar) to the ancient Jewish people, religiously and culturally. The ancient Jewish people understood themselves to be set apart by God as a priestly nation in order to mediate blessings from God to all the earth.[34] Identifying this way, the ancient Jewish people expected of themselves certain ritual and cultural distinctions that did not always "make sense" upon rational reflection (e.g., not shaving one's sideburns, or never eating shrimp). Same-sex intercourse was one kind of "mixing" that was forbidden as a matter of Jewish distinction. But we must remember: the Torah also says that it is forbidden for Jewish men to marry and have sexual relations with foreign women, eat pork, or wear mixed fabrics.

It is likely the case that same-sex intercourse violated strata of concerns with respect to the mixing-of-kinds. The reader should not be surprised that if fabrics, plant seeds, body fluids, and people were among the list of things to be kept separate from one another—or mixed correctly—sexual prescriptions and proscriptions were to abound as well. To that end, no one disputes that according to the written law, mixing men with men (sexually) violated the Jewish law, under the ritual and holiness codes. It was a violation, because it would make a Jewish man *ritually* unclean. It changed the status of his ability to participate in ritual worship or sacrifice. Same-sex intercourse would have made a man "unclean" because it involved the emission of semen (a ritually unclean substance) and the touching of an anus (a body site that daily facilitates excrement, another ritual impurity). But a Jewish man was also considered "unclean" if he had a nocturnal emission, or sex with his wife (or wives) during menstruation, or even during the time shortly after her monthly period.

Ritual cleanliness, therefore, was clearly at stake in the Torah command against male anal intercourse. But it was not the only concern. We must remember that for Jewish men, marriage and procreation were interpreted (especially through the lens of the Talmud) as obligations of the Torah. Thus, as a result of both the ritual issues and marriage duties at play in the Torah, same-sex intercourse was simply disallowed. But we should not infer from that prohibition any sense that the ancient Jewish people were responding to questions about sexual orientation, or self-identified LGBT people seeking relational fulfillment with same-sex partners. Those issues are strikingly absent from the Book of Leviticus altogether.

To be sure, there was a moral dimension that Jewish people inevitably connected to following the 613 laws written in the Torah, including the verses in question. But we have to be clear that the moral weight of these laws (where it exists) was a matter of *Jewish* people being obedient to the Torah, so as to be set apart ritually and culturally from the rest of the nations. Christians do not examine or observe the Torah very carefully, nor do Christians seem to feel the moral weight of much of it. Reform and Conservative Jewish communities also agree that many of the Torah laws are not necessarily relevant in order to be in good standing with God.[35] Therefore, to make these laws the moral standard for Christian living seems to go beyond their original purpose. That is not to say that they are wholly irrelevant or should be thrown out. But when they are drawn upon, it should be done with careful study of their various meanings, all of which only make sense in their original context—specifically, purity codes for ritual and cultural separateness.

A Comment on: Bestiality, Incest, and Adultery

Of course, it should be noted that the Torah also has sexual prohibitions concerning bestiality, adultery, and incest. Some Christians will want to know why these sexual acts are still considered "morally wrong" while the adjacent biblical statements on same-sex activity are "explained away" by context. But the reality is, when we consider the biblical prohibitions on bestiality, adultery, and incest, the biblical concerns are very different than the ones we have today. For example, the biblical command against bestiality likely concerned two issues: ritual purity (the mixing of kinds) and procreation (the lack of ability to procreate with an animal). But in our day, the problem with bestiality concerns harm to both humans and animals; the lack of informed consent between animal and human, and a concern that those people who use animals as sexual objects do so because of a failure to connect with other human beings. What is more, when it comes to incest we likewise find differences between the biblical norms and contemporary Christian sexual ethics. For example, the Torah permits a man to marry a first cousin, and yet a number of contemporary state laws would count that as an act of incest.[36] What is more, the book of Genesis tells the story of Sarah and Abraham, who have the same father, yet are married as half-siblings of different mothers.[37] By our conventional moral standards, we would call this incest. Sexual morality doesn't get any clearer, even when reading the Bible on matters of adultery. For example, the biblical laws allow for men to take more than one wife and to have concubines. These allowances definitely strain our modern and conventional understanding of fidelity and adultery.[38] What is more, it is important to remember that adultery laws in the Hebrew Bible were deeply steeped in concepts of property—in particular, women as property of men.[39]

These examples, hopefully, illuminate that people should not only read Leviticus contextually with respect to same-sex activity, but with respect to everything, including bestiality, incest, and adultery. Without the insights of cultural context to help us understand what might be going on in the text, we would default into a kind of biblical literalism that ends up being less than helpful for moral deliberation. Indeed, I fully expect that Christian conservatives who would not promote cousin-marriage or polygamy *should* appreciate that biblical context matters. I would press them to consider that context matters not only for biblical statements on bestiality, incest, and adultery, but for teachings on same-sex activity as well. Therefore, for a Christian to cite the prohibition in Leviticus on same-sex (male) intercourse as a clearly negative proof-text against same-sex relationships would be granting more to the text than what is present.

Thus, the best we can say about these passages is that they not only fit the ancient Jewish holiness/purity codes (ritually and culturally), but they also conform to the traditional duty incumbent upon each Jewish man (as explained by the Talmud) to marry a woman, or women. If we try to do anything more with the text than this, then we are foisting our moral sensibilities upon the Bible. Since Christians do not define "holiness" or "purity" according to dietary laws, obligatory marriage, or matters of mixing "kinds" of things (whether seeds, threads, or people), these laws cannot possibly function as any kind of ethical mandate for Christian living.

Remarkably, Genesis 19 and Leviticus 18:22 and 20:13 are the only passages in the Hebrew Bible that are commonly used by Christians to argue against LGBT relationships today. What it reveals to us is not only that the Hebrew Bible is absent of any explicit commentary on these matters, but that one has to literally reassign meaning to the biblical texts in order to "make" these passages opposed to homosexual orientation or contemporary same-sex relationships. Because there is so little material in the Hebrew Bible on the issue, anti-gay Christians usually do not stay in the Hebrew Bible too long, and turn instead to the New Testament collection.

The New Testament and Homosexuality

When we turn to the New Testament, it is important to understand that these texts were situated in the Greco-Roman world. Within this context there is historical evidence of a wide variety of same-sex activities and relationships. The Greek and Roman cultures (to varying degrees) expected that there would be some kind of sexual activity between men, whether that occurred between an older man and a young man (as part of the ancient Greek mentoring program, called *paideia*), sometimes between soldiers and athletes (perhaps most notably among the Sacred Band of Thebes), or between a man and a male prostitute (as it occurred in brothels, as well as in some Greco-Roman religious sites).[40] But it is also important to note that attitudes about same-sex relationships (and desires) varied between historical periods (e.g., ancient Greece appears to have held more flexible views on sex and sexual desire, while the Roman Empire sought to regulate these matters, creating dualities between public and private sexual moralities and practices).[41]

Same-Sex Desire and Patriarchy in the Greco-Roman World

While reading some of the philosophical literature that comes out of the Greco-Roman world, I often wonder if it was on its way to cultivating a rudimentary understanding of sexual orientations. For example, when I read Plato's *Symposium* I am always stunned by a creation myth as told by Socrates's philosophical companion, Aristophanes. In his attempt to explain the origins and meaning of love, Aristophanes told a creation story about three kinds of original humans. Each kind had two faces, two sets of arms, and two sets of legs. One of those creatures had two female faces, another had two male faces, and the other had the face of a male and a female. According to the myth, the gods became concerned that these human beings were becoming too powerful, and there was some talk of destroying the human creatures altogether, lest they best the gods (as the gods had once done to the Titans). But as the myth goes on to say, Zeus decided to split the humans into two. When he did this there was a deep pain of desire felt in each of the humans, and this desire was *love*. Aristophanes said, "Love is born into every human being; it calls back the halves of our original nature together; it tries to make one out of two and heal the wound of human nature."[42] Because the three types of primeval humans were halved by the gods, Aristophanes said that there are some women and men among us who are bound to seek each other, and there are those women who will look only toward other women, and there will be some men who likewise will only turn to other men.

That story is wonderfully mythic and offers a parallel (albeit poetic) understanding of sexual and relational desire, which we now see in the language of the social and psychological sciences. And yet even as this story suggests an emerging understanding about diverse sexual desires on an innate level, it was by no means used to legitimize same-sex relationships or laws of equality. Instead, the dominating model of *pater familia* (as discussed in the previous chapter) functioned as the domestic norm. This social institution located the duty of the man as the head of his wife, blood line, and household. Regardless if a man had male lovers in his life, that man would take a wife as a matter of custom for the building up of society. To say, then, that the Greco-Roman world knew homosexuality as we know it, or same-sex relationships the way we do, would be an oversimplification. To be sure, Jesus of Nazareth and the authors of the New Testament likely knew of same-sex activity among their Roman counterparts, but what they saw and knew of it would not capture the whole of gay, bisexual, and lesbian relationships today.

Christ and Queer Community

In the gospel narratives, neither Jesus nor his disciples comment on homosexuality as a sexual orientation, nor same-sex relationships grounded in mutuality or romantic love. In fact, the Jesus of the gospel narratives makes no statement on same-sex activity, and he says nothing about the sexual or relational desires a person might have for someone of the same physical sex. For all of the emphasis that many contemporary Christian communities place on homosexuality, it is strikingly disproportionate that Jesus says *nothing* on the issue. In fact, in the one place that Jesus might have commented on same-sex relationships, he did not. This is a story well worth telling.

According to Matthew 8:5–13, a Roman centurion came to Jesus asking that his servant might be healed. Jesus consented to go with the centurion, but the soldier resisted, believing that he was unworthy to have Jesus enter his home. The Roman centurion simply asked Jesus to say the word of healing, with the belief that an utterance from Jesus would make the servant whole. Jesus praised the Roman centurion for his faith and even went so far as to say that "in no one in Israel have I found such faith."[43] What is interesting about this narrative is that the gospel writer used the Greek word *pais* to describe the Roman centurion's servant. According to the religion scholar, Nancy Wilson, the Greek word *pais* was sometimes used to describe a male lover, typically the younger partner of two men.[44] This is significant because the gospel writer could have used the Greek word *doulous*, which plainly means "servant," as in one who serves or works for another.

To be sure, the Greek word *pais* does literally mean "child," and in use could have referred to the inferior place of a young servant to his master. However, it is also true that *pais* was one of the words used to describe a young male (same-sex) lover. The gospel narrative in Matthew does not tell us which meaning of *pais* the Roman centurion meant to employ. When the same story is told in the Gospel of Luke, the word *doulous* is used, meaning simply "servant." So what do we make of this? If we assume that "of course" the servant was *not* also a sexual partner for the centurion we would be whitewashing the gospel of its cultural and historical context. If we insist that the servant was absolutely the centurion's lover, we say too much. But what we can say is that in the one instance when an actual same-sex relationship could very well have been at play, Christ said nothing, but instead praised the centurion for his faith and healed the *pais* of his illness.[45]

Paul and Same-Sex Activity

Even as Jesus said nothing on same-sex activity in the gospels, very little is said about same-sex activity within the rest of the New Testament. Indeed, there is debate about which of the New Testament texts actually refer to same-sex activity and which have been mistranslated to corrupt the Bible with antihomosexual condemnations. There are three significant passages: 1 Corinthians 6:9–10, 1 Timothy 1:10, and Romans 1:18–2:1.

1 Corinthians 6:9–10/1 Timothy 1:10: Arsenokoitai

Of the many English translations of the Bible, the *New International Version* (NIV) is one that is frequently used in American churches, especially among evangelical Christians. In the NIV, one passage associated with the matter of homosexuality is translated the following way: "Do you not know that the wicked will not inherit the kingdom of God? Do not be deceived: Neither the sexually immoral nor idolaters nor male prostitutes nor *homosexual offenders* nor thieves nor the greedy nor drunkards nor slanderers nor swindlers will inherit the kingdom of God" (1 Corinthians 6:9–10).[46]

Millions of Christians have encountered these verses, whether by sitting in a pew on Sunday morning, or having read this version of the Bible (or other similar English translations) in the privacy of their own homes.[47] Such a rendering of 1 Corinthians 6:9–10 leaves little room for discussion, and paints homosexuality as an immorality. When a perceived authority, such as the Bible, appears to render a negative verdict, the burden of that moral and theological weight is not insignificant. Indeed, for many, it has been the motivation for self-harm, or, exile from religious communities.[48] A number of biblical scholars, however, have questioned whether the NIV translation of 1 Corinthians 6:9–10 is the best rendering of the text, or if it represents the preexisting judgments of those who translated the *New International Version* of the Bible.

First, the use of the word *homosexual* in an English translation of any biblical text is rather suspicious. It is a matter of historical fact that the category (and thus, terminology) of "homosexuality" was not coined until the nineteenth century. Today, the vast majority of social, medical, and psychological sciences recognize homosexuality as a natural variance of sexual orientation, and that gay and lesbian people are in no way hindered by same-sex attraction, except by societal prejudice.[49]

Insofar as the categorization of homosexuality is a modern construct, readers of the Bible should be curious as to why Bible translators would draw on the word *homosexuality* in their effort to translate ancient scripture. When biblical scholars investigate 1 Corinthians 6:9–10, the word that the NIV translation committee rendered as "homosexual offenders" is the Greek term *arsenokoitai*. The term is used once again in 1 Timothy 1:10. Translation and interpretation of this term is contested.

One biblical scholar, Richard Hays, argues that while this term may not speak to issues of innate sexual orientation, it *does* condemn same-sex activity. He writes:

> *Arsenokoitai*, is not found in any extant Greek text earlier than 1 Corinthians. Some scholars have suggested that its meaning is uncertain, but Robin Scroggs has shown that the word is a translation of the Hebrew *mishkav zakur* ("lying with a male"), derived directly from Leviticus 18:22 and 20:13 and used in rabbinic texts to refer to homosexual intercourse. The Septuagint (the Greek Old Testament) of Leviticus 20:13 reads, "Whoever lies with a man as with a woman (*meta arsenos koiten gynaikos*), they have both done an abomination." This is almost certainly the idiom from which the noun arsenokoitai was coined. Thus, Paul's use of the term presupposes and reaffirms the [Hebrew Bible's] condemnation of homosexual acts.[50]

Explanations such as this one largely satisfy the existing ideology in many Christian minds—namely, that same-sex activity is immoral and outside of God's design for humanity.

However, other biblical scholars have questioned the explanation that Hays has offered. Dale Martin, a fellow biblical scholar, notes that when translating the Greek term *arsenokoitai*, contemporary Christians might benefit from knowing the history of the word's translation and interpretation. Martin notes that in the fourteenth century *arsenokoitai* was rendered by one translator as an act of lechery with men.[51] Lechery, by most definitions, suggests a sexually inordinate act, especially of an excessive sort, and describes the kind of man (or men) who make people sexual objects for simple use, not persons of mutual regard. By the seventeenth century, the King James Version of the Bible (issued in 1611), rendered *arsenokoitai* as "abusers of themselves with mankind," suggesting that *arsenokoitai* referred to a kind of violent or injurious act. Dale Martin goes on to say that as English translations of the Bible emerged in the nineteenth and twentieth centuries, readers could find *arsenokoitai* translated as anything from the peculiar term *sodomite* to the specific term *homosexual*.[52] Martin explains:

> Between the end of the nineteenth and the middle of the twentieth century . . . the translation of *arsenokoites* shifted from being the reference to an action that any man might well

perform, regardless of orientation or disorientation, to refer to a "perversion," either an action or propensity taken to be self-evidently abnormal and diseased. The shift in translation, that is, reflected the invention and the category of "homosexuality" as an abnormal orientation, an invention that occurred in the nineteenth century but gained popular currency only gradually in the twentieth.[53]

Martin's comments are certainly illuminating.

These insights reveal that when we do a simple historical survey of the translation of this text, we see that gay and lesbian identity was never an explicit concern. What was of concern to translators between the fourteenth and eighteenth centuries was some kind of sexual inordinacy, or maybe even sexual violence. We are left, then, with an interpretive conundrum: Can anyone accurately translate *arsenokoitai* in contemporary language? Previous translations of this term did not in any uniform way suggest that it referred to innate sexual orientation, nor to mutual and/or loving sexual relationships. Therefore, the use of the (modern) term *homosexual* as a translation of the ancient Greek word *arsenokoitai* should really signal a red flag to the serious student of the Bible. At the same time, if all we had was the curious history of this word's translation, we would still not have a right to say that this text has absolutely nothing to do with same sex activity. Fortunately, there are more data for us to consider, so that we might make an informed interpretation of the text.

First, we must consider the vocabulary of the word itself. Dale Martin notes that the term *arsenokoitai* is a compound word (*arsenos*: men, *koitais*: laying). Richard Hays thinks that the conjoining of these two words points us back to a ritual/holiness code in the Hebrew Bible (Leviticus 18:22 and 20:13) that forbade male anal intercourse. But Martin disagrees that *arsenokoitai* is quite so easily understood. Martin reminds us that compound words do not explain to us the meaning of a word. He says, "To 'understand' does not mean to 'stand under.' In fact, nothing about the basic meanings of either 'stand' or 'under' has any direct bearing on the meaning of 'understand.' The etymology [origin] of a word is its history, not its meaning."[54]

What is more, Martin says that when we examine the ancient Greco-Roman world for other examples in which the term *arsenokoitai* was used, it was almost always used to describe exploitation of some kind. Martin notes that in the second-century Christian text, The Acts of John, the word *arsenokoitai* was employed to describe a sin of economic exploitation. Martin goes on to report that the same text has a list of sexual sins, and yet *arsenokoitai* was not used there to describe any sexual vice.[55] One would expect that if *arsenokoitai* was "almost certainly" a condemnation against same-sex activity (as Richard Hays says) then we would see it used consistently as such in other Christian texts. But the truth is, we do not.

The association of exploitation with *arsenokoitai* (and not homosexuality) is an important linguistic and historical insight. If the ancient world was using the term *arsenokoitai* to describe exploitation (economic, sexual, or otherwise), it is most certainly a far stretch to associate sexual exploitation with contemporary same-sex partnerships or even same-sex activities performed in mutuality between any two people. Gay and lesbian people *could* be exploitative in sexual relationships, but no more so than one's heterosexual counterparts. To that end, LGBT and straight people could be guilty of being *arsenokoitai* (generally speaking), but only insofar as any of us are being exploitative, whether violently or subtly.

So how does the word *homosexual* find its way into an English translation of the Bible? It can only get there by the hand of a translator who *already* believes that homosexuality is a perversion and then foists (or assumes) that understanding of homosexuality onto the biblical text itself. By doing so, such a translator causes certain versions of the New Testament to read (or sound) as if homosexuality is in fact immoral according to the texts themselves (1 Corinthians 6:9–10 and 1 Timothy 1:10). This obviously cannot be certain, or even implied by the original biblical language. All we can really say is that the history of how this word (*arsenokoitai*) has been translated tells us much more about the translator (or translation committee) than it does the word itself.

There are good reasons, then, to constructively critique those Christians who misuse this passage to condemn homosexuality, as if the passage is certainly clear. But we should also caution liberals against posturing themselves with any sort of complete certainty. Dale Martin rightly brings the conservative and liberal back to the interpretive table when he writes:

> I am not claiming to know what arsenokoitai meant. I am claiming that no one knows what it meant. I freely admit that it could have been taken as a reference to homosexual sex. But given the scarcity of evidence and the several contexts just analyzed, in which arsenokoites appears to refer to some particular kind

of economic exploitation, no one should be allowed to get away with claiming that "of course" the term refers to "men who have sex with other men."[56]

Indeed, no one should be allowed to get away with claiming that a text of the Bible has an undisputed meaning.

1 Corinthians 6:9–10: Malakoi

In addition to *arsenokoitai*, some Christians have also asserted that Paul used the Greek word *malakoi* (also found in 1 Corinthians 6:9–10) to condemn men who are penetrated anally, including male prostitutes. However, as Dale Martin notes, the word *malakoi* was used in the Greco-Roman world, and it literally meant "soft." It could refer to anything from fabric, gourmet food, luxury, men who made themselves "pretty" *for women*, and yes, even male prostitutes.[57] To be a *malakoi*—to be soft—was to be weak, in a qualitative sense. The term actually drew on the gender hierarchy of the day. Namely, weakness was associated with femininity, and strength with masculinity. Such gendered language applied to morality as well.

As New Testament scholar Jennifer Wright Knust has noted, that which was recognized as virtuous or having respectable status in the Greco-Roman world was usually associated with "strength."[58] Thus, to be "soft" was an indictment of any number of proclivities for overindulgence. We might imagine, then, that the first-century accusation of being "soft" (qualitatively) was one that indicted *moral* weakness. To assume that Paul was singling out male prostitutes—who were "soft," culturally speaking, by virtue of being penetrated like a female—is a reading of the text that is likely fueled by preexisting antihomosexual views. In order for that narrow interpretation to hold up, Christians would have to associate being penetrated as a "weak" act, *morally* and/or *theologically*. I'm quite certain that most Christian women and gay men would beg to differ. Thus, I suggest that Christians do well to draw on *malakoi* as an allusion for "softness" in morality—or vice, in general.

Romans 1: God Gave "Them" Up

The only other text of the New Testament that has anything to do with same-sex activity is Romans 1:18–2:1. In this section of Paul's letter to the church in Rome, he describes polytheism as "idolatry" (Romans

1:20–23), a practice that could easily have been seen by those reading his letter. In first-century Rome, the gods and goddesses were worshipped in shrines and temples. Within these sacred sites, one could find statues and images of the gods, whether as animals or human-like creatures (Romans 1:23). Paul would go on to say that idolatry actually darkened the minds of the polytheists and caused them to lose sight of the one true God, and of morality too. He wrote, "Women exchanged natural intercourse for unnatural, and in the same way also the men, giving up natural intercourse with women, were consumed with passion for one another. Men committed shameless acts with men and received in their own persons the due penalty for their error."[59] Paul doesn't stop there. He goes on to say that these polytheists were also gossipers, rebellious toward their parents, boastful, and foolish, to name just a few more instances of polytheistic vice (see Romans 1:28–32 for the complete list).

The aforementioned New Testament scholar Jennifer Wright Knust offers some illumination to this text. She notes that this kind of "vice list" was a common rhetorical tactic in the Greco-Roman world. It was called the *invective*. As Knust explains it, the invective was "a speech of blame" that "intended to malign and defame" and was "deployed in fierce struggles for identity, prestige, and power."[60] Politicians, philosophers, and religious figures drew on the invective to create a sharp difference between the good and the bad, the righteous and the wicked.

Paul's laundry list of vices in Romans 1 certainly reads like an invective. To that end we need to ask the question: Was Paul involved in theological and moral mudslinging? The answer, I think, is a qualified "no." Paul does seem to be drawing on the invective, but his use of it was for a much more clever and rhetorical purpose.

As the theologian, Jack Rogers, notes:

> It seems as though Paul is setting up his Jewish readers. It is easy at this point in the text for them, and for us, to feel self-righteous. . . . But then Paul lowers the boom on his readers by listing other sins that proceed from idolatry—covetousness, malice, envy, strife, deceit, craftiness, gossip, slander. Idolaters could become haughty, boastful, rebellious toward parents, foolish, faithless, heartless, ruthless. Now Paul is talking to all of us, speaking to those sins of attitude to which we sometimes succumb when we turn our ultimate allegiance from the true God.

Paul makes this point again, in Romans 2:1. We are without excuse, especially when we judge others. Why? Because in God's sight we are all given to idolatry. . . . Paul has been criticizing those idolatrous [Gentiles]. Now he is saying to his Jewish colleagues [who are Christian converts], and to us, no one is righteous. We are all sinners. That is Paul's point in Romans 1.[61]

With Rogers, many biblical scholars seem to agree that Romans 1:18–2:1 is really a sting operation to trap self-righteous Christians.[62] It is not a passage about gay and lesbian people, nor a treatise on same-sex relationships.

Nevertheless, Romans 1:26–27 does say that the polytheistic women exchanged "natural" intercourse for "unnatural" (even though it does not explicitly say *what* that means), and that the polytheistic men exchanged "natural" intercourse for sexual activity with one another. Some Christians take this to mean that homosexuality is just one of many sins, but a sin nevertheless. For Christians such as these, it matters not that Paul was tricking self-righteous believers into humility—the trick, they say, still draws on a list of "actual" sins.

But the Greek manuscript actually says that these polytheistic women and men went in *excess* of their nature. The Greek words Paul used are *para physin*. (In Greek: *para*, meaning "above" or "greater than," and *physis*, "nature" or "the natural"; some have said, "the customary"). If such is the case, then the sexual accusation would be sexual excess. But the question remains: Did Paul mean to condemn same-sex activity *itself* as specifically excessive, and/or unnatural to human beings altogether? Or, was he pointing to *instances* of same-sex activity that manifested sexual excess? If the first interpretive option is the more accurate, then Paul did see same-sex activity as sinful. Certain biblical scholars (such as Richard Hays) agree with that conclusion, but also note that if this is the case, then Paul treated same-sex activity on equal footing with being rebellious toward one's parents, gossiping, or being boastful.

On the other hand, we cannot dismiss that the terminology Paul used points to sexual excess, and not to any known category of sexual orientation or sexual identity. This is significant. In the first century, Roman men often took other sexual consorts in addition to their wives. The fact that Roman men sometimes took female and male sexual partners for short-term pleasure was not necessarily surprising, although *how* they did so spoke to their state of virtue. For example, it was a matter of honor and shame that adult free men were never to be penetrated. That would have counted as "unnatural."[63] And yet, it was not shameful, per se, for a Roman free man to rape a male house slave to demonstrate dominance, or to "use" a male prostitute simply to gratify a desire for sexual pleasure. What is more, from many Greco-Roman philosophical perspectives "going beyond one's nature" meant going beyond that which rational reflection allowed. In such a case, "unnatural" sex would take on the form of indiscriminate activity.

The biblical scholar James Brownson offers even another interpretive possibility. Namely, Brownson suggests that Paul could have been drawing on the example of the Roman emperor, Gauis Caligua, whose public behavior was well known as sexually vicious (whether toward women or men), not to mention murderous toward his enemies. Drawing on the scholarship of Neil Elliott, Brownson notes that Paul's "sin-list" is nearly identical to the public activities of Gauis Caligua—especially the sexual activities. Brownson notes that in the life of Gauis Caligua, "a military officer who [the emperor] had sexually humiliated joined a conspiracy to murder him, which they did less than four years into his reign. Suetonius records that Gauis was stabbed through the genitals when he was murdered. One wonders whether we can hear an echo of this gruesome story in Paul's comments in Romans 1:27: 'Men committed shameless acts with men and received in their own person the due penalty for their error.'"[64]

In Brownson's view, if Paul was indeed referring to the house of Gauis Caligua, such contextual specificity would require the modern reader to interpret the text very carefully. In particular, the reader would have to acknowledge that the sexual vice referred to in the text is aggressive and violent sexual behavior. As such, Romans 1:26–27 would not be a commentary on mutual and/or long-term LGBT relationships.

That being said, Brownson emphasizes that any interpretation of Romans 1:18–2:1 that focuses primarily on the reference to same-sex activity (albeit, same-sex sexual violence) misses the whole point of the passage—which, for Brownson, is Paul's intention to link the moral fallout of idolatry (the worship of self, or objects) with Christian judgmentalism. Brownson says, "As Paul sees it, what lustful pagans have in common with self-righteous judgmental Christians is that both are driven by the thirst for their own agenda—their own way, their own status, their own honor—while ignoring the concerns of everyone around them, particularly those of the living God." In this sense, Christians who harshly judge others can be as inhumane and violent to others (spiritually and socially) as sexual abusers are apathetic to the humanity of their victims.

Admittedly, we cannot have a definitive statement on Paul's thoughts about same-sex activity in this passage. Christians who draw on this text will have to lean heavily on interpretative judgment, and this could go in a variety of ways. Christians certainly could interpret this passage to condemn same-sex genital activity, but they would be relying on best guesses about Paul's premodern ideas about sexuality, and they could not say that "condemnation" is the *only* or most compelling reading of this text. Perhaps it is mere irony (and a function of scrupulosity) that we focus so much on this particular issue, since the primary point of this scripture passage is to avoid harsh judgments altogether.

However, if Paul did mean to indict same-sex activity as an actual sin he did not do a very good job of making that case. After all, his messiah made no comment on same-sex activity, and nowhere else in Paul's writing (interpreted well) does same-sex activity make the list of explicitly evil, inordinate, or sinful activity. That does not mean that I think Paul was a closet sexual libertarian. Paul was deeply shaped by his Jewish heritage, even as he was simultaneously negotiating what it meant to live as a follower of Christ, free from Torah observance. Thus, there were likely many things that would have struck Paul as "natural" or "unnatural," "customary" or "uncustomary" that even conservative Christians, today, would not understand.

Indeed, as Jonathan Dudley has well noted, Paul's concepts of "natural" and "unnatural" are most certainly foreign to our own. For example, in 1 Corinthians 11:14–15, Paul condemned long hair for men (and short hair for women) on the basis of what is "natural." Dudley goes on to say that "few Christians who cite Paul's writings in Romans to condemn homosexuality would cite Paul on cultural hairdressing— which as a matter of modesty or gender expression could be taken as a weighty moral subject."[65] Curiously, then, whereas some Christians insist that Paul's "nature" language in Romans 1 makes very clear the immorality of LGBT relationships, such Christians are not so quick (or even certain) about Paul's use of "nature" language in other matters. Dudley goes on to say, "Whether the topic is hair length, celibacy, when life begins, or divorce, time and again, [contemporary Christian] leaders most opposed to [gay and lesbian issues] have demonstrated an incredible willingness to consider nuances and complicating considerations when their own interests are at stake."[66] Dudley concludes that such Christians "aren't defending the Bible's values. They're using the Bible to defend their own."[67]

The Bible and the Ends of Sexual Virtue

To recall, the purpose of the previous chapters has been to examine in what ways interpretations of the Bible can shape a definition of sexual virtue. As I have said, we do not find in the Bible any clear ethical mandate for sexual activity to be located only in marriage, nor even in heterosexual unions. What we find in the New Testament, instead, are portraits of early Christian communities trying to practice the principles of the gospel within their given social contexts and personal conditions. What the New Testament authors offer, then, are not rules to follow, per se, but principles to embody—in whatever time or place Christians find themselves. Thus, if there is a sexual ethic that can be gleaned from the New Testament, it is one of principle, not law: to live according to the principles of the gospel, and to allow those principles to guide one's sexual life as one part of living in the reign of God. If there is a list of sexual vices to avoid, the New Testament steers Christians away from sexual exploitation, as well as the kind of sexual vice that objectifies sexual partners as mere instruments, instead of full moral persons.

Certainly, some Christians will say that I am being antinomian, or decentering the authority of the Bible for the sake of a "liberal" sexual ethic. That is hardly the case. I strongly encourage Christians to make the study of scripture a key part of one's religious ethic. But in my view, if we take the insights of biblical scholarship seriously, careful study of the Bible undoes a number of narrow expectations about sexual morality. That being the case, the effort to define sexual virtue, in a Christian context, will require (in part) that the ends of sexual virtue that we name are resonant with principles of the gospel that can be responsibly interpreted.

Admittedly, Christians will not likely agree with one another on what "the principles of the gospel" are. In my view, these include the oft-cited principles of unconditional love, justice, and kindness. Other Christian sexual ethicists, such as Christine Gudorf, have said that the principles of the gospel include such things as joy and inclusivity.[68] The biblical scholar William Countryman has said that the gospel includes commitments of non-maleficence.[69] Given a wide variety of perspectives on "gospel principles," I have not sought to argue what the definitive list should be, only that the most apparent (or oft-cited) principles of the gospel can (and do) show up in nonmarital, and nonheterosexual relationships—and thus, we cannot say that the principles of the New

Testament in any way demand that sexual activity must be constrained to heterosexual marriage.

In earlier chapters I have said that recreation, relational intimacy, and selective acts of procreation are three different "ends" for people to pursue in the practice of sexual virtue. I name these with reflection on Christian scripture. To my knowledge, there are no moral principles that can be *persuasively* interpreted from Christian scripture that would necessarily limit us from pursuing any one of these ends. Of course, it may be that some people will ultimately find a marital norm or a heterosexual union very meaningful. But I do not think such people can say that those norms must be followed in the same way by every person who calls him or herself a Christian.

Eight

Curious Interpretations of Nature

We cannot draw conclusions from what is to what ought to be, from the presumed biological structure of the sexual act—for example, to moral obligation—for even after determining what is, we still have to determine whether it is right or wrong.

—Todd Salzman and Michael Lawler

Natural and Unnatural Sex

When defining sexual virtue in a Christian context, theologians have drawn upon interpretations of nature in order to define the proper "end" to which sexual activity should be directed.[1] As we have already seen in previous chapters, a number of influential Christian theologians interpreted procreation as the natural end of human sexuality, and thus, the goal to always seek when engaged in licit sexual activity (which is to say, sex between a man and his wife). No contraception—*of any sort*. No oral sex, and especially not to orgasmic completion. No heterosexual anal sex. No masturbation. And certainly: no same-sex activity. As the religious ethicist Mark Jordan has said it, "Forget what you think you know about which acts constitute 'sins against nature' or 'sins of Sodom.' It is bound to be too restrictive."[2] Jordan notes that "unnatural sex" is a category that has

> included . . . *every* erotic or quasi-erotic act that can be performed by human bodies *except* penile-vaginal intercourse between two partners who are not primarily seeking pleasure and who do not intend to prevent conception. Every other erotic act, desire, or wish has been deemed a sin against nature by one Christian theologian or another.[3]

Thus, if nothing else, the procreative norm is the great moral equalizer.

If you masturbate, if you use contraception, if you enjoy oral sex, if you are inclined to same-sex activity, then according to the "natural" procreative norm, *all* such performances are "unnatural," and thus, "immoral." By the standard of the "natural" procreative norm, we're all sexual perverts—or at least, most of us. Even happy, churchgoing, heterosexual married couples, with their two or three children (which apart from fertility issues usually reveals their dastardly use of contraceptives)—even these good Christians fail the test of sexual morality, according to the "natural" procreative norm.

And yet, many of these churchgoing, contraceptive-using heterosexual "perverts" make stinging accusations about the "unnatural" sexual habits of their fellow citizens. Fingers are pointed at same-sex relationships, masturbation, or even the use of pharmaceutical methods for birth control. For Christians such as these, the category of "natural sex" is controlled by visible heterosexuality (in marriage), "decent" marital sexual practices, and a concern that nothing disturb a fertilized egg.[4] But theirs is not the only voice on matters of "natural" sexuality. A plethora of communities have resisted such claims—from scientists to theologians, as well as liberals and conservatives.

What counts as "natural" and "unnatural" sex, then, amounts to a competition of interpretations and definitions. On the one hand, it is a competition to describe what is natural to human beings, in terms of what is innate to our creaturely nature. On the other hand, it is a moral and theological debate about what (if anything) is the intended purpose of sexuality. However—and as we saw in chapter 2—the fact that Christians have revised what counts as "natural" and "unnatural" sex clearly indicates that there is no "one" Christian view on sexual nature. Thus, how Christians might draw on nature to define sexual virtue is wide open to debate.

In this chapter, I focus on diverse concepts of natural and unnatural sex in Christian discourse. I do so in order to demonstrate that any time a religious community offers a definition of "natural" and "unnatural" sex, these definitions are theological constructions. Therefore, what one church defines as "natural sexuality" will not function as the norm for other Christian churches, nor for society as a whole. However, from the perspective of critical realism, I will end the chapter considering what might count as more accurate descriptions of sexual nature on the basis of investigations in the natural and social sciences. Upon this information, I believe that moral and theological interpretations about sexuality are better informed.

Frameworks for Describing Natural/Unnatural Sexuality

Natural Law

Interpreting norms of morality from nature is not unique to Christianity. We see this most explicitly in what is called natural law thinking—a form of moral reasoning that Christian and non-Christian thinkers have used to argue social and moral norms. In particular, natural law thinking seeks to discern principles of morality from the perceived "order of nature." As most scholars tell it, natural law thinking has its origins in Greek philosophy.[5] One natural law scholar, James Luther Adams, has suggested that the origins of natural law can be traced to the intersection of ancient Greek cultures and their growing awareness of the diversity of laws and customs among different societies. Adams notes that "contact with foreign societies possessing very different [laws] served to make [the ancient Greek] aware of the transient character of all laws."[6] Realizing that not all people shared the same customs or rules, they began to wonder if there was a law of nature itself that might provide for a universal code of morality and social order.[7]

While some Greek thinkers had appealed to the ordering of the world by the gods, and derived a sense of human morality and social order from religious-mythological narratives, many Greek philosophers imagined instead a transcendent, nonpersonal, rational power that gave order to all things. This they called the *logos*. Many of the Greek and later Roman philosophers further postulated that if all things were indeed *rationally* ordered by a transcendent intelligent power, then human beings—as rational creatures—have the special capacity to figure out if a thing is in good or poor working order. But the key here is not that nature itself reveals moral norms, as if those are simply given. Natural law, at least for the ancient Greek and Romans, was an exercise of practical reason. For them, utilizing the natural law was a matter of discerning what was best, or in good working order—not merely accepting what is "given" of human nature. Thus, natural law thinking provided (for them) a foundation for ethical discourse on the basis of practical reasoning about ideal human nature. Believing that this kind of thinking revealed dependable moral and social norms, many Greek and Roman philosophers drew on the natural law as a serious moral authority.

Although originating with and developed by Greek and Roman philosophers, natural law thinking was eventually incorporated into the Christian religion by various influential theologians. It continues to play a significant role in the moral theories of the Roman Catholic Church, and less formally (sometimes accidentally) by certain Protestants who appeal to "nature" to substantiate their moral arguments.[8] The adoption of natural law thinking into Christianity is not surprising. Given the preference of many Christian theologians to turn to the ancient Greco-Roman world for philosophical insight, Christian ethics and natural law thinking were all but destined for synthesis.[9] As Greek and Roman thinkers appealed to the logos as the intelligent power that ordered all things, Christians imposed the biblical God in that place.[10] In turn, Christian natural law thinkers reflected on the "nature" of our rational, embodied, social existence, albeit as creations of God.

In its Christianized form, natural law perpetuates the idea that all things are intelligently created by God. Because humans are rational creatures, many Christian theologians have accepted that human beings can discern (by reason, in part) what it means for something to be properly ordered, morally speaking. Because Christian natural law thinkers arrive at moral norms in light of faith in the biblical God, Christian natural law reflection is deeply theological. It is usually employed with considerable reliance on the Bible and church teaching.[11] Thus, what a Christian says about proper moral ordering from the perspective of natural law is usually filtered through biblical interpretation and preexisting theological commitments.

With respect to the moral authority of natural law thinking in Christian discourse, the religious historian John Boswell notes that it was "Thomas Aquinas, whose *Summa theologiae* became the standard of orthodox opinion on every point of Catholic dogma for nearly a millennium."[12] What is more, Boswell notes that Aquinas's ideas about ideal nature "permanently and irrevocably established the 'natural' as the touchstone of Roman Catholic sexual ethics."[13] And as we saw in chapter 4, when Aquinas reflected on sexual activity, he discerned "procreation of the species" as the natural function (and thus, what God intended) for human sexual activity. As Boswell summarizes the theologian's teachings on sex and nature, the historian notes that Thomas Aquinas advanced the idea that "semen and its ejaculation were intended by 'nature' to produce children, and that any other use of them was 'contrary to nature' and hence sinful, since the design of 'nature' represented the will of

God."[14] But as Boswell points out, even Aquinas knew that this "natural" procreative standard was problematic, philosophically and theologically speaking.

> [S]aint Thomas realized that this argument had fatal flaws. He himself raised the question of other "misuses" of "nature's" design. Is it sinful for a man to walk on his hands, when "nature" has clearly designed the feet for this purpose? Or is it morally wrong to use the feet for something (e.g., pedaling an organ) which the hands ordinarily do? To obviate this difficulty, he shifted ground and tacitly recognized that it was not the misuse of organs involved which comprised the sin but the fact that through the act in question the propagation of the human species was impeded.
>
> This line of reasoning was of course based on an ethical premise—that the physical increase of the human species constitutes a major moral good—[but this] bore no relation to any New Testament or early Christian authority and which had been specifically rejected by Saint Augustine. Moreover, it contradicted Aquinas's own teachings. [For example] nocturnal emissions "impede" the increase of the human race in precisely the same way as homosexuality—i.e., by expending semen to no procreative purpose—and yet Aquinas not only considered [nocturnal emissions] inherently sinless but the result of "natural" causes. And voluntary virginity (*Summa theologiae* 2a.2ae.151, 152), so clearly operated to the detriment of the species in this regard that he very specifically argued in its defense that individual humans are not obligated to contribute to the increase or preservation of the species through procreation; it is only the race as a whole which is so obligated.[15]

While Boswell's comments gloss over the differences between unconscious nocturnal emissions and conscious participation in nonprocreative acts, he nevertheless points out, quite well, that what seems certain about "natural sexuality" in one instance (the "naturalness" of procreation to human sexuality), requires qualifications and alternate explanations when applied to other matters, whether those concern "natural" nocturnal emissions or voluntary celibacy.

Thus, what Boswell revealed for contemporary Christian sexual ethics, is that what came to be the "traditional" reading of natural law thinking in Christianity (i.e., Thomas Aquinas's) is itself a shifty argument, dependent on slippery (and multiple) concepts of "nature." Boswell is correct that these shifting definitions of the "natural" more or less functioned to confirm what the church had already accepted (in Aquinas's time) about sexual morality.[16] What is more, Boswell notes that a number of Aquinas's judgments about "natural sex" appear to borrow also from "civil legislation and popular diatribe before the *Summa* was written."[17]

These insights from Boswell should lead the reader to appreciate a certain problem about traditional natural law thinking and its use in moral reasoning. Namely, much in the same way that preexisting ideas can (and do) shape interpretations of Christian scripture, so too, preexisting, fixed, ideas about sexuality have shaped definitions of "natural sex" within Christian renderings of natural law. But in contest with natural law traditionalists are those whom Todd Salzman and Michael Lawler have designated as "natural law revisionists."[18] While revisionists share a belief with the traditionalists in a creator God, and thus a cosmos in which some order can be discerned (respecting that evolutionary theory does challenge how one talks about "natural order"), the revisionists do not agree that the natural goods we can discern from "nature" are necessarily good to pursue in *every* case.[19] According to Salzman and Lawler, revisionists are said to emphasize "historical consciousness, the particularity of basic goods and the human person, norms that reflect this particularity, and a relational-centered morality."[20] For the revisionist, what one counts as natural/human goods is deeply informed by context and individual circumstances; thus, prudence is given priority over "laws" of nature.[21]

With respect to sexual morality, natural law revisionists argue that procreation is not so primary that it overrides other natural/sexual goods that can be pursued for their own sake. Thus, natural law revisionists argue that procreation need not be *the* good that every person must remain open to in every sexual act. Rather, revisionists tell us (and I think rightly so), that *people* are what come together in sexual relationships, not simply our bodies, or our genitals. Of course, contemporary natural law traditionalists respect that interpersonal relating is important, but they nevertheless understand that the norm of sexual morality should observe, very strictly, a bifurcated (i.e., male/female) view of sexual compatibility and complementarity, and then toward a procreative end.[22] But according to natural law revisionists, "natural sexuality" should primarily concern "relational compatibility"—in particular, our relational compatibility defined, in part, by sexual orientation (which is a part of our given human "nature"), and then with respect to the compatibility between individual persons. As Salzman and Lawler say, this includes the ways in which people are compatible intellectually, emotionally, physically, and socially, without the regulation of a heterosexual norm.

Natural Law and Virtue

With respect to sexual virtue, natural law thinking is relevant if it is drawn upon to set the "end" or "ends" of legitimate sexual activity. That said, the use of natural law thinking in Christian discourse on virtue is deeply shaped by preexisting sexual theologies about the "purpose" of sex. Natural law traditionalists will clearly require openness to procreation in every sexual act called "licit." Official Roman Catholic teaching represents this view. But because natural law revisionists depend on prudence to discern what is best to pursue (of all natural/sexual goods) no such strict reading of "natural sexuality" would be expected. However, this does not mean that the revisionist view of natural law will accept just any sexual relationship as licit. Revisionists take very seriously that prudential reflection on what is "natural," and thus "good," is about recognizing discernible sexual goods that contribute to a life well lived. To be clear, revisionist natural law thinking is not the postmodern acceptance of "whatever feels good."[23]

In light of my previous comments (in chapters 2, 3, and 4) about the multivalent nature of human sexuality, I find that natural law thinking is best exercised when drawing on the revisionist approach. Revisionist natural law thinking appears to account, more accurately, for what is "natural" and good for human beings—insofar as we are social/sexual creatures with psychological, emotional, and interpersonal needs. Such natural needs can be met, in part, through sexual relations that have nothing to do with reproduction. For example, it may be that a couple wishes to draw upon sexual activity in order to promote their relational flourishing, but they cannot chance pregnancy because of certain health risks to the woman, or because of a lack of material resources to take care of potential offspring. The revisionist approach would allow us to defend why "relational closeness" is a natural interpersonal good worth pursuing, while at the same time avoiding reproduction through contraceptive use (we will address the prudent use of contraception in more detail in chapter 12).

Thus, the revisionist view of natural law could also allow, theoretically, for a more flexible definition of sexual virtue, insofar as a revisionist approach to natural law could justify a number of "ends" to pursue.

But in order to know when we ought to pursue these ends, or hold back—and then, how to do so well—belongs to the virtues of prudence and temperance. Ultimately, then, revisionist natural law thinking will have to depend on a theory of virtue in order to help mediate more specific questions: not only about whether sexual activity is best had at a given place or time, but also how our sexual relationships contribute to a whole life well lived.

However, it is not my intention to reconstruct a revisionist natural law theory in order to support my overall argument about the ends of sexual virtue (i.e., recreation, relational intimacy, and selective acts of procreation). That said, natural law thinking is central to many Chris-tian thinkers when it comes to sexual ethics, and thus, it is an important category for us to attend to theoretically. At the same time, the revision-ist form of natural law thinking depends so heavily on prudential think-ing (as well as prudential flexibility) that I do not find it necessary to repeat what I have already argued about prudence, prudential flexibility, and sexual virtue (see chapters 3 and 4). What is more, in chapters 10, 11, and 12, we will look more specifically at why recreation, relational intimacy, and selective acts of procreation are justifiable "ends" of sexual virtue, especially when relying on prudential reflection on contemporary descriptions of human/sexual "nature." I turn our immediate attention, instead, to other relevant examples of Christian discourse about "sexual nature" that can shape ideas about sexual morality.

Curious Interpretations of Sex, Sin, and Nature

Even as Christians have drawn on very different concepts of the natural law to talk about "natural" and "unnatural" sex, so too Christians have engaged in quite a bit of theological speculation about the nature of human sexuality in light of doctrines of "original creation" and "sin." Sometimes this kind of theological speculation is in coordination with natural law thinking; sometimes it is engaged on its own.[24] This type of thinking speculates, in particular, on what "ideal" or "perfect" life was like "in the beginning," but also speculates about how the introduction of "sin" has corrupted the created order (not only in terms of humanity's relationship to God, but also creaturely effects, such as sickness, death, disorder, etc.). However, many modern Christians (whether tradition-al, mainline, or progressive) may be surprised to learn that for several of the early Christian theologians, either sex itself or the desire for it were believed to be entirely absent from God's original creation. As the religious ethicist James Nelson notes, many early Christian theologians "typically assigned sexuality not to the good order of creation but to the results of the Fall."[25]

Throughout this book we have already encountered a number of examples of Christian thinkers who wed much of sexuality to the presence of sin. Recall that St. Augustine regarded all desire for sex a manifestation of lust (i.e., inordinate sexual desire) and a sure sign that human beings had fallen from grace.[26] Remember also that when St. Gregory of Nyssa interpreted the Genesis creation narratives, he could not imagine sex as part of the "perfect" human life.[27] What is more, Nelson notes that the fourth-century bishop of Milan, St. Ambrose, would strike a similar chord, but more specifically, to denounce sexual pleasure as the "enticement" of the serpent, not a "gift" from God.[28] Even when such theologians would accept heterosexual marriage as the one relational context in which sex could be had (toward procreation), suspicions about sex and sexual pleasure still reigned. As Nelson points out, for example, St. Jerome "could accept marriage, reluctantly, only because from marriages virgins were born."[29] Jerome would say, "I praise marriage and wedlock, but only because they beget celibates; I gather roses from thorns, gold from the earth, pearls from shells."[30]

Protestants have also struggled to interpret the status of sexual nature in a world of "sin." On the one hand, the sixteenth-century Protestant reformer Martin Luther accepted that marriage was "natural" to the human being, admitting that God created it for humans before the notorious "fall."[31] But in light of Luther's concerns about human sinfulness, and sin's motivation of sexual immorality, Luther also described marriage as an "emergency hospital for the illness of human drives."[32] Protestant suspicions about "sex after the fall" were not limited to figures such as Luther or Calvin. For example, one contemporary Protestant denomination, the Reformed Church in America (RCA), agrees with Luther that sexuality is natural to human beings (i.e., part of God's original intent for humans), but only insofar as human sexuality is of a particular kind. Namely, when addressing the issue of homosexuality (morally and theologically), the RCA teaches that homosexuality is a sad consequence of the "fall" of human beings into sin—and that homosexuality is much like any other kind of physical or mental disorder. In fact, the RCA teaches:

The homosexual invert (one who does not decide to become
homosexual, but for whom genetic, hormonal, or psychosocial
factors have influenced his or her sexual orientation) is not
more to be blamed for his/her condition than a retarded child.
It follows, then, that the church's ministry to the invert may
best begin with the attempt to lift a burden of guilt that need
not be carried. Inverts may not idealize their orientation as a
legitimate alternative, but neither should they blame themselves
for their sexual orientation.[33]

On the one hand, the comparison between an "invert" and a "retarded
child" will likely strike a number of readers as an outdated (and offensive) form of speech. But on the other hand, the comparison demonstrates the complexities that modern churches face when attempting to
sustain premodern church judgments about the effects of "sin" on the
"nature" of sex and sexuality within a larger culture that is conversant
with scientific data on human sexuality.

Let's consider again the statement on homosexuality by the RCA.
In it, the church is tacitly willing to draw on scientific vocabulary in
order to describe the genetic, hormonal, and psychosocial factors in the
makeup (or "nature") of sexual orientation. However, the RCA then
shifts to a *theological* conclusion that homosexuality is a defect (compa-
rable to cognitive disability), which they say manifests in humans (now)
due to the fall of creation into "sin." Arguably, that arbitrary shift away
from the sciences to denounce homosexuality conceals information that
might otherwise be helpful for both prudential and theological reflection
on the nature of human sexuality.[34] In short, the sciences (especially
the psychological and psychiatric sciences) do not regard homosexuality
as a disorder or psychopathology. The comparison of homosexuality to
general cognitive disorder suggests that an innate same-sex inclination
disadvantages a person in a similar way that a cognitive disorder disadvantages (to varying degrees) a person with limited use of his or her
mental faculties. And yet, the American Psychological Association notes
that the only disadvantages LGBT people face—by virtue of having a
homosexual orientation, or, nonconforming gender identity—are disadvantages that result from prejudice and discrimination inflicted upon the
LGBT community by members of the wider society.[35] Turning away from
the sciences on this point, the RCA grounds its judgment in another
authority: theological speculation about "original creation."

Leaning on its theological speculations, the RCA takes the negative evaluation of homosexuality a step farther, suggesting that the gay or lesbian person is guilty of some kind of moral failing should he or she act on that inclination. The RCA teaches that "homosexual acts" are "against nature," believing that "human sexuality was created for heterosexual expression," and thus, the church condemns same-sex relationships as "contrary to the will of God for human sexuality."[36] Although this position is disputed by many practitioners, pastors, and theologians in the RCA (most notably by the organization *Room for All*), it is the position that has persisted (to date) by the majority voice of the denomination. Given the church's official views on sexuality, we can see that the interpretive choice of the RCA (sometimes reflected in other denominations, too) is to weight premodern theological and moral presuppositions about "sexual nature" over scientific reports on natural sexual diversity. And yet, the church is also, very clearly, willing to draw on the vocabulary of modern science to describe the innate experience of same-sex desire. The problem, then, turns out to be a selective use of science, drawing on premodern theology as the referee of science in moral arguments on, or about, "sexual nature."

But not all churches make reference to "natural" and "unnatural" sex by privileging premodern theologies on sex, creation, and sin. In recent years, for example, the Episcopal Church, the United Church of Christ (UCC), and the Evangelical Lutheran Church in America (ELCA) have revisited their theological teachings about "natural sex" in light of what the natural and social sciences have discovered about human sexuality. This has led the denominations to accept a wide range of sexual relationships as licit (whether straight or LGBT). But even these more progressive views are nevertheless shaped by theological reflections about creation, sin, and sex.

For example, the ELCA accepts many of the full reports from the sciences on the naturalness of diverse sexual orientations. Sexual diversity, the church accepts, is simply part of creation's diversity. Even so, in its most recent document on sexual ethics, *Sexuality: Gift and Trust*, the church qualified its thoughts about sexuality (whether for straight or LGBT people) in terms of "sin" and "grace."[37] In the document, the ELCA acknowledges that while "sin" does permeate human sexuality, "grace" can nevertheless uplift sexual relationships, so long as Christians commit responsibly to the gospel principles of mutuality, trust, and love in their sexual relating.[38] For the ELCA, then, the effect of sin on sexuality is a matter of discernment—namely, the church teaches that sexual activity is only sinful (and thus goes against the creator's intent for human nature) when it results from inclinations or choices that do not reflect (or participate in) the reign of God.

Thus, the official teachings of the ELCA do not require Christians to accept heterosexuality as an idyllic norm—like the one sustained by the Reformed Church in America. Instead, the ELCA allows Christians to consider "natural sexuality" (i.e., what is "given," or what God has created) as a range of innate sexual inclinations. Sexual morality and immorality, however, are more specifically conceived in terms of principles. For the ELCA this means pursuing wholeness, self-giving love, and trust when thinking about "God's will" for human sexuality; or, exploitation, alienation, and selfishness when thinking about sin.[39]

Of course, these brief descriptions of church teachings are but mere gleanings of the discourses about "sexual nature" among some contemporary Christian communities. We could certainly explore a number of other Christian positions on the "nature" of sex before and after the fall in more detail. But I think that even a short (and selective) look at Christian teachings on these matters reveals that there is quite a bit of disparity on concepts of "sexual nature" in the Christian religion. And of all the areas of theological speculation in Christianity, the speculation about sexuality has surely demonstrated the influence of presuppositional commitments. Consider: celibate clergy such as Augustine, Gregory of Nyssa, and Jerome anticipated that perfect humans were also nonsexual. But other Christian views, especially traditional Protestant ones, as well as contemporary Vatican teachings, have more or less imagined our first parents as embodying heterosexual and marital norms. What is more, twenty-first-century progressive Christians have accepted the "naturalness" of sexual diversity in light of descriptions from the sciences, as well as contextual theological reflection on the Bible and natural law. In other words, Christians have often interpreted what is "natural" from what they experience (now) as normal, or normative.

Creation, Sin, and Virtue

The implications of such diverse Christian views for a definition of sexual virtue are fairly straightforward. Namely, those Christians who paint a theological portrait of "original creation" as one in which sexuality was absent, or one that only manifested heterosexuality, tend also to articulate theological narratives that condemn those sexual activities and relationships that do not reflect their beliefs about life before the "fall." On the other hand, Christians who accept that sexual diversity is a natural good of creation are likely to anticipate the need for prudential flexibility when discerning ends of sexual virtue, if not also when thinking theologically about what counts as sexual sin.

Thus, the way in which Christians construct the relationship between "creation" and "sin" will shape the way one talks about virtue and vice in a religious context. Namely, accepting the category of "sin" suggests that human life is not the best that it can be, and that consequences of sinfulness have negative effects both corporately and individually—including all sorts of complications and consequences in life, as well as in death. However, not all concepts of sin are helpful for contemporary moral reflection. I have specifically in mind those doctrines of sin that suggest there have been radical ontological changes in the human species (i.e., like the kind of radical change St. Gregory of Nyssa suggested when he said we "fell" in sin from asexuality to sexuality). These notions of sin rely very heavily on peculiar theological assertions about prehistoric human life—and I find such theologies to be rather unreliable for practical moral reflection. If for no other reason, those who construct such primeval theologies of "perfect nature" set themselves up as the sole arbiters of all disputes about human nature and morality now. We cannot engage in true dialogue with them, because such religious characters are often unwilling to consider any other explanation about our human origins, fiercely defending their literal conception of an idyllic genesis—and we are simply wrong because we do not hold their views. Such theologians fail to see their own potentiality for error—and as a result, they tend to speak in monologues and eschew the need for dialogue and mutual critique.

Instead of constructing a primeval theology about "perfect nature," from which to deduce ideas about sin, I suggest Christians might read the category of "sin" as a relational state of being, in reference to all thoughts, actions, feelings, and relationships that do not participate in the "reign of God" (as that is interpreted by the Christian community). If that view of sin is advanced, then a Christian investigation into what is "natural" or "unnatural" for human beings (in light of doctrines of creation and sin) really amounts to a search for what is "better" or "worse" for the human being, as one who is simultaneously a given kind of physical creature, a moral agent, *and* a spiritual being. Thus, I suggest that meaningful Christian statements on the "natural" and

"unnatural" (so defined) will require the synthesis of at least three bodies of knowledge. First, it requires detailed descriptions of given human
"nature"—not theological speculations about primeval "original" human
life, but scientific (i.e., descriptive) analyses of human beings now, which
can provide a basis for rational scrutiny of all other moral or religious
claims about human nature. Equipped with scientific knowledge about
human nature, the Christian community can then turn to two other
bodies of (speculative and practical) knowledge: theology and ethics.
Such an approach to understanding "human nature," however, does not
mean to subordinate theology and ethics to the sciences. Rather, this
approach equips us with as much information as possible about human
beings in order to reason well about what leads to human flourishing.

For the rest of this chapter we will focus on descriptions of "given"
human nature from the sciences in order to better understand our subject
of human sexuality. From this information, we will be able to better
reflect on virtue and vice prudentially, with greater insight into the
kind of creatures that we are. And for the Christian thinker, data from
the sciences will provide a body of knowledge with which theological
speculation might have more fruitful intercourse.

Scientific Views on Sexual Nature

As we discussed it in chapter 2, the perspective of critical realism allows
us to accept that the world is knowable and relatable, and that through
critical reflections on human living we can dare to uncover reasonable
goods that contribute to happiness and diminish suffering (i.e., living
and doing well). What is more, I have also affirmed that the pursuit of
the "good" (morally) can be informed by scientific data about what does,
and does not, contribute to our *creaturely* flourishing. Indeed, creaturely
flourishing should be anticipated when thinking about what it means
to live and do well, morally. If for no other reason, the pursuit of the
"good" life is usually predicated upon having a life at all, and to the
extent that we can have it, a life that is in well-working order—which
is not to say "perfect," but at least functional (intellectually, emotionally, physically, and so forth, but with mindfulness to various levels of
ability). Thus, scientific insight is helpful. In particular, it helps us to
think about what is possible for us given the kind of creatures that
we are (or are now). In other words, the sciences provide a portrait
of our "given" human nature, in light of which, moral and theological

reflections about that which is (and is not) natural to human beings can be compared, contrasted, or tested for rational integrity. This is especially important when it comes to describing the "nature" of human sexuality.

That said, there are far too many scientific studies about sexuality for me to offer an adequate description of them here. What is more, I choose to reserve some of these studies for later chapters, when we examine recreation, relational intimacy, and selective acts of procreation as "ends" of sexual virtue. Allow me, then, to summarize just two scientific insights that bear on descriptions of human sexuality, relevant to our discussions on sexual morality. The first explores the "nature" of sexual attraction. The second concerns the "naturalness" of nonprocreative sexual activity. I choose these two subjects insofar as traditional Christian reflections on sexual morality have cast "natural" sex as heterosexual and procreative. But when we turn to reports from the sciences, neither heterosexual desire nor reproduction of the species captures all that is "natural" to human sexuality.

The Science of Sexual Desires

Whereas many conservative churches (today) teach that heterosexuality was God's sole intent for human sexual orientation (and thus desire), scientific reports tend to agree that there is a spectrum of sexual orientations, or inclinations (from homosexual to heterosexual, generally speaking), and that these orientations are innately experienced, not something chosen, or perverted, from some "original" heterosexual state.[40] For example, as Wysocki and Martin first demonstrated in 2005, when people are subjected *only* to sexual pheromones (naturally excreted chemicals that can arouse sexual attraction), it is possible to show which bodies (male or female) subjects are innately attracted to apart from conscious apprehension of an aesthetically/sexually appealing body.[41]

And yet, sexual attraction is not only a matter of innate sexual orientation to male or female bodies. As creatures with the intellective capacity to consciously value others, we are also attracted to people on the basis of what we value of them (whether personally, socially, or otherwise). But this has to do with general intellective attractions, which are distinct from sensory sexual attraction, and yet can, and do, intersect with our sensory sexual attractions as well. And as psychologists tell us, we experience general intellective attraction on the basis of "rewards."

The most fundamental assumption about interpersonal attraction is that we are attracted to others whose presence is rewarding to us (Clore & Byrne, 1974). Two different types of rewards influence attraction: noticeable direct rewards we obviously receive from our interaction with others, and more subtle indirect benefits of which we're not always aware, that are merely associated with someone else. Direct rewards refer to all the evident pleasures people provide us. When they shower us with interest and approval, we're usually gratified by the attention and acceptance. When they are witty and beautiful, we enjoy their pleasing characteristics. And when they give us money or good advice, we are clearly better off. Most of the time, the more direct rewards that people provide us, the more attracted we are to them.

But attraction also results from a variety of subtle influences that are only indirectly related to the obvious kindness, good looks, or pleasing personalities of those we meet. For instance, most of us like ourselves, and anything about new acquaintances that connect them to us, however tangentially, may make them seem more likable. . . . Rewards like these are indirect and mild, and we sometimes don't even consciously notice them—but they do illustrate just how diverse and varied the rewards that attract us to others can be.[42]

Thus, we're not just horny creatures that like "hot" bodies. We are deeply complex creatures that find psychological reward in certain persons for reasons that are conscious and unconscious; sexual as well as social.

What is more, it is also our "nature" to find some people more physically pleasing (or attractive) than others. Psychologists report that most human beings are constantly evaluating (consciously and subconsciously) our level of sexual attraction to everyone we meet. While some of this is culturally relative, owing to certain aesthetic fads, it also appears that there are some innate "givens" about physical/sexual attraction between human beings, which have been tested across time and cultures. Such "givens" include facial features, waist-to-hip ratio, and the symmetry of body. These, according to scientific study—across cultures and fads of aesthetics—signal (both consciously and subconsciously) levels of sexual viability, health, and compatibility.[43] And yet, in spite of certain "givens" about which bodies are generally more sexually attractive than others, many times a person's general intellective attraction to another is more important (personally or relationally) than a primary sexual attraction—and thus, our general intellective attractions are also very important to us when choosing, or navigating, sexual relationships.

Therefore, if the sciences are right, we experience sexual attraction as simultaneous sensory and psychological inclinations toward specific sexual objects. These attractions (or desires) are generated from innate inclinations borne of complex biological and psychological dispositions, and these allow us to consciously discern what is suitable for us sexually (i.e., a body with which we feel naturally attracted) as well as what is intellectively good for us interpersonally (i.e., a person with whom we want to relate for any number of reasons). Understood this way, sexual attraction ends up being an inclination not only of a basic sensory sort ("Wow! Look at him!"), but *also* an intellective inclination that informs our sexual desires in reference to particular people. Namely, our intellective capacity allows us to assign conscious meanings to our sexual desires (e.g., desire to express love, to pursue play, or to engage in fantasy, etc.), as well as to draw on sex as a means of interpersonal communication. Thus, our "natural" sexual attractions can "orient" us to a variety of sexual relationships. To that end, we have desires not just toward certain bodies (although that is part of it), but also toward various people for complex intellective and emotional reasons. That we have such sexual attractions is more or less given. However, how we reflect on these attractions, how we "unpack" them, and how we act on them is a deliberate matter—and thus belongs to our moral agency.

For example, studies in psychology and sexuality show that the adult who is innately disposed toward children as sexual objects (the pedophile) can in no way act upon that desire without harming a child physically, psychologically, emotionally, and/or socially.[44] Morally speaking, we can say that pedophilia is wrong insofar as it lacks reasonable standards of mutuality, equality, and rational consent—and thus cannot, in any reliable way, lead to human happiness when actualized (i.e., living and doing well). The example of pedophilia, then, is a helpful reminder that what is "natural" to human beings might not always be "good" to act upon (morally), and thus the moral community has the difficult task of discerning between what is simply given, and then when (if ever) it is good to act on a given sexual inclination. To that end, science helps us to better understand what is good for us in terms of creaturely flourishing. Ethics then apprehends that data and interprets (morally) what of our given "nature"—when actualized—leads to our living and doing well. In some cases, such as pedophilia, what is "given" can in no way be actualized to a reasonable end. In other cases, what is "given" of human nature may very well be actualized in such a way that it results in genuine happiness.

The "Purpose" of Sex

If it is "natural" for human beings to experience different kinds of sexual attractions—whether in terms of orientations to certain kinds of bodies or in terms of attraction to particular people for personal/intellective reasons—then it ought to follow that we can name a variety of "purposes" of human sexuality. Recall, however, that this has not been the attitude held about sex by many Christian churches. Time and again we have been told that sex is only for procreation, but only so long as that sex is also an expression of love between (well-sanctioned) heterosexual spouses. While that view has been nuanced and challenged throughout Christian history, many Christian churches have nevertheless retained marital, or monogamous, or heterosexual norms for sexual morality. And yet, our "natural" sexual attractions do not always lead us to marital, monogamous, or heterosexual encounters. Traditional Christians might tell us that this has to do with "sin." The sciences, however, suggest that a plethora of sexual attractions and sexual scenarios are quite "natural" for human beings—especially for nonreproductive purposes.

According to the psychologist Christopher Ryan and the psychiatrist Cacilda Jethá, human beings, as well as our nearest primate relatives (the bonobos), draw on sex in ways that many other creatures do not. In particular, Ryan and Jethá note that these two species

> use eroticism for pleasure, for solidifying friendship, and for cementing a deal. . . . For these two species (and apparently only these two species), non-reproductive sex is "natural," a defining characteristic. The animal world is full of species that have sex only during widely spaced intervals when the female is ovulating. [In fact] only two species can do it week in and week out for non-reproductive reasons: one human, the other very humanlike.[45]

Thus, in their view, having sex "like an animal" is having sex for repro-ductive reasons—while nonprocreative sex might be the most "human" sex of all, revealing our distinctive capacities for meaningful social inter-actions, if not creativity too.

In fact, insofar as early humans were hunter-gatherers (not agricul-turalists), Ryan and Jethá suggest that the capacity to draw upon sex for reasons other than reproduction is one part of what likely helped the early humans to bond with one another, cultivate tribal interdependence, and provide care for multiple offspring. They hypothesize:

> Without frequent [social-erotic experiences, or, S.E.Ex.] it's doubt-ful that foraging bands could have maintained social equilibrium and fecundity over the millennia. S.E.Ex. were crucial in binding adults into groups that [also] cared communally for children of obscure or shared paternity, each child likely related to most or all of the men in the group (if not a father, certainly an uncle, cousin, etc. . . .).[46]

Their hypothesis of a "promiscuous" human past may be evidenced in our very own bodies.

For example, the head of the human penis is shaped in such a way that it can scrape out "other" sperm from a woman's vagina. Ryan and Jethá suggest that this is actually an evolutionary marker, which reveals that sexual exclusivity was absent or rare among early humans, and fur-thermore, that competition for reproduction happened on the cellular level, not between adult males. What is more, Ryan and Jethá note that the human penis is longer and thicker than any other primate's, and that the human male is capable of longer duration of sexual activity, which suggests an emphasis on pleasure, albeit with a positive reproductive util-ity.[47] On the other hand, most primates can only endure sexual activity for a short time (seven seconds for chimpanzees), and thus are ordered toward immediate ejaculation for reproductive purposes.[48]

Human females also have such markers of a "promiscuous" human past. Ryan and Jethá note that the human female's breasts are unlike most other mammals—in particular, for their (comparatively) large size and shape. This, Ryan and Jethá postulate, is a form of genital echoing. Whereas other female mammals have swelling vaginas that signal sexual viability and immediate readiness for reproduction, Ryan and Jethá sug-gest that human/female breasts echo that function, but only to signal sexual viability, not to indicate immediate fertility.[49] What is more, Ryan and Jethá also highlight the fact that human females have the capacity to orgasm through clitoral stimulation—which of itself does not have a direct reproductive benefit (unlike male ejaculation).

Ryan and Jethá argue that such bodily "evidence" points toward a human species that originated in "promiscuous" (or multi-mating) tribes. In their view, exclusive sexual relationships only arose with the advent of agriculture—a system that not only introduced the idea that land can become the property of an individual but also that our sexual mates—and the children we make with them—are "our" property too (which is to say, women and children became the property of men).

However, their hypothesis does not mean that relationships ordered toward relational commitment are "unnatural" to the human being. The human capacities for emotional and relational commitments are facilitated, in part, by our intellective capacities.[50] Thus "relational commitments" are "natural" to us too. However, what may not be "natural" to us, Ryan and Jethá suggest, are codes of sexual morality that deny us access to multiple sexual partners (should we desire them)—recognizing that it is natural for humans to desire multiple sexual partners for reasons *other* than reproduction or exclusive romantic love.[51]

Thus, their argument suggests that it is "natural" for human beings to find ourselves drawn to many and various kinds of sexual relationships, precisely because our species was originally "promiscuous." In their view, it is part of who we are as human beings to seek out social erotic experiences not merely for the sensory pleasures of sex, but also as a symbol of what we might call basic friendship or tribal loyalty; if not also to exercise and enjoy novelty (through new and multiple sexual partners) in the face of life's doldrums. Those "capacities" of sex, they say, are what drove our ancient ancestors, shaped our very bodies, and *still* steer many of our basic sexual inclinations. But as we well know, that description of sex runs counter to the traditional cultural message we often hear: that "sex is for love, romance, monogamy, or marriage." But just as a kiss can signal a greeting from a family member or lover (and thus communicate different meanings), and just as eating can be utilitarian or sacramental, so too, Ryan and Jethá invite us to consider (on the basis of scientific study) that the "nature" of sex is multivalent—and that even as it can be about romance or purposeful reproduction, it can also facilitate basic human connections (such as friendship), as well as satisfy the "natural" want for novel sexual experiences or fantasy fulfillment.

Concluding Thoughts on "Sexual Nature"

Although this has been but a brief glimpse into what the sciences are revealing about the nature of human sexuality, the sources I have cited suggest that human "sexual nature" is: diverse, always active (consciously and subconsciously), ordered toward physical/sensory fulfillment, capable of symbolizing relational bonds, meaningful on emotional and psychological levels, and, innately ordered toward multiple mates for reasons both reproductive and nonreproductive. Individually, each insight is interesting, perhaps illuminating of sexual experiences and/or feelings that any of one us might have had (or will have) at various points in our lives. And yet, as we have noted, scientific insights into human "sexual nature" do not tell us (straightaway) what is "good" for us to pursue.

For example, that human beings can experience strong sexual desires toward multiple people (for distinct reasons) does not—of itself—mean that we should abandon committed relationships. After all, we might have reasons for choosing a natural good like "relational intimacy" via sexual monogamy at the expense of pursuing the natural good of "sexual novelty" through sexual "promiscuity" (or vice versa). What is "natural" to us only indicates what is possible. I want to reiterate that, as moral agents, we must choose which of our options is best for us, for those we love, and in light of wider social issues too.

Recall, then, that virtue ethics promotes habits of doing the right thing, at the right time, and for the right reason. Recall, also, that virtue ethics considers our creaturely nature before turning to evaluate what of our options is best for us to pursue. To do that well, I am convinced that we need to consider the data we have about human sexuality from the sciences. From them, we can imagine a number of different ways of navigating our sexual lives, whether in celibacy, monogamy, or some kind of "open" sexual relationship (whether in tandem with a spouse or partner, or on one's own when "single"). But these are just the possibilities. Virtue ethics will help us to think about these, insofar as prudence will aide us in considering when acting on our sexual desires will contribute to our living and doing well. Virtue ethics will also help us to discern when sexual activity is best held back, at a given time or place, or held back from particular people.

However, when engaged in Christian ethics, drawing on the sciences can lead us back to debates about "nature" before and after the "fall." In particular, some Christians will fall back on the theological argument that any scientific description of human sexuality is merely a description of what human sexuality is like, now, "after the fall." From this theological perspective, one can say that science only studies *corrupted* sexuality, and thus the conclusions that the sciences reach only describe imperfect human nature. But let's clear our heads about this kind of defense. Privileging speculative theological interpretations of "nature" over the descriptions of science is precisely what led many Christians to believe in a flat earth at the center of the universe. In more recent years, such privileging has led to fundamentalist Christians teaching that dinosaur bones were put in place by God to test the faithful (i.e., a test of whether we would believe in a literal six-day creation, or, if we would succumb to the "deception" of evolutionary science).[52] Likewise, other contemporary Christians (with fundamentalist leanings) have actually argued—from a theological view of nature—that demons inhabit sexually transmitted diseases.[53]

Such claims will likely strike many readers as incredibly unfounded. But I cite these examples to make a point—not to belittle fundamentalists. Namely, I invite the reader to consider having an actual debate with such fundamentalists about the intersection of science and religion on topics such as dinosaur bones or STDs. You would likely draw upon science to convince your fundamentalist friend that dinosaur bones are actually remains of creatures millions of years deceased. What is more, you might show them scientific evidence from the World Health Organization that STDs are not the domain for demons, but various forms of virus and bacteria. However, if your fundamentalist friend responds with literal interpretations of the Bible, or unsupported fringe theologies, you (in turn) might likely feel stonewalled and stalemated (even with the preponderance of evidence on your side). In many ways, this is the same kind of frustrating stalemate that faces the Christian community today when certain Christians (or churches) deny reports from the sciences, in favor of premodern understandings of sexuality—whether they derive those from plain-readings of the Bible, or from theological speculations about "nature" before and after the "fall."

It is my hope that such obviously erroneous Christian judgments about the "nature" of a flat earth at the center of the universe—or speculations about the "nature" of STDs as demon domains—will help Christians (now) to carefully examine how they have come to their own conclusions about "sexual nature"—and what of that, may need revision. While science may not be able to comment on "what God has willed" in Christian ethics, science can describe (with increasing accuracy) how human life has developed, and how a given creature has (or can) operate according to its given "nature." Thus, with respect to "sexual nature," the sciences help us to sketch "what is" so that we might finally consider more carefully, and ethically, what is best to pursue as part of a whole life, well lived.

Nine

Church Teachings Revisited

Must we not, in all humility, acknowledge that all orthodoxy is semi-orthodoxy—meaning that none of us can claim to have captured the infinite and inexpressible in our feeble human definitions and expressions?

—Brian McLaren

Belief: A Matter of "What" and "How"

Any careful examination of Christian teachings on sexual ethics will reveal that there is very little agreement among the churches about norms for sexual morality. I have already cited a number of these differences in the last several chapters. For example, it has been noted that the Roman Catholic Church has upheld the procreative norm, demanding that all loving married couples engage in sexual activity in such a way that it does not contravene the potential for new offspring.[1] Twentieth and twenty-first-century Protestants, on the other hand, have accepted the use of birth control (or at least, certain forms of it). But they are divided over the question of whether marriage is necessary for sexual expression, and they are further divided over debates about same-sex relationships.[2]

The churches disagreements about sexual morality are, on the one hand, differences in biblical interpretations and readings of human nature. On the other hand, the differences also reflect shifts in how the theological enterprise of "faith seeking understanding" is engaged. As the religion scholar Diana Butler Bass has suggested in her book *Christianity After Religion*, the Western Christian theological imagination has historically centered on three questions: "*What* do I believe? *How* should I act? And, *who* am I?" (i.e., what is my religious affiliation).[3] Answers to these questions have usually been controlled by denominational dogmas, passed on through well-regulated catechesis and maintained by privileged castes of "orthodox" church leaders (pastors, bishops, seminary professors, denominational leaders, church publishers, etc.).

However, as sociologists of religion have noted, this old system of dogma and theological privilege has suffered considerable strain in the last few decades. When we look at Christianity, specifically in America, we see that church membership has been steadily declining among the denominations.[4] Whereas some Christians have left mainline traditions for independent mega-churches, new data suggest that the exodus from the churches has not been for one church over another. Instead, we are finding that as many as one-fifth of the American population has abdicated organized religion altogether. The Pew Forum on Religion and Public Life has designated this group: the "nones."[5] However, by all accounts most of the "nones" are not atheists, or even agnostics.[6] Diana Butler Bass has called them the "spiritual not religious"—people who maintain a spiritual identity, but who will not abide by narrow dogmatism. The "nones" of the spiritual-not-religious variety retain a theological imagination, but as Bass suggests, their questions present four new religious inquires: "*How* do I believe? *Who* do I believe? *What* do I do? And, *why* do I do it?"[7]

These new questions not only empower people to think more carefully about what they believe, but they also motivate people to evaluate whether or not church teachings actually illuminate the life that one is living, or if these teachings have circumscribed one's views to an intellectual or personal disadvantage. Bass suggests that the embrace of "spirituality" over "organized religion" amounts to a search for meaningful concepts of God, as well as a search for satisfying answers to pressing theological questions, which the old paradigms and old dogmas may not be able to address. She says:

> In a wide variety of guises and forms, spirituality represents an important stage of awakening: the search for new gods. As the old gods (and the institutions that preached, preserved, and protected the old gods) lose credibility, people begin to cast about for new gods—and new stories, new paths, and new understandings to make sense of their new realities. In the process, the old language fails, and people reach for new words to describe the terrain of their experience.[8]

The search for "new gods" and "new stories" to understand "new realities," however, does not necessarily entail an abandonment of particular deities, but a shift in how one understands their God.

Shifting the questions from "what" one believes to "how," and perhaps "why," is the effort of reform and renewal. Catholic and Protestant churches are not opposed to reform and renewal, generally conceived. And yet, many churches today are adamant about preserving "old" concepts of divinity and sustaining "old" theologies, by which certain church officials can demonize notorious sinners and venerate their preferred saints. It is no wonder, then, that ideas about sexual morality have become so entrenched. Set within the context of churches keeping vigil of old gods and old stories, old ideas about sexuality prevail as well. But we are learning that archaic traditionalism is beginning to crack under a new reformation of people who are willing to challenge (or leave) the churches without fear of condemnation. Without question, this reformation movement is relevant to moral reflection on human sexuality.

Consider, for example, what is happening in Roman Catholic communities. Namely, while it may be true that the official teachings of the Roman Catholic Church paint a "traditional" portrait of sexual morality that resonates with some, it does not resonate with all. Indeed, many Catholics have objected that the official church monologue about celibacy, marriage, and procreation does not reflect the breadth or depth of sexual experiences among a great cohort of wise, faithful, and loving people (both in and outside of the church). The discrepancy between "what the church teaches" and the lived experiences of decent—nontraditional—people strikes many thinkers as an indicator that dogma has failed to speak meaningfully to reality. Fran Ferder and John Heagle have articulated this concern well. They write:

> In each of our parishes, there is a wide diversity of backgrounds, life experiences, and love stories. In our church, we have tended to speak of and listen to only two of those love stories: marriage and consecrated celibacy. But consider for a moment all of the people who do not fit neatly into either of those categories: single adults, the separated and divorced, those who are celibate not by choice but by circumstance, gay and lesbian persons, together with all the other people who wonder if there is a place for them at the table.[9]

While this statement may read as gentle and respectful, it is also an expression of critical resistance to the monologue of official Catholic teaching. It is indicative of a larger movement—in particular, a movement to analyze doctrine, not simply to preserve it—which many Christians (both Protestant and Catholic) hope can lead to theological renewal, including new theological approaches to human sexuality.

In this chapter, I invite the reader to consider the relationship between church teachings and sexual morality in general, through the critical questions that Bass has identified: *How* do I believe? *Who* do I believe? *What* do I do? *Why* do I do it? With these questions as our guide, we will look in the aggregate at why the shift from "what" to "how" churches believe can change the way one engages in moral and religious discourse. In particular, we will consider how Bass's critical questions bear on actual Christians' engagement with sex and sexuality, whose faith is a central component of their daily living.

"How" Have I Believed?

When people of faith say that they "believe" in this or that, they are indicating what they sense to be true or really real—metaphysically or spiritually—and how that "truth" can (or should) bear on everyday living. But *how* Christians "believe" is another matter altogether. The pastor, and author, Maurine Waun offers one description of "how" Christian belief comes in different forms. She writes:

> How do you hold truth? Do you hold it with hands clenched and close to your body, or do you hold it with hands open, palms facing upward, away from your body? That fist clenching grip is the one we use when we are determined to hang on—to hang on for dear life—because we are afraid that if we don't, we will lose hold of our truth and be washed away into oblivion and moral chaos. And so that we will not abandon all that we have come to believe, we cling tenaciously and fiercely as others bring their truths to share.
>
> The second way—to hold tenuously—is more like offering. I offer you my piece of truth so that you and others will share yours with all of us, and together we will arrive at a greater picture of the truth. My vision isn't the whole picture, nor is yours or anyone else's. It is only in the sharing that we come

to see the value in others' truth, and even after we give and receive what we have to offer in this company, we will still not have a completed portrayal of what *really* is.[10]

I suggest that Waun's comparison of belief "hands clenched" and belief "palms open" is a poignant (and telling) illustration.

Namely, it matters not only "what" Christians believe (insofar as belief shapes one's life and lifestyle), but also "how." As Bass suggests, "*How* [one believes] is a question of meaning and purpose that pushes people into a deeper engagement in the world, rather than memorizing facts."[11] Thus, asking the question "How do I believe" calls into question the very theological frameworks that support articles of belief. It creates the space to investigate the wider religious system before committing oneself to particular religious answers.

For example, imagine any number of LGBT adolescents who are raised in Christian churches with "sin-lists" that include homosexuality. These young people are told in their formative years that their capacity for intimate love and physical companionship—central to most human lives—is, in their case, "sinful" and condemned by God. From the time that they become aware of their sexual feelings, these LGBT youth are shaped to believe that the Bible is very clear about the immorality of homosexuality—and furthermore—that if they reject their home church's teachings, they are, in effect, rejecting God.[12]

But imagine that those LGBT adolescents grow up, move away from home, and attend churches, colleges, or universities where sexual diversity is respected, and religious teachings are approached contextually. Our LGBT young adults (now) start to realize that there are a whole host of interpretive choices to make—and that various churches make interpretations in significantly different ways. In other words, our LGBT young adults come to realize that they too must make interpretive decisions about "how" faith is best conceived at all, not simply "what" they have been taught to believe on any given issue.

Obviously, then, "how" one believes (e.g., contextually or literally) can profoundly shape both "what" a person accepts theologically, as well as how one lives one's life morally. Let's consider another example. Think for a few moments about a conservative evangelical Christian who believes that marriage is a relationship that should only be entered by a man and a woman. It is likely (to various degrees) that this person will live and act (and maybe even vote) in such a way that marriage (whether civil or religious) is denied to anyone who does not fit the heterosexual mold. To reach that conclusion, our conservative evangelical friend will have to read the Bible in a particular way (i.e., a plain reading), perhaps drawing on proof-texts, or even certain "traditional" interpretations of "nature."

But suppose we asked that Christian if he or she treats faith in the same way when it comes to other issues? For example, we might contrast the debate about marriage equality with a debate about gun control. Would the evangelical Christian take verses in the Bible about non-violence just as literally as he or she does with passages about same-sex activity? As it turns out, many conservative evangelical Christians in America trump the Sermon on the Mount with the Second Amendment of the United States Constitution. According to studies conducted by Pew Research, conservative evangelicals in America are overwhelmingly in favor of rights to gun ownership (and their use).[13] However, the same evangelicals are overwhelming opposed to marriage equality for same-sex couples—because the Bible "says so."[14]

Pause for a moment to consider what that example reveals, in terms of "what" and "how" Christians believe. An American evangelical Christian is more likely to defend gun ownership (and use) on the basis of promoting a broad reading of the Second Amendment, and thus rejecting a "plain-reading" of those biblical verses that promote nonviolence. But with respect to marriage equality for same-sex couples, American conservative evangelicals are more likely to condemn legal marriage equality on the basis of a *plain reading* of a few passages in scripture, at the expense of constitutional precepts such as equal protection under the law. Of course, the conservative evangelical embrace of guns and condemnation of same-sex marriage is more complex than what I have only sketched. But the disparate approaches by which some Christians settle social/moral issues does suggest that examining "what" and "how" one believes is important when analyzing Christian moral perspectives. This is true not only for conservative Christian churches, but for liberal ones too.

For example, when the United Church of Christ (UCC) teaches about human sexuality, it explicitly acknowledges that "what" people decide about sexual morality will result directly from "how" they think about sexual relationships in light of their particular Christian faith. The UCC affirms, "When faced with ethical decisions, each of us needs to be accorded the freedom and responsibility to choose. We may turn to the scriptures, call upon the Spirit in prayer, and invite the counsel of trusted people as we seek to discern what is right to do."[15] Without this freedom, the UCC warns, "our power as self-defining moral agents is undermined."[16]

Pause again and consider what this example reveals, in terms of "what" and "how" Christians believe. For a member of the UCC, sexual morality will not be decided, necessarily, by citing a biblical text, or even looking to the thinking of past theologians, or even to traditions of Christian history. Instead, the UCC encourages the Christian to reflect carefully on a wide variety of sources, and to do so in light of one's faith in God. The UCC highlights for its members that "how" one approaches questions of faith is important to consider before making comments about morality. But this, in turn, means that denominations such as the UCC are more or less centered on a polity of individual conscience, which for many other Christians sacrifices the central authority of historic cardinal doctrines. Thus, if, or when, the UCC stakes a theological claim, it may do so as a matter of conviction, but never certainty.

Ultimately, then, the positions churches take on "how" to believe, and "what" to believe, are a reflection on how one weights religious authority. But in our time, religious authority is not a settled issue. Diana Butler Bass notes:

> Once upon a time, Americans would have deferred to the clergy, a teacher, or a parent on issues of belief. When it comes to questions of meaning and purpose, however, it no longer seems adequate to say, "The church teaches," "Christians have always believed," or "the Bible said it, so I believe it." External authorities do not carry the weight they once did. Thus questions of belief have not only morphed from *what* to *how*, but they necessarily include the secondary dimension of *who*. . . .
>
> As the question of *how* is experiential, so is the question of *who*. In the early twenty-first century, trustworthiness is not simply a matter of an expert who holds a degree or a certain role in an institution. Rather, authority springs from two sources: one, relationship, and two, authenticity. . . . Authority comes through connection, personal investment, and communal accountability, rather than submission to systems or structures of expertise. . . . Although certain people will always hanker for authoritarian or charismatic leaders, there is a much broader longing for authentic leaders in these times—those whose message and actions validate their deepest beliefs.[17]

Bass's insight captures, from a bird's eye perspective, a major fault line that (arguably) is defining churches in twenty-first-century America: those that are committed to hierarchal and clerical authority so as to control "what" one believes; and those that are open to new insights about "truth."

As I read the differences in religious beliefs—in terms of "what" and "how"—there are obvious implications for Christian sexual ethics. Namely, churches that emphasize ongoing reflection on "how" people believe, *without* narrow expectations for "what" people *should* believe, will likely offer considerable flexibility on matters of sexual morality. Readers can find this kind of flexibility (to various degrees) within a number of contemporary Christian churches, including the United Church of Christ, the Episcopal Church, the Evangelical Lutheran Church in America, the Presbyterian Church (USA), progressive Reformed congregations, and the Metropolitan Community Church, to name a few. On the other hand, churches that emphasize the "what" of belief (i.e., preserving denominational orthodoxy) over critical reflection about "how" they might otherwise believe, will likely sustain older norms about sexual morality that are now regarded as "traditional."

Who Do I Believe? What Do I Do? Why Do I Do It?

A Protestant friend of mine once confided in me that when he was a teenager he had a rather peculiar masturbatory ritual. After discovering masturbation, he also discovered the onslaught of religious-laden guilt. He reported that upon ejaculation, his teenage mind would immediately recall the damning lessons that his church had taught him about sex (at least, sexual acts outside of marriage). Given that his sexual fantasies were about men, not women, he felt doubly damned. His solution was to sing Christian songs and hymns as an offering to God, within moments after orgasm. For him, "clean-up" was both physical and spiritual.

Most people of faith have likely encountered a similar scenario: the enjoyment of an activity that the church otherwise says is wrong—followed by confession, forgiveness, and then a repetition of the so-called sin. In his letter to the church in Rome, the apostle Paul described a similar pattern of behavior. He wrote:

> So I find it to be a law that when I want to do what is good, evil lies close at hand. For I delight in the law of God in my

inmost self, but I see in my members another law at war with the law of my mind, making me captive to the law of sin that dwells in my members. Wretched man that I am! Who will rescue me from this body of death? Thanks be to God through Jesus Christ our Lord![18]

Thus, whether with Paul or with my friend in his teenage years, there is—in the mind of many Christians—a "war" between what one thinks is right and what one actually does.

In his letter to the Romans, Paul referenced an unnamed personal struggle, which he resolved by surrendering to grace (apart from achieving perfection himself). But for Christians in our time, the "war" between "the good" and "evil" is often prepackaged in the moral teachings that people have inherited from the churches. To that end, churches are morally responsible for the outcome of their teachings in peoples' lives, and thus are not above moral reproach. In particular, I believe that there are (at least) two matters that should be critically addressed before accepting any church norm on morality. The first draws on Bass's question: "Who do I believe?" Namely, we need to investigate whether the moral and religious content of various church teachers actually contribute to our happiness, or conversely, promote suffering. The second matter draws on Bass's remaining questions: "What do I do?" and "Why do I do it?" In particular, we also need to explore how human experiences might signal the credibility of church teachings on moral issues.

With respect to moral norms advanced by Christian communities, I want to be clear that "church teachings" should always be critiqued for their viability and credibility. Where certain moral norms about sexuality have been sustained in the churches, difficult (and real) consequences have followed. Indeed, some church norms have set certain people up for moral, psychological, and spiritual crises. Take for example, my friend's early-life faith crisis. While he's now a well-adjusted, successful man, as a teenager he anguished alone over substantial matters of salvation or condemnation—because of masturbation. He did not know that masturbation was common, and from many perspectives, morally permissible. His church's teachings left him alone in a room with the image of a God who condemns people who touch their bodies. His only recourse was to create a ritual that might somehow appease a vengeful God, so as not to be cast into eternal hell for a few moments of sexual pleasure. That kind of psychological war was not necessary—nor was his emotional or psychological suffering, to whatever degree he experienced it.

The suffering that church teachings can inflict on people is not limited to a teenager's anxieties about masturbation. There is, as Maurine Waun notes, much "pain in the church" because of the inability to perform certain traditional norms, or to consistently "fail" by them. For example, in reference to the suffering of LGBT people in the church, she writes:

> It's all around us. And most of the time, we do not, will not, or cannot see it. The pain of feeling excluded, unwelcome, condemned, is what keeps countless men and women—alone in their struggle, alone in their spiritual journey—from entering the doors of the church, when they need it more than anyone can imagine. What would make them want to come? What would make anyone want to come to a place where they would be spotlighted, singled out, and asked to deny or change who they are, or to be absolutely silent about all of it? And so, in order to find a welcoming, supportive community, some gay, lesbian, bisexual and transgendered persons end up [consigned to] a gay bar or bathhouse, or they may choose to escape the pain by turning to self-destructive behaviors. Alcoholism in the gender community is 300 times the national average; suicide is four times as frequent, according to PFLAG (Parents and Friends of Lesbians and Gays). The root cause of these evils is not homosexuality or other sexual orientation, but a church and society that force gay, lesbian, bisexual, and transgendered persons to want to escape hatred and judgment. Most of the time the church is totally unaware of the toll in human suffering and ecology.[19]

This pain also extends to heterosexuals—especially among those whose sexual relationships (in some way) arouse the condemning arm of their church: whether because of divorce and remarriage, or children before marriage; or the use of certain contraceptives that the church deems illicit, or some other "transgression." Indeed, heterosexual couples have been denied marriage rites, their families rejected from particular congregations, and their very character deemed "immoral," all because of alleged sexual offenses against official church teachings.

I emphasize the pain that church teachings can inflict, because it draws our attention to the moral norms that churches promote—and, in particular, it draws our attention to whether those moral norms actually contribute to human flourishing or suffering. Thus, it raises the question whether we should believe a church when it advances such norms. If for no other reason, we know that churches have been—and can be—wrong about their definitions of morality and immorality.[20] In the last century, churches have apologized for egregious past mistakes in moral and social teachings (e.g., for supporting slavery, segregation, gender discrimination, homophobia, etc.). Apologies, however, always come after an offense. And while privileged clergy can make those apologies looking back on history, the offense is almost always carried on the backs of real people who suffer considerably when churches make gross mistakes in moral judgments.

So as to avoid unnecessary suffering, I believe one way in which church teachings can be tested is to ask the critical question Bass has posed: "Who do I believe?" If in the exploration of that question we find that certain church teachings lead to human suffering, we will have very good reason to resist the teaching(s) of that church. But by this I do not mean that we should consider a moral norm of a church "faulty" just because it may be difficult to attain, or because there is some discomfort in reaching it. Sometimes pursuing the "good" requires struggle. What is more, sometimes moral norms are difficult to follow for people having certain addictions or psychopathologies. Such exceptions noted, there are some moral norms (set by the churches) that are certainly questionable, if not ill-advised to pursue. Thus, it is important to ask the remaining questions that Bass has posed: *What* do I do, and *why* do I do it? Namely, if in the struggle to achieve the ideals of a church's moral norms we find that frustration and suffering are systemic, demonstrable, and diminishing aspects of a person's life (i.e., induced fear, depression, or self-loathing), these outcomes might signal that there is something wrong about the norms that the church has set before us. With negative outcomes such as these, it seems reasonable for Christians to question "what they are doing" and "why they are doing it." In other words, the experience of Christians needs to be considered when reflecting on the moral teachings of the church.

This is not a radical suggestion for Christian ethics—in fact, it's quite standard.

For example, contraception has long been accepted into most Protestant churches, but not because the Bible praises condoms or pharmaceutical methods—it does not. Rather, twentieth-century people in Protestant churches brought their lived experiences to bear on this particular matter of sexual ethics, and the churches changed accordingly. Indeed, when we consider every shift in Christian teachings about sexual ethics, Christians (especially Protestants and pew Catholics) have changed their minds about sexual norms by considering their experiences of happiness and suf-fering in relation to sex and sexuality. In effect, such Christians explored the questions: *Who* do I believe? *What* do I do? and *Why* do I do it? Thus, it seems to be a foregone conclusion that when a church is open to careful reflection about "what" and "how" one believes, and when the church also incorporates the lived experiences of people in the pews, change—where prudent—comes, whether eventually or in earnest.

Of course, it may seem to some readers that I am esteeming "expe-rience" as a superior source of moral authority in competition with scripture or church tradition. However, I am not actually seeking to subordinate these venerated sources of religious authority, I am merely accepting (ethically) what appears to be part of the Christian religion itself: the integration of human experience in the moral vision and appli-cation of Christian ethics. Namely, the practice of the Christian religion, morally, has always required prudent (if not pastoral) application of its principles to real peoples' lives. What is more, real peoples' lives have helped Christian theologians and ethicists consider the merit of various teachings that the churches have (at one time or another) sustained. As the theologian James Tunstead Burtchaell has said, "The church is a community of moral wisdom accumulated, passed on, challenged, and revised. The primary font of that savvy is our own experience and observation."[21] Burtchaell goes on to say:

> It is inevitable that some elements of the wisdom handed down would give us pause, and that a few might even stick in our throats. It is inevitable, and it is good. For as [caretakers] of a vital tradition we must re-construe and improve on those few matters on which our particular generation may have been given further light. The tradition is not inert. But our reconsideration of it is a nervous task, for it is as likely to be astigmatism or blindness which puts us in stress with our elders in the faith as it is their backwardness and our enhanced vision. Still, we must take our misgivings out to the plaza of human experience for newly inquisitive study. If it goes well we shall either disagree more articulately with the tradition because we know better why we must revise it, or we shall appreciate the older wisdom more than ever because we did take a second look.[22]

In other words, we must finally admit that the church is a human institution, even as it dares to be a font of divine truth. Furthermore, Christians need to recognize that in its well-intended hope of being an ark of salvation, the church, in its human judgments, can be quite wrong. Thus, whom Christians "best" believe about moral matters may not always be the church (or a church leader) with which they are accustomed. In cases such as these, Christians may find it helpful to seek multiple perspectives on matters of morality in order to better understand the breadth and depth of ethical insights that are available to the Christian religion (as a whole). What is more, questions about "what" Christians do, and "why" they do it (or what they don't do, and why they don't do it) may better be answered in light of testimonies of human experiences, rather than the cold application of rigid orthodoxy.

Conclusion

In this brief chapter, we have looked at church teaching from the perspective of the critical questions: How do I believe? Who do I believe? What do I do? And, why do I do it? The goal was not to describe church teachings in detail, but to look at how these questions can (and do) shift Christian thinking about matters of faith and life—and what implications these questions have for Christian sexual ethics. When Christians think carefully about "how" they believe, and why they do what they do, they open the intellectual, moral, and theological spaces to imagine if there are better ways of conceiving and living their faith. In relation to a Christian argument about sexual virtue, these questions likewise allow the Christian to entertain how new concepts of sexual morality lead—or not—to "living and doing well," especially in light of their faith in the Christian God.

In the next three chapters we will turn, at last, to consider more detailed analyses of the "ends" of sexual virtue that I have named: recreation, relational intimacy, and selective acts of procreation. Now that we have examined the Bible contextually, nature and natural law thinking from new perspectives, and church teachings in light of shifts in questions about religious authority, it is finally possible to consider my proposed ends of sexual virtue with insights from these critical analyses.

Part IV

Ends of Sexual Virtue

Ten

Recreational Sex

We live in a world where we have to hide to make love, while violence is practiced in broad daylight.

—John Lennon

Misgivings About Recreational Sex

"Sex," "recreation," and "virtue" are not common word associations.

What is more, when one thinks of *sexual virtue*, it is probably rare to find someone who associates it with "recreational sex." Usually recreational sex falls somewhere else on the moral chart: whether as something condemned, or as something that does not have serious moral value—at least not in the way that "morality" is conventionally conceived. In fact, for many people, "recreational sex" is just "casual sex"—something easy to enjoy when the mood strikes. However, others find it troublesome, morally, and potentially dangerous, physically and emotionally.

Whatever one thinks of its moral value, recreational sex is often said to be sex "for fun." When it is pursued outside of long-term committed relationships, it is often with "no strings attached," having no romantic or exclusive relational commitments. Modern slang for it is usually blunt, and if there is a common moral value associated with recreational sex, it might be inferred by the names we assign to it—like a "hookup" or a "one-night stand." What is more, general social thinking about recreational sex might also be inferred by the names we give to those who practice it: "swingers," "players," and "fuck-buddies,"—just to name a few.

Since social slang can shape our moral intuitions, let's consider a little more of the "unofficial" discourse about recreational sex that pervades the public square. For example, if so-called hookups happen too often, that allegedly makes one "slutty." If a person seems to enjoy frequent "no strings attached" sexual encounters, that person is usually demoted to the rank of the "whore"—especially if that person is a woman. Men, on the other hand, tend to get away with "promiscuity" with a badge of honor. "He" is just "sowing his oats"—a "red blooded man"—and to draw on an older term, a "stud." Unless, of course, that man is gay—gay men, like women, do not get to publicize their sexual "promiscuity" without also being rendered a "slut," if not also slandered as one who is a "carrier" of disease.[1]

But what is a "slut," really? On the one hand, the charge of "sluttery" is a tool of shame to criticize others because of their audacity in taking pleasure in sexual activities with multiple sexual partners, and then, without any exclusive relational attachments. But take away the intent of an accusation, and a "slut" is just someone having more sex than you.[2] Whether or not the person who enjoys frequent sexual encounters is really engaging in immorality is something that requires careful moral analysis.

As with all human activities, recreational sex has potential risks and benefits. In this chapter, I am going to argue why I think there are moral benefits to recreational sex (well defined.) But there are indeed risks. So as to signal my appreciation for the risks involved in sexual relating, let me name just a few of these up front. First and foremost, if sexual activity is going to happen, and especially if it is going to happen with more than one person, we cannot ignore those real relational, personal, and health matters that bear directly on human well-being. For instance, there is no question that in the navigation of sexual pleasures, sexual abuse and exploitation are all too frequent, and such abuses have led to incredible suffering. What is more, impulsive sexual decisions have led to unintended indiscretions and infidelities; and sometimes, impulsive decisions have resulted in serious health issues. Additionally, when our sense of worth is disproportionately informed by how many people are willing to have sex with us, we shift our self-esteem externally to potentially detrimental ends (psychologically and socially).[3] Thus, we need to be mindfully vigilant of human well-being when engaging in sex, recreational or otherwise.

However, while prudential caution is necessary, we need not also assume that sexual abuse, exploitation, immorality, and disease are all but inevitable outcomes in the lives of people who incorporate short term episodes of sexual play—with multiple partners—as part of the enjoyment of life. When we take the time to understand what recreation is, and how sexual activity might be ordered toward it, the threats of exploitation, sickness, and immorality can be accounted for, and hopefully disarmed. As we will see, true recreation is neither blindly impulsive nor selfishly hedonistic. But in order to understand the potential value of recreational sex, we must have a better understanding of recreation itself.

Reframing the Relationship Between Sex and Recreation

Due to advances in the social and psychological sciences, there are now articulate definitions of recreation that point toward the important, if not necessary, role of play. As we shall see, true expressions of recreation are far from exploitative or meaningless. In fact, recreation (defined correctly) provides necessary interruptions in our day-to-day activities that allow people to renew their personal resources, both mentally and physically. However, there is no "one" way to recreate. We know this, practically speaking, through any number of our recreational activities: the enjoyment of good company, throwing a party, playing sports, going to the movies, camping, or some other leisurely activity. We know this, and yet, some people still have a difficult time admitting that sexual activity is one way that human beings can recreate.

The moral opposition to recreational sex comes from a number of sources. Some find that "sexual play" with multiple partners can actually lead to feelings of isolation, especially when sex is pursued impulsively and without self-respect or respect for one's sexual partners. This is a valid concern about thoughtless "sex play," but one that I believe can be addressed by defining recreational sex properly, and by formulating moral criteria for discerning when recreational sex is best pursued. However, there is another kind of moral opposition to recreational sex that is often advanced by a number of Christian communities, whose official teachings regard sexual activity with multiple partners as excessive, morally bankrupt, dangerous, and/or destructive to one's character.

For example, in the Roman Catholic Church, sexual activity that is nonmarital and/or closed to procreation is associated with the sin of "lust." The church describes lust not only as "disordered" desire for sexual pleasure (i.e., desiring sexual pleasure for its own sake, or wanting it through "illicit" activities), but also as "inordinate enjoyment" of sexual pleasure (wanting too much of it).[4] Thus, for the Roman Catholic Church, the problem with recreational sex (as an end in itself) is that it violates their marital and/or procreative norm, and it does so through the pursuit of sexual pleasure in the "wrong" way, whether through masturbation, contraceptive sex, nonmarital sex, homosexuality, and/or prostitution.[5] Likewise, many Protestants also reject sexual activity outside of marriage. In fact, a number of Protestant manuals on sex (though certainly not all) teach that nonmarital sex pollutes the body, spiritually—if not physically too.[6] Therefore, whether Roman Catholic or Protestant, such teachings lead a number of Christians to believe that sexual activity is only "good" (morally) when it is a unique gift to another person, who must also be one's spouse.

Thus, when Christian communities condemn recreational sex, they are claiming that there is nothing praiseworthy about it—often associating it with those things morally "dirty," spiritually "polluting," and sinfully "distant" from God. But if we sift through the moral invectives laid against recreational sex, and if we think carefully about sex, play, and human happiness, I do not think that true recreational sex should be denigrated this way. In fact, I find it quite unconvincing when Christian communities categorically condemn sexual activity as wholly immoral for simply taking on a recreational nature. To be fair, perhaps what many Christians are concerned with is sexual activity that proceeds from a brutish pursuit for pleasure, which can lead us into the cold objectification of fellow human beings. But as we will see, with a better understanding of what recreation is, and how sex might be ordered toward it, such a concern can be alleviated, and thus we can open the possibility for Christians to accept that recreation is one "end" by which people can practice sexual virtue.

Reconstructing Recreational Sex as Virtuous

Recreation and Happiness

A variety of specialists tell us that recreation, or leisure, is important for cultivating a well-balanced life.[7] Researchers have formally defined recreation as, "personally expressive discretionary activity, varying in intensity of involvement from relaxation and diversion . . . through personal development and creativity . . . up to sensual transcendence."[8] Without it, the human life is overburdened by stress, which generally deteriorates the quality of life. As "personally expressive discretionary activity," recreation allows us to engage our creative interests, which in turn help us to endure ordinary life burdens—including any life activity that becomes tedious or stressful, and thus depletes us of those positive affective states that nourish our sense of happiness (socially and psychologically).[9]

However, respect for recreation has not always been shared. Indeed, some of our cultural definitions of recreation have cast it as nonnecessary activity, or a luxury. As recreational specialists have noted, it was only in the early part of the twentieth century, in America, that "recreation and play [were] accepted as integral parts of our social system," and access to it became more available.[10] Because recreation has only more recently been established as a genuine human good, it is important to recognize that it has often been thought of as less than praiseworthy. This is especially true for those people shaped by the so-called Protestant work ethic, which has promoted the idea that material successes are sure signs of God's blessing, and poverty a likely sign of sin and laziness. For those who equate productivity with blessedness, recreation is hardly a virtue. In fact, it has been noted that those who hold such a view have "equated leisure with idleness and idleness with sin."[11] It has only been in the twentieth and twenty-first centuries that Americans have more boldly embraced the importance of recreation in human living.[12] Thus, if one holds moral reservations about the "goodness" of recreation, it may be that those suspicions come from a particular cultural inheritance—and, as we will see, such suspicions may be detrimental when thinking about living and doing well as human beings.

Of course, we can certainly imagine a kind of excessive recreational life that could be rightfully challenged as selfish or unjust. Indeed, throughout the world many people are enraged by the lavish displays of affluence by the supremely wealthy in the face of profound poverty—whether at home or abroad. This is not the only example of excessive "leisure" that could be critiqued. However, even though recreation (or leisure) can be taken to the extreme, there is broad agreement among the psychological and social sciences that recreation, well defined and well pursued, contributes to our *creaturely* flourishing as human beings. Central to these studies is a thesis that recreation is "a means to healthful living" and not essentially "a form of idleness."[13] These studies tell us that while recreation is a mode of leisure, it is not something as narrowly defined as a game, or time away from work or study. Recreation concerns personal re-creation through activities of leisure (generally conceived) that nurture and nourish our mental and physical resources.

According to the studies, there is something about the human psyche that requires a level of recreation (in some fashion) to maintain a happy life, socially and psychologically. Central to our cultivation of social and psychological happiness is a need to attend to our affective states. Psychological studies have indicated that people who do not engage in activities that lead to positive affective states tend to be less happy, as well as less productive in their work (or study), and have lower levels of "success" in life, whether in terms of professional development and advancement, or the maintenance of personal relationships. One relevant report from the American Psychological Association explains why:

> Numerous studies show that happy individuals are successful across multiple life domains, including marriage, friendship, income, work performance, and health. . . . the happiness-success link exists not only because success makes people happy, but also because positive affect engenders success. . . . The results reveal that happiness is associated with and precedes numerous successful outcomes. . . . [Thus] the evidence suggests that positive affect—the hallmark of well-being—may be the cause of many of the desirable characteristics, resources, and successes correlated with happiness.[14]

This is not an insignificant insight into human psychology. It tells us that activities generating psychological happiness are not irrelevant. In these studies, one of the often-cited examples of activities that cultivate positive affective states was (and is) recreation. The researchers noted that there is a correlation between recreational activity and the psychologically happy life.[15] Indeed, there was a general consensus among the specialists that enjoying recreation—of a variety of sorts—is part of actualizing our full human potential.

Rrecreation, Sex, and Virtue, in General

I propose that there are moral insights to glean from the psychological and social sciences on this matter. While generating positive affective states is not the sum of living and doing well in the moral sense, we can certainly imagine how such affective states contribute to the pursuit of a life well lived. Namely, positive affective states can accompany good choices. And as we have learned from a study of virtue, it is good to take pleasure in the right thing, at the right time, and for the right reason. Indeed, pleasure belongs to the practice of virtue and the enjoyment of the good life, generally speaking. It is important, then, to consider the insight from the sciences that recreation provides positive affective states that are *necessary* for human happiness (psychologically and socially). If for no other reason, living and doing well (morally speaking) attends to flourishing as the kind of creatures that we are, and thus, recreation is not optional, it amounts to a particular "end" to pursue in life—at the right time, in the right ways, and for the right reasons. To that end, when seeking out recreation (morally) we will need the light of prudence to know the right reason of things to be done, such that a person pursues recreation by cultivating good habits of enjoying that which is genuinely recreational (and thus constituent of human flourishing), while avoiding the extremes of excess and deficiency.

Of course, there are many ways in which human beings can engage in recreational activities that generate positive affective states. Sexual play is one such activity.[16] In fact, if we reconsider the specialists' definition of recreation, we see that sexual activity can manifest each part. Namely, sex is an activity that is discretionary. It is personally expressive. It can involve both relaxation and diversion. It can contribute to personal development, as well as creativity, and it most certainly can provide for sensual transcendence. While we might argue about what counts as legitimate acts of sexual recreation, I believe we can say, theoretically, that sexual activity can manifest qualities of recreation (as it is formally defined). However, that is not to say that anything called "recreational sex" (in common parlance) is actually recreational (morally or actually). What is more, I am not suggesting that recreational sex is always best pursued, or that it must be pursued by all. Rather, I am proposing that recreation (as defined) is one human good—one "end"—to pursue, by which humans might practice sexual virtue.

Because recreation is a genuine good conducive to human flourishing, true recreational sex could not in any sense be meaningless sex, excessive sex, or sexual activity that is somehow apathetic to physical and psychological health. We can be wrong about what we identify as recreational sex, but we should not confuse counterfeit examples of virtue with the real thing. While recreational sex may be "fun" in many regards, from the perspective of ethics, we can approach recreational sex with the intention to live life well as the kind of creatures that we are—creatures that need to relax and divert our attention through discretionary activity. We do this in sexual activity when we take the time to intentionally play well with ourselves, or with other people.

To recreate sexually is a good act. It is to enjoy sexual pleasure as a matter of directing one's sexual desires and activities toward a reasonable end that contributes to comprehensive human happiness—morally, psychologically, and socially. Proposed this way, recreational sex—as an end of sexual virtue—can be defended according to the genuine positive affects we experience from the recreational activities we engage in (which we need on a creaturely level), as well as by its contribution to our living and doing well (morally), recognizing that the habit of "playing well" is itself a character strength.

Of course, the above statements are certainly general, and therefore are in need of further explication. Indeed, I fully expect that some people will need more convincing about the possibility of recreational sex as an expression of virtue. In particular, my critics will want evidence that pursuing recreational sex—on its own—is something that will actually contribute to our flourishing as moral beings. I propose that there are three central issues we must address in order to alleviate a variety of critics' concerns. First, we must examine whether recreational sex attends to sexual justice. As I said in chapter 2, we cannot call any sexual relationship "good" if it violates the basic criteria of sexual justice. Second, we will have to name the kinds of relationships that can realize recreation as an end of sexual virtue. In particular, we will have to consider what kinds of human relationships allow us to "play well" with others, so that we avoid exploiting people in our sexual relations. Third, we must consider whether recreational sex fits within a Christian framework for sexual morality. In light of the many centuries in which heterosexuality, marriage, and procreation have been reigning norms in Christian communities, it will be necessary to explain why Christian sexual ethics should accept recreation as a separate and complete "end" of sexual virtue.

Recreation and Sexual Justice

Recall from our exploration of sexual ethics (in chapter 2) that I defined sexual justice as the fair treatment of sexual partners who—as human beings—deserve equal regard. I further noted that whereas traditional Christian source materials (e.g., the Bible or church teaching) do emphasize the importance of justice (as a principle), the ancient source materials do not give us definitions (or examples) of sexual justice that presume the social equality of persons (i.e., women and men) or anticipate natural sexual diversity. However, even if the traditional Christian source materials do not provide adequate definitions of sexual justice, interpreters of the tradition do. To that end, I suggest that the Christian sexual ethicists

Margaret Farley and Carter Heyward provide helpful criteria for defining sexual justice. In particular, these ethicists articulate criteria for sexual justice that if absent in any sexual relationship would result in violent or exploitative sexual acts—and therefore, their criteria give us a common foundation to work with, even if we come to disagree with one another in the application of those criteria. What is more, I propose that their criteria for sexual justice function well as guidelines, or "rules for play" when pursuing recreation as an end of sexual virtue. Given that Margaret Farley has constructed a more detailed list of criteria for sexual justice for Christian ethics, I will highlight her argument primarily, and then draw on Heyward to augment and gently critique Farley's work.

No Unjust Harm

First, Margaret Farley says that we ought to *do no unjust harm* to ourselves or our sexual partners.[17] Certainly, this means avoiding malicious physical harm in sexual activity. But for Farley, it also means that our sexual activity should promote "psychological, spiritual, and relational" well-being.[18] Her point is that when we engage in sexual activity with another person, we are vulnerable to them (and they us) in a variety of ways. This is true in any sexual scenario, including sexual activity that is ordered toward recreation. Thus, if a person senses that playing sexually will lead to emotional difficulties for oneself or another, or, that it might lead to physical harm—through particular difficult sex acts or unwanted sexually transmitted diseases—then it ought to be avoided. But when a person is reasonably sure that he or she is entering a recreational sexual relationship, where all parties are in good conscience and sexual health is not an issue (or is addressed and dealt with through safer sex practices, or informed decision making), then moral agents will have done well not to harm self or other people.

Free Consent

Second, Farley says that there should always be *free consent* of partners in sexual activity.[19] Free (and informed) consent is an obvious quality that must be present in order for sexual activity to be licit at all. Apart from free consent, sexual acts would amount to molestation, assault, and/or rape. It is simply impossible to play well with other people, sexually, without respecting their autonomy, and they ours.

Mutuality

Third, Farley names *mutuality*. This, she says, concerns "mutuality of participation."[20] Namely, that sexual partners have a reciprocal esteem for one another as active agents, each fully respected for their contributions to the sexual encounter. To promote mutuality requires that sexual partners not essentialize sexual hierarchies. Sexual hierarchies tend to hold in place dualisms that demoralize people. For example, when patriarchal thinking demoralizes women (and certain men) for being on the "receptive" end of sex, the penetrated partner is thus imagined as utterly passive and somehow less valuable, while at the same time privilege is accorded any man who performs the role of the "penetrator." Of course, there are some sexual encounters that intentionally perform submissive and dominating roles for a variety of socioerotic reasons. An appeal to mutuality is not to dismiss that some sexual play may engage in fantasies of bondage and discipline. But these could not be called "just" or well-performed (morally) if the persons in sexual play did not recognize each other as like participants. That is to say, sexual partners should not be treated as essentially less than fully equal in personhood and worth, even if in some forms of sexual play fantasies of subordination are enjoyed.

Equality

Fourth, and related, Farley names the criterion of *equality*. She argues that it is morally troublesome to engage in sexual acts if we have not considered the equality of our sexual partnerships—especially taking into consideration issues of social power differentiation. Farley notes, "Major inequalities in social and economic status, age and maturity, professional identity, interpretations of gender roles, and so forth, can render sexual relations inappropriate and unethical primarily because they entail power inequalities—and hence, unequal vulnerability, dependence, and limitation of options."[21] She goes on to say, "Equality need not be, may seldom be, perfect equality. Nonetheless, it has to be close enough, balanced enough, for each to appreciate the uniqueness and difference of the other, and for each to respect one another as ends in themselves."[22] Defined this way, "equality" is a criterion of sexual justice that should speak to a number of moral concerns.

In particular, some critics of my argument might suggest that accepting recreational sex is stepping onto a slippery slope that will inevitably lead to the promotion of *any* sexual behavior. Some people will warn that what might seem like a "small" step of sexual liberation now will only result in demands to tolerate other forms of sexual activity and relationships, until we tolerate everything (e.g., pedophilia, bestiality, incest, etc.).[23] This is simply not the case. Opening definitions of sexual virtue to include recreational sex in no way operates as part of an agenda to advocate any or all sexual activities that one might have a proclivity to pursue. As Farley rightly notes, sexual relations that are truly just cannot tolerate merely *any* activity. For example, the use of a child for sexual gratification clearly violates any reasonable standard of equality between sexual partners, and it certainly renders harm to the child. Recreational sex, as I am defining it, would also never tolerate such activities. True recreation must be play that satisfies the criteria of sexual justice, even as it also leads to demonstrable positive affects for self *and* sexual partner(s). Sexual manipulation and abuse have no ground in recreational sexual activity that is in any way virtuous. Indeed, if we think in terms of virtue ethics, sexual manipulation and abuse would count as vices of deficiency—insofar as they lack the necessary criteria of sexual justice.

Turning back to Margaret Farley's criteria for sexual justice, she names three other qualities of "just" sexual relationships. These are: *commitment, fruitful love,* and *social justice.* With respect to practicing recreational sex as a virtue, I do not define commitment and fruitful love in the same way that Farley does. However, I still find them important for moral reflection in our attempt to find guidelines for sexual play.

Commitment

Consider, then, the quality of *commitment.* Farley believes that one of the best places for sexual activity is within a committed relationship of some sort. However, this does not mean that she thinks we should reject short-term sexual relationships as wholly immoral. In fact, Farley accepts that "discrete moments of [sexual] union are not valueless."[24] At the same time, she is concerned that these discrete and temporary sexual relationships have the capacity "to isolate us from others and from ourselves."[25] I interpret Farley to mean that people who navigate their sexual lives solely in the realm of short-term sexual relationships could cultivate habits of using people instrumentally for sexual gratification. Just as it is possible to slip into blind hedonism in other pursuits of pleasure (e.g., wealth, food, or drink), so too sex without mindfulness could slip into the instrumental use of others. That is a possibility when right reason and virtue are abandoned. However, I am not convinced that it is the only outcome that will result for those who enjoy short-term sexual relationships. In particular, recreation is an end that can be pursued in short-term sexual relationships, and its value is (demonstrably) a positive one. At the same time, in order to pursue recreational sex, it does seem to require a level of commitment.

Namely, there must be commitments to acts of true play between persons. That is no small thing. When we embrace recreation (as defined) for its contribution to our human flourishing, recreational sex acts become a means for living and doing well. Without this kind of intentional commitment, true play in sexual activity could not be had. While Farley and I may not be able to imagine a life of sexual virtue limited to its expression in recreational activities alone, we need not demote the kinds of play-commitments necessary for recreational sex, even if they are short term. In particular, I propose that the basic criteria of sexual justice would count well as "play commitments" to be taken seriously. When manifested in short-term sexual relationships, these criteria of sexual justice demonstrate that any number of adult, mutual sexual relationships can attend to some of our deepest moral concerns about sexuality—and thus, "sexual play" does not have to be conceived as a matter of selfish gratification. In order to expand on these ideas, I turn to the sexual ethicist Carter Heyward, who offers additional comments on sexual justice and does so explicitly embracing the value of short-term sexual relationships.

Boundaries and Accountability

Like Farley, Carter Heyward argues that "mutuality" must be present in any relationship that we call just. However, Heyward does not share Farley's sense that sexual justice is best expressed in long-term, committed sexual relationships. Instead, Heyward respects that people can realize sexual justice even in short-term sexual relationships. But to do so well, Heyward argues, sexual partners (whether short or long term) must establish boundaries and accept accountability. Without boundaries and accountability, Heyward says that sexual relationships can easily slip into abuse and exploitation. Indeed, Heyward admits that "sex relationships are often abusive. [And] this is the case whenever the bodily integrity of any person—woman, child, or less frequently in heterosexist patriarchy, adult man—is violated."[26] In order to avoid sexual abuse, Heyward teaches that we need to establish boundaries. She says:

> A sense of boundaries can enable us to be confident of our bodily integrity. It can enhance our ability to participate in mutually empowering relationships. Boundaries can help us know ourselves in relation, what we enjoy and what we don't, what we want and what we don't. . . .
>
> Without a boundaried sense of ourselves, we are likely to experience sexual energy as a rush into which we simply get sucked and swallowed up, or as an addictive commodity that we have to get more of in order to feel good about ourselves. In the first instance, we lose touch with ourselves. . . . In the second case, we grab "sex" wherever we can get it and wind up with little or nothing that enables us to enjoy or respect ourselves very much.[27]

Thus, in order to "establish boundaries" we need to share with our sexual partners where our "limits" are, why those are important to us, where we might be willing to test our limits (perhaps to expand or loosen them), but also, to hear from our sexual partners and to respect what they reveal as their limits too.[28]

Therefore, if we accept Heyward's call for "boundaries," then sexual relationships that are intentionally ordered toward true recreation would be those that are not rushed into, as well as those in which we do not get mindlessly "sucked and swallowed up." Indeed, without such boundaries, it would be difficult to protect ourselves or other people from sexual exploitation or abuse. What is more, Heyward says that we can only respect our boundaries when we are accountable to one another, through "fidelity to our commitments."[29] For Heyward, however, "fidelity to our commitments" does not imply the imposition of certain norms, such as monogamy or marriage, but instead, she says, it only requires fidelity to what we have promised to a given sexual partner. For example, if a person was seeking recreational sex—but one's sexual partner wanted a deeper emotional or relational commitment attached to the sex act—it would be unjust to feign love or relational attachment in order to gratify the desire to play with "no strings attached." In fact, even if both partners received sexual pleasure in that scenario, it would not count as genuine recreation, because it would be an unjust act on the basis of the deception involved and the lack of true mutuality.

Indeed, the need for establishing boundaries and accountability not only alerts us to matters we must navigate personally but also alerts us to the need, as Margaret Farley says, for "social justice." In particular, to have in place civil authorities, and "just" codes of law, that can incapacitate those people who would grossly infringe upon the sexual boundaries of others, whether in terms of outrageous manipulation (e.g., pedophilia), assault, molestation, or rape.

Love?

Heyward's suggestion that sexual partners need only be faithful to the commitments they've negotiated—even if those are short term—is a proposal that is contrary to many Christian articulations of sexual fidelity. For many Christian communities, sexual fidelity is tied very closely to commitments of monogamy (one partner at a time), and usually in relation to marital vows. For Christians such as these, sexual activity is primarily an expression of committed love. And indeed, where such vows are made, fidelity to that vow would be important for the realization of sexual justice—and thus sexual virtue. However, with Heyward, I am not convinced that long-term exclusive love commitments are necessarily in order for sex to be virtuous.

Even so, love is a cardinal virtue in Christian ethics—and so it must have a shaping role to play in recreational sex, if recreation is to count as a legitimate "end" of sexual virtue in a broad Christian framework. Indeed, I argue that there is a relationship between recreational sex and "love," provided we define what kind of love is appropriate to Christian ethics, and how that love can be expressed between sexual partners. To the point: if Christians appeal to the theological virtue of love (agape or charity), then I believe it is possible to conceive of loving recreational sex in short-term relationships.

To be clear, the theological virtue of love is not romantic, nor exclusive. It is the love of "agape," which has been described by the Christian ethicist Gene Outka as the unconditional regard for a person's total well-being.[30] In fact, even Farley notes that if love is indeed a criterion of justice—especially in a Christian framework—then it must be of the theological sort, which she describes as a "fruitful" self-giving love that inspires others to produce the same love in their lives.[31] Of course, Christians have disagreed about how "agape" love is rightly described and expressed. However, there does not seem to be a question among

Christians that "agape" love involves loving one's neighbor, recognizing that "the neighbor" (a fellow human being) is an object of God's love. From a Christian perspective, then, the command to "love your neighbor as yourself" cannot be absent when considering sexual relationships—long or short term. Indeed, Christians could express this kind of love (i.e., unconditional regard for a person's total well-being) in short-term sexual relationships without also having long-term romantic feelings or exclusive monogamous commitments.

What is more, within the gospel narratives the command to "love the neighbor" is applied to friends and enemies alike—seemingly to everyone, as the opportunity to love others is made available.[32] Gospel love, therefore, is a promiscuous and prodigal kind of love. Thus, I think it would be difficult for Christians to say that Christian love cannot be expressed to sexual partners, even of the short-term kind. Christians will likely argue about whether people *should* be in short-term sexual relationships, but I do not think they can deny that when short-term recreational sexual relationships are intentionally pursued, people *could* express "agape" love—and that this is no small matter, insofar as "agape" orders us toward the care, concern, and unconditional regard for others, and thus fulfills a criterion of justice. Which is to say, even if there are Christians who disapprove of short-term sexual relationships for particular religious reasons, they should at least be able to praise (morally) wherever the criteria of justice are met, and they should be able to honor, theologically, wherever their chief virtue is exercised with intentionality.

Short-Term Sexual Relationships and Sexual Virtue

However, if we are going to accept that recreation is an end of sexual virtue, then we need to explore the kinds of relationships in which recreational sex (as defined) is possible to realize. Where people are lovingly partnered or married, I take it for granted that such partners will have recreational sex, with one another, from time to time, and that these episodes of play cannot help but support the larger relational goal of special intimacy. What is more, I also recognize that some spouses and partners choose to open their sexual relationship to other (i.e., multiple) sexual partners for purposes of recreation.[33] That said, it is not my intention to give an analysis of such open relationships, except to reiterate the need for sexual justice and to encourage such partners to think about sexual virtue in terms of reasonable "ends" to pursue, and how the ends they seek (sexually) contribute (or not) to their flourishing. But that is an argument for another project.

I want to keep our focus on sexual experiences had with short-term sexual partners in the absence of conventional committed relationships. Where such happens, I have already suggested that the criteria for sexual justice will help us to "play well" with others. However, it is also good for us to think in advance of those who might make the best kinds of short-term recreational partners, so that we might seek out the best (morally) in our recreational sexual experiences.

Of course, I can no more tell you who that is, specifically, than you can tell me. But we might be able to think about the kinds of sexual partners who could help us to realize sexual virtue when seeking the "end" of recreation for its own sake, especially when sought outside of the context of a long-term, committed relationship. Thus, we need to think about a variety of sexual partners, and which of these might make for good recreational partners—if that is something that we have decided to enjoy.

First, let's start with a character type we do well to avoid. In their now famous text *The Ethical Slut*, Dossie Easton and Janet Hardy give some practical advice about whom to avoid in episodes of sexual play. They note that "[s]ome people treat sex as a big-game hunt—trying to conquer the unwilling and unwitting victim, as though the object of their attention would never decide to share sex with them unless tricked into it."[34] They go on to say:

> Such people often approach open sexual lifestyles as if keeping score. Set collectors and trophy fuckers treat their partners like prizes in a contest they have set out to win—only what happens after the prize is collected? Is it time to go after the next one? . . . Sex that means treating your partners as collectibles does not meet our requirements for mutual respect.[35]

At the core of Easton's and Hardy's concern is not only mutual respect, but self-respect. Namely, when the basic criteria for decent human relating, such as mutuality and respect, are absent, we easily become a depersonalized notch in someone's bedpost, or we do so to others. While there might be certain bedposts upon which we wouldn't mind becoming a proverbial notch, disregarding how others treat us (or we them) diminishes self-respect. With diminished self-respect, we might also disregard the need for boundaries and accountability, not to mention mutuality and equality—which increases the probability of allowing ourselves to be violated, or to violate others. In terms of sexual justice, the lack of respect (for self or others) is something that can lead to the injustice of exploitation.

As the queer theologian Patrick Cheng explains it, of the many problems with exploitation is that it often turns a sexual partner into a "mere object of gratification." Cheng explains:

> Some people, particularly those who struggle with sex addiction and/or low self-esteem, engage in anonymous, unsafe, and/or drug-fueled hook-ups in which self-gratification is the primary if not only concern. The sex addict's partner or partners are reduced to objects for stimulation and are not seen as full human beings in themselves.[36]

Thus, when a sexual partner no longer regards the other as "a full human being," it is impossible to say that matters of justice or mutual regard are respected. What is more, we could not expect such a sexual partner to respect our sense of sexual boundaries, or to accept accountability for crossing those personal boundary lines.

Indeed, it is in light of those who would "hunt" or "exploit" others that social and moral warnings against "hooking up" are well heeded. When "hooking up" means anonymous sex without actual concern for the total well-being of self or other; and where such "hooking up" happens without establishing play commitments basic to the criteria of sexual justice, then "hooking up" is indeed morally problematic, and quite distant from the "end" of recreation that I am advocating. However, I am not suggesting that anonymous "hookups" will always result in exploitation, or the objectification of others. I am quite certain that people of good will sometimes find one another in such "anonymous" scenarios and still manage to be just with one another. But such a roll of the dice is not conducive to virtue—nor to our overall well-being.

But when we turn away from the extreme of the "trophy fucker"; when we avoid anonymous sex that is potentially dangerous; and when we eschew sexual exploitation, we can better consider those short-term sexual partners that might help us to practice sexual virtue toward the "end" of recreation. My proposal is that those in our established social networks—our acquaintances and friends—are likely our best nonmarital and/or nonromantic relationship options for pursuing recreation as an end of sexual virtue. Of course, the suggestion that we might have sex with our friends is not revolutionary. But how we talk about it, morally, can be. While our society flirts with the possibility of sex with friends through the rhetoric of "friends with benefits," I am suggesting that we can negotiate nonromantic and nonexclusive sexual relationships with friends as an expression of sexual virtue.

While I am quite serious about this proposal, I am not suggesting that all friendships can, or should, pursue recreational sex. But where friendships are capable of negotiating sexual relationships for recreation, these relationships seem pre-poised to help us attend well to the criteria of sexual justice (which are our requirements for genuine sexual play); to avoid the extremes of excessive hedonism and/or exploitation, and thus allow us to seek out—in mutuality—recreation for its own sake.

Friends are people with whom we have cultivated the habit of exercising mutual regard for one another's total well-being. Indeed, if the designation of "friendship" means anything, it is that friends are people who do not intend to exploit, hurt, or use one another (self-ishly). Thus, friends that can negotiate sexual relating toward the "end" of recreation can do so in ways that avoid the pitfalls of "hooking up" while still allowing people to enjoy a genuine human "good" (i.e., rec-reation). What is more, I am not suggesting that recreational sex with friends should be ongoing when people establish other romantic and/or domestic partnerships, in which monogamous commitments might be made. But as human beings who are also sexual beings, recreational sex with our friends would allow us to actualize an aspect of our human/ sexual potential with people whom we can trust, and, then, toward a reasonable end that promotes genuine happiness (socially, psychologi-cally, and morally).

Of course, many people tend to define friendships as "nonsexual" relationships. I believe that this is often true. But I am not convinced that "friendship" and "sex" are mutually exclusive categories. The idea that sex should only be expressive of romantic love, or uniquely within exclusive/monogamous relationships, is itself a disputable norm. How-ever, that is not to deny that sexual activity can be expressive love or facilitate relational closeness—it can. Rather, I am arguing that sexual activity can be ordered toward different "ends," in different relational contexts, for different reasons—including sex for nonromantic and non-exclusive reasons. Ethicist Richard Wasserstrom describes this well:

> The first thing that might be said is that the account of the connection between sexual intimacy and feelings of affection

is inaccurate . . . in the sense that there is substantially more divergence of opinion than the account suggests. . . .

To be sure, sex is probably better when partners genuinely like and enjoy being with each other. But sex is basically an intensive, exciting sensuous activity that can be enjoyed in a variety of suitable settings with a variety of suitable partners. The situation in respect to sexual pleasure is no different from that of the person who knows and appreciates fine food and who can have a satisfying meal in any number of good restaurants with any number of congenial companions.[37]

While Wasserstrom's analogy to eating glosses over the qualitative differences between sharing a meal and engaging in sexual activity, I believe he points us in the right direction (morally) for thinking about enjoying sexual pleasures, with a variety of people, especially for the purpose of recreation.

Namely, Wasserstrom helps us to think about cultural assumptions about sexual activity. One such assumption is that sex must always be connected to romance or marriage. Another assumption is that having sex with people who are not our beloveds actually cheapens the meaning of sex. Yet another assumption is the idea that sexual activity signifies the intention to pursue a romantic relationship.[38] While it may be true that sex can be an indicator of romantic intent, to say that sex is only best suited for (or indicative of) exclusive romantic relationships denies what we know about sex itself. Recall, for example, the insights from chapter 8 about what the sciences are revealing about the "nature" of human sexuality. According to Ryan and Jethá's evidenced hypothesis, nonprocreative, nonexclusive sexual relationships are "natural" to human sociality. In fact, Ryan and Jethá noted that even our bodies are "designed" to attract and enjoy many sexual partners, and then through sexual encounters that emphasize the enjoyment of sexual pleasure for purposes of friendship or kinship—not necessarily reproduction. And as I argued in chapter 8, that kind of information should inform our moral reasoning. However, to be clear, I am not suggesting that the data they collected require people to give up on concepts of romantic relationships, marriage, or monogamy—but I do think that it indicates that humans are capable of a wide variety of sexual relationships, ordered toward a variety of natural human "goods."

Thus, the expectation that certain friends cannot also be sexual partners, especially when seeking the "end" of recreation, is an assertion, or a personal preference. That assertion, or preference, may not be true in all friendships—especially where friends are capable of pursuing recreation as an "end" of sexual activity. Indeed, recreational sex (well defined) does not confuse the line between romance and nonromantic friendships. Recreational sex (well defined) only requires that we play according to the criteria of sexual justice, and then in order to enjoy the pleasures of sex for the human goods that true recreation provides. For some people, this will mean enjoying recreational sex with a number of friends, whether of the same sex or opposite. For other people, it will mean drawing on recreational sex with a trusted friend only now and then. If such scenarios are possible, I see no reason to forbid such activity (morally), insofar as it provides for an expression of sexual virtue—and consequently, the cultivation of human happiness.

There will, of course, be people who do not pursue sexual relationships outside of committed partnerships or marriages, and we can admit that they do so for good reasons. Namely, some people are not interested in opening themselves up to the vulnerabilities (whether emotional, psychological, or physical) that are involved in sexual relations. For people like these, waiting to engage in sexual relationships—in which the many "ends" of sex can be coordinated carefully and lovingly— is an understandable and respectable choice. But I do not think that such people can deny that others in the wider moral community might be capable of negotiating sexual relations toward the end of recreation alone—and where that happens with friends (justly and prudently), no moral condemnation is necessary.

Christian Ethics and Recreational Sex

However, even if people might accept that recreation (well defined) is achievable in sexual relations, and even if some people also accept that recreational sex can attend to matters of sexual justice and the promotion of natural human happiness, it may also be true that some Christians will find that their faith does not permit them to seek this "end," whether outside of marriage or on its own (in marriage) with the aid of contraception. Without question, critics could very well counter my proposal with interpretations of scripture, centuries of church teachings, as well as traditional interpretations of the natural law. But as I noted in the last chapter, I am inviting people to turn from "what" has been believed about sexual morality, in order to reconsider "how" we can approach sexual ethics with new insights into human sexuality, as well as new approaches to Christian sexual ethics. Indeed, the need for new approaches to sexual ethics is perhaps more important than ever, insofar as "traditional" speeches about sexual morality often advance premodern notions of sexuality, morality, and social order that are highly disputable—scientifically, morally, and religiously. To that end, I agree with the Christian sexual ethicist Christine Gudorf, who commented:

> After many centuries, it still remains tragically ironic that a religion which holds as its central belief that divinity became fully and humanly embodied and then endured bodily suffering even unto death in order to redeem all embodied human persons is, among world religions, perhaps the most ambivalent about the goodness of the human body, its development, its activities, and its appetites.[39]

However, if that ambivalence is going to change, we will need accurate (and up-to-date) descriptions about sexuality, as well as new approaches to sexual ethics that better allow us to incorporate sexual and gender varieties into our larger moral vision. I suggest one such approach is to open up the definition of sexual virtue to account for many "ends."

But in order to defend recreation as an "end" of sexual virtue, I admit that I cannot turn to explicit scriptural references, nor to the official teachings of Roman Catholicism; nor even to the majority of teachings on sexual ethics within mainline Protestant Christianity. As I have noted throughout this book, the traditional source materials of Christianity are deeply embedded in social contexts that had very different views on human sexuality than we do—and therefore, these do not speak to (or anticipate) a number of relevant moral issues related to sexual ethics today. Thus, we're not going to find many positive statements in scripture or church teaching that validate my proposal about recreational sex.

But such is the case with many issues in Christian sexual ethics today.

Recall, there are no explicit or positive references to the use of contraceptives in scripture, or in historic church teachings, and yet many Protestants (and pew Catholics) draw on contraception as an exercise of prudence. What is more, there are no detailed descriptions about the relationship between sexual and relational intimacy in the scriptures, nor in church dogma. To fill this void, Christians have to turn to counselors

or relationship specialists—whether in or outside of the church. Likewise, there is nothing in the New Testament literature that describes how
to navigate divorce and remarriage, and yet Christians find themselves
doing so all of the time.

In other words, contemporary Christian sexual ethics—even among
some "traditionalists"—defers to reason and experience, set within the
wider context of Christian faith. And as I noted in the last chapter, I
find that both reason and experience are valuable sources for engaging
in Christian ethics. Namely, sometimes, in the face of new realities,
people of faith must learn to creatively apply principles of their faith
where scripture and/or church teaching lacks sufficient details.

Therefore, if by the light of reason and experience we can acknowledge that "recreation" (well defined) is good to pursue in sexual relationships, and we can also imagine a variety of relationships in which
recreational sex could be well pursued (so long as we fulfill the criteria
of sexual justice), then I also invite us to imagine—within a broad
Christian framework—how the themes and principles of Christianity
might support my proposal that recreation is a valid end of sexual virtue.

Recall, then, the interpretive conclusions we reached in previous chapters on the Bible, natural law, and church teachings. When
we approach these sources of authority contextually, we find that the
Christian faith is not a complex set of narrow rules to follow but, rather,
principles to embody. Christians call this participating in the reign of
God. While I have not sought to give a definitive list of those principles, we have seen that a broad range of theologians have identified
love, inclusivity, joy, and nonmalfeasance as principles of the gospel
message. Jesus of Nazareth summarized the reign of God as the actualization of two principles: to love God and to love your neighbor as
yourself.[40] The apostle Paul gave a slightly longer list, including: "love,
joy, peace, patience, kindness, generosity, faithfulness, gentleness, and
self-control."[41] Indeed, the apostle Paul wrote: "There is no law against
such things."[42]

If these are defining principles of the Christian faith, then I submit
that my description of recreational sex is fully capable of embodying
these principles. Consider again, then, my claims: First, recreation is
not only good for humans in terms of our creaturely well-being (as the
social and psychological sciences suggest) but it is also good for us morally when we pursue it virtuously, in the right way, at the right time,
with the right people, and for the right reasons. What is more, insofar
as recreation is a human "end" that promotes our happiness, I have

suggested that we can pursue it through sexual activities, and then in a number of sexual relationships, but not necessarily requiring romantic commitment or a procreative result. However, I also said that we can only "play well" in sexual relationships insofar as we attend to the criteria of sexual justice. When we account for all of this, I do believe we can say (confidently) that recreation is an "end" of sexual virtue that can align with all the oft-cited principles of the reign of God.

I anticipate, however, that there will be disagreements about "who" should engage in recreational sex, and, then, in what kind of relationships. But these disagreements—if they are couched in Christian theologies—will take us back to biblical interpretation, natural law thinking, or church teachings. I cannot settle all of those disagreements. But I propose that this new way of thinking about recreational sex (through an ethic of virtue) is one way that Christian communities can think anew about sexual ethics—not only theologically, but also in light of all the insights that the sciences report, as well as all that critical moral and religious discourses reveal for contemporary Christian ethics.

Surely, my proposal about recreational sex requires prudence and responsibility. I am not suggesting that "recreation" is a catchall category for any kind of sexual relationship outside of a romantic or marital partnership. Thus, if there are other "ends" to pursue in short-term, and/or nonromantic sexual relationships, I do not pretend to account for them here. I am only focusing on what appears to be a reasonable connection between recreation (formally defined), "just" sexual relationships (i.e., those that satisfy the criteria of sexual justice), and notions of human happiness—as these are set within a broad Christian framework and a theory of virtue. From this perspective, I suggest that it is possible to ingrain in oneself a habit (a virtue!) to respect sexual play (recreational sex) as part of the good life (naturally speaking), and that this view can be harmonized with many of the major theological principles of the Christian religion.

Eleven

Relational Intimacy

I love you as certain dark things are to be loved, in secret, between
the shadow and the soul.

—Pablo Neruda

Agreements and Disagreements

One of the things that Christians tend not to disagree about is that
sexual activity can be an expression of relational intimacy. Catholics
and Protestants, conservatives and liberals seem to share a common
knowledge (likely borne from experience) that our sexual relating can
be a form of knowing and being known, loving and being loved. To
that end, there seems to be a broadly shared sense—in the moral community—that many human beings have a natural inclination to engage
in pleasurable sexual activity for the purpose of relational closeness.[1] It
is an inclination that arises from some of our most distinctively human
capacities, including our cognitive, emotional, relational, and spiritual
modes of interpersonal connection.

Our inclinations toward intimacy sometimes motivate us to engage
in sexual activity not only because we find others physically appealing
but also because we wish to accept, care, and love one another through
sexual encounters.[2] Sexual activity, therefore, has the remarkable capacity of expressing interior relational goods. Indeed, it can be a way of com-
municating deep feelings and strengthening the bonds of a relationship.

The good of relational intimacy is recognized by religious and secular figures alike. Take, for example, the following statement on sexual
intimacy by justices of the Supreme Court of the United States. It was
written as part of a 2003 ruling on the legal permissibility of same-sex
intercourse. Their legal ruling waxed psychological and ethical when the
majority opinion justices wrote:

As this Court has recognized, sexual intimacy is "a sensitive, key relationship of human existence, central to family life, community welfare, and the development of human personality." The human impulse for sexual intimacy, as well as the importance of this impulse to the self and to the development of close relationships with others, have been observed and chronicled for centuries. The mental health professionals have also long recognized the importance of the desire for sexual intimacy in the development of the self, in the establishment of close relationships, and in the maintenance of family units. And the most recent study of the sexual behavior of the American population has found that sexual satisfaction in intimate relationships is linked to satisfaction with those relationships and with general satisfaction with life.

Of course, many individuals lead productive and psychologically healthy lives in which sex or an intimate partner does not play an important role. The importance of sexuality in relationships also varies considerably across individuals and throughout the life span . . . [criminalizing same-sex acts thus] impinges on the ability of . . . [some people] to participate in activities that have long been recognized as important aspects of humanity: to develop the emotional self, to build a supportive relationship with a partner, and to create a family unit.[3]

What the justices describe in the above statement is something that many of us hold to be deeply true and morally good. And yet, we have also seen throughout this book how (and in what different ways) Christians have accepted or rejected the good of sexual intimacy for its own sake.

For example, whereas the Roman Catholic Church now teaches that intimacy is a legitimate end of sexual virtue, they still maintain that it is indissoluble from procreation—and only to be pursued in sanctioned heterosexual marriages.[4] But we also know that a number of mainline Protestant churches disagree with the Catholic procreative demand, and sometimes the marital norm as well. For many Protestants (and some "rebellious" Catholics too), intimacy is a good that can be pursued through sexual activity, by gay and straight people alike, with contraceptives if necessary.

In this chapter I seek to demonstrate why intimacy should be regarded as a distinct and complete end of sexual virtue. In particular, a separate end from procreation. In the last chapter I attempted to do

something similar with respect to recreation. Namely, I made the argument that sexual activity can be ordered toward recreation (well defined)
and that this can take place outside of long-term committed relationships
when the criteria of sexual justice are met. However, I also acknowledged
that recreational sex could be pursued by people in long-term committed relationships, and thus, I signaled that recreational sex can be one
constituent of a couple's life of sexual intimacy.

In this chapter I will consider relational intimacy as a distinct
"end" of sexual virtue in the context of long-term committed relationships. My goal is to suggest why relational intimacy can be regarded as
a separate end from procreation. I do so as a critique of any Christian
argument (Catholic or Protestant) that insists "good sex" requires either
a heterosexual pairing or a procreative possibility in sexual relations. To
that end, I argue that sexual virtue can be practiced when sexual partners
aim at relational intimacy, apart from a procreative intent or possibility
(and then with the use of contraceptives where needed). Such a position is not new to many progressive Protestant Christians (nor to the
Catholic laity who disagree with Vatican teaching); even so, I invite the
readers to consider this as a matter of virtue—something to be imagined
as choice-worthy and emblematic of the "good."

Intimacy: A Separate End

Defining Intimacy

In order to set relational intimacy as an "end" of sexual virtue, it is first
necessary to define what it is. To do so within a Christian framework is
somewhat problematic. Little about relational intimacy is written in the
Bible—at least not formally—and most of what we read about relational
intimacy in church teaching is the product of theological and moral
innovation, which usually includes insights from the social and psychological sciences.[5] In fact, it is really only when we turn to the sciences
that we find sophisticated analyses of intimacy that show us how sexual
relationships demonstrably encourage relational closeness.

In one of the more explicit studies on the subject in the psychological and social sciences, Barry Moss and Andrew Schwebel provide
a detailed analysis of intimacy.[6] In particular, they delineate the components of relational intimacy, and show the connection of intimacy
with sexual activity. I ask the reader to consider a summary of their

findings in order to better think about intimacy as a matter of human flourishing.

According to Moss and Schwebel, there are seven characteristics to intimacy that are widely acknowledged by researchers in the relevant sciences. The first is that intimacy requires *mutual interaction* between persons.[7] Intimacy is not accidental. It must be nurtured through intentional and affectionate interpersonal engagement.[8] It also consists of *sharing ideas*.[9] As rational creatures, reciprocal expression of our thoughts is important to the bonding of intimate partners. When we do not share what we are thinking with others, it is difficult to feel connected to them. Indeed, it can feel as if we are being denied access to the deepest parts of our friends and partners when they refuse to share the thoughts that they have with us. Third, the specialists note that intimacy concerns the *reception or expression of physical acts,* including (but not limited to) sexual activity.[10] In addition to these characteristics, they find that intimacy requires degrees of *relational commitment, feelings of solidarity,* a strong degree of *communication,* and finally, a general sense of *closeness* to one another.[11] Synthesizing these component parts, Moss and Schwebel conclude that relational intimacy is best achieved (according to their studies, and the studies of a wide variety of their professional peers) when human beings express "commitment, affective intimacy, cognitive intimacy, physical intimacy, and mutuality."[12] Not all intimate relationships are sexual, but where they are, the specialists agree that sexual relating can nurture the quality of relational intimacy itself, so long as it is coordinated with the other intimacies too. Thus, relational intimacy (well defined) is not something sought or achieved in every mutual sexual encounter (for example, in short-term sexual relationships ordered more toward recreation). But I suggest relational intimacy can be realized within intentional relationships that integrate sexuality into the overall goal of relational flourishing (as described above).

The Benefits of Sexual Intimacy

In recent years, a number of studies have overwhelmingly shown that the sexual dimensions of relational intimacy benefit human life. Researchers have found that sexual intimacy has an integral relationship not only to self-reports of being happy, but also to psychological maturation and the ability to sustain loving and satisfying relationships. Of course, science cannot of itself settle the moral issues of sexuality that we have been focusing on throughout this book, but it can show that a human activity, such as when we engage in sexual activity for relational intimacy for its own sake, contributes to many people's abilities to participate in human relationships that they (and we) judge to be morally fine. Where we find this correlation between scientific study and moral reflection, the gap between what is "natural" to humans and what we call "good" narrows considerably.[13]

In particular, the sciences have helped us to understand why—and in what way(s)—sexuality contributes to human life, beyond biological generation. Of primary interest to many researchers are the personal and interpersonal benefits of sexual activity, especially when procreation is avoided.[14] Indeed, I have yet to find a peer-reviewed psychological study in the last three decades that argues against sexual relationships ordered toward intimacy alone. The studies repeatedly agree that relationships tend to flourish where sexual intimacy is regularly pursued, even when procreation is not possible, or is prevented.[15] This is true in straight and LGBT relationships alike, whether partners are married or not. There is also evidence that where *any* couple is mindful of cultivating sexual intimacy there are secondary mental and physical health benefits.[16]

While the studies show that marriage is not necessary in order to cultivate relational intimacy through sexual activity, there is agreement among the specialists that the advancement of relational intimacy requires time and commitment. However, whether or not we choose to pursue advanced levels of intimacy through a long-term sexual relationship does not make us (ultimately) better or worse off. Knowing the benefits of long-term committed relationships merely allows people to choose which personal, sexual, and moral goods they wish to cultivate as a matter of being happy.

Thus, for those who wish to nurture greater levels of relational intimacy in long-term, committed sexual relationships, there is also broad agreement among the specialists that the quality of sexual intimacy is important to consider. In the literature, psychologists sometimes refer to "ideal" or "healthy" sexual relating as a goal for couples to attain. Consider, for example, the following description of ideal sexual relating from the psychological sciences:

> In an "ideal" sexual encounter, partners would proceed naturally from one plateau of arousal to the next undisturbed by negative thoughts about their bodies, their sexuality, their performance, or their partner. Both partners would tend to be spontaneous in

> their sexual responses, and neither person would try to inhibit
> or control any aspect of the sex act. Because both individu-
> als would take responsibility for their own sexual desires and
> needs and indicate their wants, there would be a feeling of
> equality inherent in their interaction that would contribute
> to their overall sense of well-being and individuality. Ideally,
> there would be an absence of guilt, self-critical ruminations, or
> hostile attacks on one's partner about the experience. Following
> a gratifying sexual encounter, partners would tend to experience
> a mixture of happiness, sadness, relaxation, and fulfillment, and
> they would probably express their mutual appreciation, verbally
> and nonverbally, for the pleasure they received. . . . Although
> there is a wide range of sexual experience that men and women
> enjoy, many have described their ideal experience as one that
> combines tenderness, warmth, friendship, and sexual satisfaction.[17]

Of course, none of us manifest the "ideal" sexual encounter in every
intimate experience we have with our beloveds. To reiterate, the above
description is a goal to work toward, not something we can immediately
perfect. However, what is striking about this description of "ideal" sexual
relating is that procreation does not play a prominent role.

Procreation (or openness to procreation) is not, from a psychological perspective, a necessary component of sexual relating that is done
well. The prevailing psychological model for ideal sexual relating recognizes (or privileges) the goal of relational intimacy, which may or may
not include a shared intention to procreate. What is more, this model
implies that if procreation is a goal of a committed couple in a sexual
act, then the navigation to that goal is best done respecting the end of
intimacy first, and then procreation. I believe these insights from the
psychological and social sciences translate well into moral principles,
especially with respect to the practice of sexual virtue.[18]

Sexual Intimacy and Virtue

According to an ethic of virtue, the enjoyment of human happiness is
a matter of living and doing well as the kind of creatures that we are.
If we accept that relational intimacy is one of our capabilities as rational, embodied, social, and spiritual beings, then practicing virtue with

respect to relational intimacy can be part of our moral outlook. Indeed, part of our task in life, from the perspective of ethics, is to develop the strengths of character that form good relationships—the kind we find life-enhancing and satisfying. This is true in our sexual relationships as well. To that end, there are particular character strengths that concern our flourishing in sexually intimate relationships. I believe that the strengths of character that are necessary for being a good long-term, committed sexual partner are elements of sexual virtue. Intimacy is one end to which our sexual desires and actions can be directed that nurture some of our character strengths as sexual beings. For the person of virtue, the chief end of sexual intimacy will be relational intimacy. To pursue intimacy as an end of sexual virtue is to desire to cultivate the characteristics of interpersonal intimacy in our sexual relating, and to do this in coordination with all the other means of growing and sustaining relational intimacy with our partners.[19]

But from a Christian perspective—especially a Catholic one—questions arise. Can we separate relational intimacy from procreation? After all, sexual activity culminates in an orgasm, which not only provides for pleasure and relational closeness, but also the reproductive cells necessary for biological generation (at least in male orgasm). The traditional reading of natural law interprets this biological function as an indicator of God's intent for human sexuality. On the one hand, then, Christians need to acknowledge, practically speaking, the connection between sexual activity and reproduction. This they must do in light of their theological understandings of "creation" and/or "creator's intent." On the other hand, Christians need to recognize that an emphasis on male orgasm, sperm, and reproduction is a remarkably narrow perspective on human sexuality, sexual function, and sexual relationships. For example, such does not take into consideration the nonreproductive social/sexual benefits of "social erotic experiences" (see chapter 8) or relational intimacy. Nor does such take into consideration the nonreproductive function and pleasures of clitoral stimulation and orgasm, anal/prostate stimulation and orgasm; nor does a "penis-centric" view of sexuality take into consideration all of the many other erogenous zones and pleasures "natural" to human beings. Thus, even if it is a matter of intellectual honesty to admit there is a correlation between sex and reproduction, that correlation cannot be accepted as the norm for sexual morality except by privileging one natural aspect of sexuality (reproduction) over many others (intimacy, recreation, natural pleasures, etc.).

Separate Ends

Thus, disagreements about the priority of procreation in Christian sexual ethics take us back to disputes about the Bible, church teaching, and natural law. For example, scripture does contain the command to "be fruitful and multiply," but it does not qualify that imperative. Many Jewish and Protestant communities have said that there is nothing about that scripture (interpreted well) that would disallow the use of contraceptives. In stark contrast, the Catholic Church has argued that contraception violates the laws of nature—set in place by God.[20] For this reason, the Catholic Church continues to teach that procreation and intimacy are inseparable ends for married partners to pursue.

But we now have access to a variety of professional studies that clearly indicate that intimacy is not only desirable for adult psychological and social development, it is necessary for successful relational development. We cannot ignore these studies when reflecting on the morality of sexual intimacy. In particular, the scientific studies point us toward what we need to know about human development in order to make relevant and compelling moral judgments. It is important to note, then, that these studies indicate that the need for (or inclination toward) intimacy is usually a part of the most satisfying adult romantic relationships—most of which include some sort of sexual relating that has nothing to do with procreation. And as the studies have shown, the most satisfying of those relationships are those in which people can be themselves as sexual beings and enjoy their own and each other's development, sexually and morally—without needing to worry about procreation as a moral demand.[21]

And this is the pressing point: Relational intimacy is a good that is sought by sexual partners, through sexual activity, whether or not they also seek the good of procreation. As the natural law theorists Todd Salzman and Michael Lawler have explained, while people may have reproductive capacities, and while reproduction is often facilitated by an act that is also sexual, the "sexual" and the "reproductive" capacities should be distinguished. Recall their analysis:

> Reproduction is achieved *via* a human activity, but it is not itself a human activity. Though humans achieve reproduction through a sexual act, that act itself is not an act of reproduction. If reproduction were the purpose of the sexual act, then all reproductive-type sexual acts would have the possibility of realizing this purpose. Women who have had a hysterectomy,

however, or infertile men continue to have and to use *sexual* organs, but they are without reproductive organs. All sexual human beings have sexual organs, but not all sexual human beings have *reproductive* organs.[22]

Thus, when procreation is not sought (and responsibly restrained through contraceptives), the moral good of relational intimacy is still achievable through sexual, nonprocreative, relations—and when it is, it contributes to the enjoyment of true human happiness.

This view is not necessarily contrary to a Christian worldview.

Where two people participate in a long-term, loving, and committed relationship, the love that they extend to each other has, and can be imagined as having, a spiritual dimension. The Jewish theologian Yoel Kahn communicates this point well. He says:

> We believe that sexuality, at its core, is a yearning for connectedness, intimacy, and relationship. Sexual intimacy, an expression of intimate human meeting, can be a route to, and expression of, "knowing" another, to borrow from Hosea, "in justice, in truth, and in faithfulness." It can therefore be a primary mode of both spiritually—knowing God, as Carter Heyward has taught, and of justice-making—making God known.[23]

Arguably, there is nothing about Kahn's description that is antithetical to a Christian perspective, generally conceived.

Indeed, Kahn's description likely captures what many Christians have experienced in intimate sexual relationships. But notice, in no way does Kahn's description of licit sexual relationships make procreation a necessary criterion for knowing God, or doing justice, when people are at the same time, *making love*. Khan is not alone in his theological judgment. Other religious ethicists, theologians, and religious communities have already made the prudential judgment that nonprocreative sexual activity, ordered toward relational intimacy, is in fact good (morally) for human beings. But what we have not heard much about is how such activity might be imagined as an expression of sexual virtue.

Intimacy as an Expression of Sexual Virtue

Let's imagine, then, that a partner in a long-term, committed, romantic relationship looks upon his or her beloved and is moved with sexual desire. The partner has the ability to reflect on this sexual urge and to consider some of the meaning it has for himself or herself, as well as the beloved. The person might judge, upon reflection, that indulging this desire would amount to a delightful sharing of selves, a way of expressing and receiving love, a way of knowing one another deeply so as to celebrate their relational bond, or the like. Mindful of the potentiality of reproduction (in some cases), the couple might open themselves boldly to that generation, accepting that they will be able and happy to provide for any children that might be conceived. Or, they might equally boldly try to forego procreation, while being aware that few forms of birth control are 100 percent reliable. Thus, they might engage in contraceptive sex with the central intention of revealing their hearts to each other in a special way that sexual intimacy makes possible.[24]

Ideally, the partners serve as a means of disclosure, by which each of them learns to understand himself or herself, and the ways in which he or she can best excel as the person that he or she is. In such a relationship, partners encourage in each other a wide range of virtues. Sexual virtue is one of them. Over time, good partners help each other apprehend the meaning and value of sexual desire, pleasure, and activity as a powerful aspect of human existence that can deepen and encourage relational wholeness, a giving and receiving of selves—and religiously (in some cases), a way to experience divine love or grace. Thus, sexual virtue can dispose us not only to desire intimacy as a good end of sexual activity, but also to participate well in our sexual relationships, in which virtuous sexual activity (which is, at the same time, pleasurable and uninhibited) will contribute to the enjoyment of genuine human happiness.[25]

However, we might also imagine a virtuous response to sexual desire in which we consider the good of relational intimacy, but decide against pursuing sexual activity for the sake of this end. It could be, for example, that one's partner has a need for some time and physical distance. He or she might wish to be alone to sort through some emotional or spiritual difficulty. Or take another example. Both partners may desire sexual relations but recognize that their present situation, in which they are sharing close quarters with two other couples, does not allow them to enjoy sexual relations while honoring the wishes of their friends. The couple (and the others) may all have a need to observe a culturally conditioned expectation of respect for privacy, unless some other understanding has been negotiated.[26]

Of course, we cannot consider all the possible situations in which sexual virtue could be realized by relational intimacy. But it is the point of an ethic of virtue to show that such cases can be imagined, one by one, even if no two cases are identical. As we do this, we will be able to add even more practical evidence that relational intimacy is a complete and separate end of sexual virtue—and to its corollary, that the procreative norm will be increasingly difficult to defend.

Twelve

Selective Acts of Procreation

It would be one of the greatest triumphs of humanity, one of the most tangible liberations from the constraints of nature to which mankind is subject, if we could succeed in raising the responsible act of procreating children to the level of a deliberate and intentional activity and in freeing it from its entanglement with the necessary satisfaction of a natural need.

—Sigmund Freud

Not Anti-Life

Procreation *is* good.

To borrow words from the Book of Genesis, procreation is "very good."[1] It is important that I begin an ethical reflection on procreation this way. If for no other reason, critics may assume otherwise. Namely, those of us who argue for the permissibility of birth control and reject the procreative norm are sometimes regarded as people who do not value life. That is simply not true. And yet, the anti-life accusations pile up. For example, in a very strong indictment, Pope Paul VI once said that anyone who intentionally contravenes procreation in sexual activity "contradicts the will of the Author of life."[2] I take it that he meant to indict those who use birth control, and those who advocate it as well.

But Pope Paul VI never spoke with the eldest Catholic matriarch in my family, who in her mid-nineties once slapped my hand and recoiled when I told her what the Vatican authorities demanded of marital sexual activity. She looked at me for a moment, and then said quite plainly, "That's not natural." There was only a beat of silence before we all laughed that familiar laugh, the one we let loose when we know that the institutional authority is clearly in the wrong. To be sure, my Catholic grandmother is not the only practicing Catholic who finds pontifications on the procreative norm to fall well short of practical reason.

In this short chapter, I seek to establish in what ways we can aim toward procreation as a matter of sexual virtue, without demanding its potentiality in every sexual encounter that we call "good." As an exercise of virtue, I wish to show why making prudent decisions about realizing our reproductive powers is important morally, especially in light of the real delights and demands of parenthood—as well as the real problems facing the human community on a global scale. To that end, I will argue that procreation is good, but that as an end of sexual virtue it must be sought after selectively and, thus, prudently.

The Virtue of Procreation

The Delight and Demand of Procreation

Without question, procreation is a high responsibility to be respected. In the basic sense, procreation concerns the perpetuation of the species. But more than that, it concerns the formation of new people through personal, moral, and spiritual education and care. That is no small task— and in my view, it is best sought after with a great deal of deliberation, preparation, and commitment. Thus, procreation, well defined, is not only something necessary to perpetuate the species; more broadly, it is a matter of shaping the kind of species we are qualitatively.

Therefore, if we are going to assign procreation as an end of sexual virtue, we need to keep in mind the full definition of it: bearing and rearing children. In my view, many of the current debates about abortion are responsible for hollowing out our understanding of what it means to procreate life well. If for no other reason, many of the current debates have reduced our understanding of procreation to the biological minimum: conception and the biological gestation of a fetus.

With an intense focus on biological generation, we have all but forgotten that the most complete definition of procreation includes the bearing *and* rearing of children. Conception and gestation are matters of reproduction. Procreation, arguably, is what comes next. To procreate a child is not simply to engage in the kind of sexual activity that can lead to conception, nor is it even to bring a fetus to term. To procreate is to knowingly commit to the nurturing of an offspring, as it grows through childhood and into adulthood. Procreation requires meeting an offspring's physical needs, yes, but it also concerns moral and social nurturing—and for people of faith, spiritual formation, too. To "procreate" a person is to help another human being become a fully flourishing individual. It is to help an offspring become a person who has full confidence in him or herself, and who is prepared to live in the world as a contributing member, according to his or her innate gifts and acquired skills. It is also to prepare a human being to live and do well, morally speaking, by helping that person become a mature moral agent who cultivates a truly happy life through prudence and all the other virtues.

It is a profound irony, then, that those political forces that are most adamant about the government making sure that every fetus is brought to term are, at the same time, the very ones who tend to reduce governmental aid for women who need help when raising their children. The 2012 Catholic organization "Nuns on the Bus" made this point well when one of their representatives, Sr. Monica McGloin said: "We believe life begins at conception and ends with natural death. . . . And [thus] pro-life means that we do concern ourselves with living wage, just wage, access to healthcare, education, food, housing, care for our seniors, Medicare and other kinds of healthcare programs that are supportive. [For example] providing daycare for children so their parents can work . . . that's what pro-life is."[3]

Thus, while the pro-life movement alleges to protect the sanctity of life, the same movement has political allies who work against the procreation of life in the fullest sense of the term—i.e., raising new offspring well. This is especially true when "pro-life" political allies treat children as burdensome and dispensable once outside of the womb. Making the matters of "life" and reproductive choices all the more confounding, there is a very clear historical record that reveals religious and moral disagreements about when personhood begins. This is relevant because if procreation is ultimately about raising a child well, then it does matter at what point the moral community recognizes the emergence of personhood in the reproductive process. Namely, if personhood is not present, then the termination of a pregnancy cannot be likened to "murder," nor would supporting women's rights to abortion diminish the value we place on procreation (properly defined). For example, in traditional Judaism, personhood was historically assigned at birth. What is more, even the revered Catholic theologians Augustine and Aquinas both taught that personhood came about after "ensoulment" (at least thirty days after conception). And when we look to contemporary Christian views on this matter, we find that Christians share virtually no agreement on this issue:

some say that personhood comes with conception, other Christians say personhood develops sometime later in pregnancy—or at birth. It is good to avail ourselves of many such moral and religious views on reproduction and procreation. If we don't, we can easily forget that "procreation" has much more to do with raising a child than it does making sure a fetus comes to term. Indeed, while a fetus must be brought to term in order to be procreated well, it is not also true that every fetus brought to term counts as the complete act of procreation—nor is it necessarily true that every fetus must be brought to term, given the variety of moral and religious perspectives on personhood and fetal life.

But what we can say with certainty is that procreation (as defined) is both a delight and a demand. To procreate *well* is to work hard at being a good caretaker. But it is also to delight in the process of helping an offspring flourish as a full moral person. Defined this way, the task of procreating a child requires more of us than being a biological mother or father. Indeed, we know that a number of biological parents do not actually "procreate" their children, either by delivering their offspring into the hands of adoptive parents or, in tragic cases, when the biological parents neglect or abandon their children altogether.

Given the comprehensive caregiving necessary to procreate well, the task of procreation will benefit from the involvement of parents, guardians, extended family members, friends, teachers, and a wide variety of other people who must assist in the task of cultivating a child's moral, intellectual, and spiritual development—if we are to do so well. But before we get that far, it is imperative that we reflect on how best to procure new offspring through reproduction, since it involves other persons to make it possible.

Most notably, it requires women.

In order to discuss reproduction with any moral maturity, we must respect that the moral agency of a woman is at least equal to that of her partner, and in pregnancies, her moral status is at least equal to that of the fetus. However, because women bear a remarkable responsibility in the reproductive process, and because there is no question about their status as full moral persons, women's decisions about reproduction are primary and final. The demands on her body, mind, and spirit are—without question—more than the few moments necessary for a man to exercise his reproductive capacity. She, therefore, has every right to exercise the virtue of prudence in order to decide when it is the right time, and the right reason, to welcome new life through her reproductive faculties (her body!)—and when she does not. Thus, when not seeking reproduction, some women will find that sexual activity is still good to enjoy, pursuing other ends, and using contraception when necessary. Indeed, the key here is to recognize that when women make these decisions about reproduction, they can do so with the virtue of prudence—the virtue of knowing the right reasons for things to be done. Specifically, prudence will help women to determine when reproduction is best to pursue given the personal and bodily demands of pregnancy.

When women pursue biological offspring with a partner, the exercise of prudence will be a joint effort, and it will require mutuality. This is true for heterosexual fertile couples, as well as infertile straight couples or gay and lesbian couples. In particular, whether or not a woman, or a couple, requires reproductive assistance through technology, or perhaps a surrogate, does not diminish the necessary role of prudence—by which people will know when it is best to reproduce, and then how best to procreate that offspring.

Of course, not all people are well suited for every aspect of procreation. Some may choose not to reproduce themselves biologically, but to assist with procreation as a matter of teaching, counseling, or some other form of caregiving. What is more, where any one of us might bring our own biological offspring into the world, we ought to be mindful not only about our own ability to procreate well, but how the reproductive and procreative processes will bear on others, with whom we share life. As with all other human activities, we must consider how potential acts of reproduction and procreation bear on social justice.

Practical Issues Concerning Procreation

At issue, then, is not whether procreation is an important human good. At issue is whether particular acts that yield biological offspring are good. Also at issue is the value of procreation for a particular person and couple, within a given context, at a given time in their lies, in the present time of the world. What is more, we must also think about when procreation might not be a good choice for a woman and/or couple. When (or if) this is the case, the couple might nevertheless do well to seek and enjoy sexual relations for the sake of recreation or relational intimacy (relying on artificial contraception to do so). Many Christian churches (except for the Catholic Church) hold that such a choice can be morally good. I suggest that such intentionality about procreation (or its avoidance) can be conceived as an expression of sexual virtue.[4]

Indeed, there are often good reasons to aim at procreation selectively or not at all in our sexual activity. The finite nature of global, national, tribal, family, and personal resources demands that particular acts that could lead to reproduction be considered carefully in light of the needs of (the rest of) one's family and community, as well as the broader requirements of social justice.[5] While it is a difficult truth to articulate, when people engage in sexual activities that add to the population of their communities and the world, their actions run the risk of causing ecological and social harm.[6]

Children are, in many cases, occasions of joy. I want to make clear that I am not arguing that procreation is no longer an important personal and social good. However, our thinking about our own (and each other's) acts of procreation cannot rest on romanticized views of parenting and family life, irrespective of the needs of the rest of humanity. People of virtue living in the twenty-first century cannot ignore the sobering realities of life on our planet. A few examples may prove helpful.[7]

According to the World Health Organization, malnutrition is the cause of death for 53 percent of children under the age of five throughout the world.[8] Co-morbidity factors include the treatment or manageable ailments of diarrhea, measles, malaria, pneumonia, and basic injuries.[9] As of 2003, 3 percent of global child deaths under the age of five were attributed to HIV/AIDS.[10] And as many of us are well aware, the number of suffering children increases each year.

With such numbers of actual children suffering, one must seriously consider whether compassion and justice require more selective procreation, not only on the part of persons who live in poverty but also on the part of people who live in wealth, who expend (and whose children also expend)—and hoard—a disproportionate amount of the world's natural resources. With respect to the number of deaths related to HIV/AIDS, this number continues to rise most noticeably in countries where contraception is not practiced, often for complex reasons, but which tend to include a religious component. I have in mind Catholic countries (or communities) in which HIV/AIDS is epidemic among heterosexual populations, but in which condoms have been denounced by the Vatican in favor of an ideal of abstinence. The following selection from a recent article in *Catholic News* reflects this point well:

Catholic leaders in Africa have pledged to step up their involvement in the fight against the AIDS pandemic, while continuing to reject the use of condoms to fight the disease. "The church says one must be faithful in marriage and save oneself for marriage," said Senegal Bishop Alexandre Mbengue. [The bishop went on to say] "We cannot cave in to the current trend."

[And yet,] according to the UN agency UNAIDS sub-Saharan Africa is hardest hit by AIDS, being home to more than two-thirds of those infected with HIV worldwide—29.4 million out of 42 million. Congo's Kinshasa Archbishop Dominique Bulamatari said: "Using condoms as a means of preventing AIDS can only lead to promiscuity."[11]

In spite of these traditional rulings, however, Pope Benedict made an announcement in 2010 that condoms might be used to stop the spread of disease.[12]

Benedict's comment caused a flurry of reaction throughout the Vatican, and indeed, throughout the world.[13] It would seem the pontiff was not reversing the course of church teaching with respect to contraception per se, but did acknowledge that if people were engaging in sexual activity (however licit or illicit) and the risk of disease was present, the use of a condom was a "lesser evil," and a way to protect a person from infection, and thus one step toward cultivating sexual responsibility and justice, in a moral sense.

Of course, this is not the place to debate complex issues of global population, resources management, or the HIV/AIDS epidemic. I simply want to point to some of these complexities and encourage people to take greater responsibility for investigating the issues and making moral choices in light of what they discover.

Namely, determining what is required of oneself as a person who has the biological power to further populate the planet requires serious reflection and deliberation. This we do individually or with a partner, but it is also something that we should do in community. As we deliberate on procreation, there are a number of relevant matters we must consider. First, we need to consider the biological and psychological inclinations of many people to procreate as a matter of living a happy life. Second, we have to consider the sexual desires many people have to engage in sexual activities that could lead to conception, even if that is not the goal. Third, we need to consider the habits of many men who enjoy sexual intercourse without condoms—especially with women—as well as the sexual habits that often drive people to have unprotected sexual relations first and to think later. In light of all of these, it is critical to find ways to promote reproductive responsibility. In my view, teaching people to get some distance on their various drives and helping them to reflect critically on the goodness of acting (or not acting) on these drives, will be enhanced by opening up a dialogue on sexual virtue that respects selective procreation as an end to pursue, rather than reproduction and procreation in an unqualified sense.[14]

What is more, it is morally irresponsible to insist on procreation as the single justifiable end of sexual activity in a world in which most people will engage in sexual relations with great frequency (and for good and bad reasons), many of them in communities that are plagued with HIV/AIDS, poverty, and overpopulation. Preventable human suffering is the issue. The romanticized vision of a woman and man being fully open to conception at all times, or of a woman who brings an unplanned pregnancy to term as the paragon of virtue, are kinds of ideals lacking in compassion for real people in specific (and often tragic) situations, not to mention inconsistent with the demands of justice, or the insights of prudence. Ideally, each child who is brought into the world ought to be brought into it by parents who have fair access to adequate nutrition, health care, and education. Sexual virtue illuminates that one not pursue sexual activity without first considering carefully the implications of one's actions for actual people, and potential people, not only in one's own neighborhood but around the world.[15]

The global realities of overpopulation, malnutrition, and poorly distributed resources expose the undeniable truth that reproduction, like any other human activity, can be in excess. Reproduction must be pursued, if at all, prudently, and it must not overshadow other sexual goods. The primacy of reproduction may seem obvious, natural, or rational to certain religious leaders (such as those in the Catholic Church), but such arguments make sense only in the context of a religious ideology, which does not (currently) correspond with what is possible and beneficial for most human beings. An ethic of sexual virtue calls attention to the biological, psychological, and interpersonal dimensions of sexuality, and to the many health, social, and ecological crises that the human race faces as a result of excessive reproduction. If we had created a more just world we might be able to say that our societies (and even the planet) can sustain our current numbers. However, within the context of disproportionate economic systems, tyrannical government structures, and so forth, many places in the world are rightly said to be "overpopulated."

Thus, with so many people suffering under the burden of the procreative norm, there is no compelling reason to believe that obedience to this norm contributes to true human happiness.[16]

Certainly, those who advocate the procreative norm could simply respond that it does not dictate unlimited reproduction, it merely demands that if one engages in sexual relations that a person does so intentionally accepting the reproductive potential. Furthermore, they might tell us that if there are situations in which procreation is a bad choice, then a person need only commit to abstinence. I argue, however, that practicing abstinence every day of one's life when a person is not in a good position to bring a child into the world denies human beings important human/sexual goods, such as recreation and relational intimacy (see chapters 10 and 11).[17] To that end, the procreative norm denies people the right to exercise the virtue of prudence, in light of all the other natural/sexual goods that human beings might choose (well)— and then as a matter of practicing and cultivating sexual virtue.

Religious Perspectives on Procreation

With respect to Christian sources of moral authority on the subject of procreation, we already know that the teachings of various churches disagree with one another. Most notably, the Catholic Church demands openness to procreation in every marital sexual act, while most Protestant churches do not. With respect to scripture, we can only point out that procreation is not always demanded of sexual activity when we interpret the texts themselves. For example, biblical scholars have pointed out that in the *Song of Solomon* we find a description of sexual activity that celebrates non-reproductive sex as revelatory of the creative goodness of God. For those not familiar with the text, let me offer a few sample verses of the biblical erotica:

> Open to me, my sister, my love, my dove, my perfect one; for my head is wet with dew, my locks with the drops of the night. . . . My beloved thrust his hand into the opening, and my inmost being yearned for him. I arose to open to my beloved, and my hand dripped with myrrh . . .[18]

One scholar, Phyllis Trible, has said, "in this setting, there is no male dominance, no female subordination, and no stereotyping of 'either sex.' She works, keeping vineyards and pasturing flocks. Throughout the Song [the woman] is independent, fully equal the man . . . never is the woman called a wife, nor is she required to bear children."[19] Thus, what many scholars interpret in this scripture is a fitting celebration of the goodness of sexuality, devoid of a reproductive concern.

Of course, those familiar with the Hebrew Bible will not be surprised by the non-reproductive sexual activity described in the *Song of Solomon* (or elsewhere). When we reflect on how the Hebrew Bible has been interpreted on matters of sexual morality, especially by modern Jewish communities, we find that the procreative norm is curiously missing. That is not to say that procreation did not (or does not) play a significant role in the sexual ethics of Judaism at various points in its history. Indeed, traditional Judaism has ascribed great value to procreating (deeming it a commandment or religious obligation for the Jewish male). But all traditions of Judaism have also ascribed great value to sexual relations that are enjoyed simply for the sake of intimacy, friendship, and mutual pleasure—albeit, usually within a marital context among the traditionalists. Jews have deemed this so important for the quality of life that they have found good reasons to permit certain kinds of birth control, so that heterosexual couples who have procreated can turn their attention to sexual relations for the sake of bringing each other pleasure or intimacy.[20]

It is helpful to contrast the Catholic view on procreation with Jewish views. It allows people to realize that one can—and many people do—draw on some of the same biblical texts to reach quite different insights into the will of God for human relations. As I have been saying all along, the diversity of interpretations makes clear that the Bible does not itself "say" that there is something inherently problematic about sexual intercourse that is not ordered toward reproduction.[21]

Of course, we could also consult natural law thinking when it comes to moral reflection on procreation within a Christian framework. But here too we already know the disagreements between the traditionalists and the revisionists. Therefore, all we can say when reflecting on religious sources of moral authority is that there are no unambiguously clear reasons to promote procreation as the only good of sexual activity. Indeed, when we reflect on religious sources anew, there are good reasons to promote recreation, intimacy, and selective acts of procreation as ends of sexual virtue that are supported rationally, but also in accord with one's vision of God.

Sexual Virtue as Selective Acts of Procreation

There is at this point in the argument, then, only a repetition that can be made. Namely, that human beings can do well (morally speaking) when we are mindful of the reproductive powers of our sexual capacities. If we are engaging in sexual activity that can lead to reproduction, then I argue that we do so well if we intend it, fully prepared to engage in procreation. What is more, we do so well when we choose to contravene reproduction for other good reasons. Finally, for nonheterosexual couples, or for those who are infertile, there is still a practice of sexual virtue toward procreation. If (or when) a person decides to reproduce with the aid of technology or a surrogate, one will donate or produce the necessary sexual reproductive cells only after considering what it means to procreate, and to procreate well.

Therefore, whether we are LGBT or straight, married, coupled, or single, the task of procreation ought to be highly respected. In this sense, we are all "on the side of life." I fear that current conservative attacks on abortion and certain religious condemnations on contraception are distractions that divide and weaken what could otherwise be a common goal to raise our children well. So long as we keep our eyes only on sexual acts and their capacity to generate biological life, we lose sight of what it means to really procreate. Demanding that every sexual act lead to biological generation, or that every pregnancy should come to term, has resulted in real children suffering. A better practice of sexual virtue toward selective acts of procreation would allow us to hold back our reproductive powers as a matter of justice and prudence. Sexual virtue described this way expresses our respect not only for our sexual reproductive powers, but for the longer life strategy of raising our children well (or waiting to have children). It is my hope that as individual Christians practice (and churches praise) selective acts of procreation as a matter of virtue, those who demand the procreative norm will see that selective procreation can yield recognizable strengths of character, and true human happiness.

Conclusion

The trouble with changing the world is . . .
. . . you don't.
Not all at once.
You just inch it forward,
a bit at a time, and watch it slip back,
like the Greek guy with the rock.
And you hope that when you're done, you've moved it up a little,
changed it just a little.
You hope.
. . .
Let's go to work

—Joss Whedon, *Last Gleaming*

Shortly after his death, on August 31, 2012, Archbishop Cardinal Carlo Maria Martini's final interview was published. In it, he accused the Roman Catholic Church of being "200 years out of date."[1] For the cardinal, this included the church's stance on homosexuality, divorce, and contraception.

Earlier that same week, the multibillionaire "conservative" financier of many U.S. Republican candidates, David Koch, came out in support for gay marriage. He went so far as to say, "I believe in gay marriage."[2] But his view would be in direct opposition to the Republican Party platform, whose anti–marriage equality position was formally accepted at the 2012 Republican National Convention (RNC). Meanwhile, conservative LGBT groups such as the Log Cabin Republicans and GOProud worked behind the scenes in an effort to shift the RNC toward more amiable positions on LGBT issues.

A few days later, the first lady of the United States, Michelle Obama, would take the stage of the Democratic National Convention (DNC). She not only defended the right of women to reproductive

choice, but also advocated for LGBT Americans to stand at the altar
with those that they love. The 2012 DNC would mark the first time in
U.S. history that one of the major political parties would include "gay
marriage" as a platform plank.

I mention these public figures to indicate that when it comes to
sexual ethics, the world is changing. It's changing for those who think
of themselves as "conservative," and it's changing for those who understand themselves as "progressive." We are beginning to move beyond
the assumption that everyone is heterosexual, and we're beginning to
move beyond sexual norms tied ever so closely with procreation. By "we"
I especially mean those of us participating in the political and social
discourses of the Euro-American West.

Indeed, many sectors of the West have already moved beyond
heterosexist and/or procreative norms. What is more, for many LGBT
and straight people alike, the liberation of sexuality requires much more
than the recognition of diverse sexual orientations; and certainly much
more than the acceptance of LGBT relationships by state, federal, and/or
religious authorities. Namely, for some people, sexual liberation requires
embracing queer positionality, which, in part, is to dwell in the liminal spaces of the social/sexual margins, where essentialist concepts of
sexuality are eschewed in favor of "queer" identities; accepting also that
notions of gender and sexuality are in a constant state of flux.

But in this book I have advanced the perspective of critical realism, seeking to uncover real human goods in sexual relationships, and
doing so through an ethic of virtue. While I believe that the insights
of queer theory are often prophetic, and they do help us to test the
fragility of certain customs and norms, I have suggested that a practical
investigation of human sexuality (with insights from the sciences and
critical moral and religious discourse) reveals some goods that appear to
be constitutive of human flourishing (or happiness).

From the perspective of virtue, I have suggested that these goods
are not a matter of defining what kind of sexual activities we engage
in, but what "ends" we pursue in our sexual relationships. My suggestion has been that there are at least three ends by which sexual pleasure is well enjoyed: recreation, relational intimacy, and selective acts
of procreation. I do not deny that there are other ends that could be
named, but I draw on these to show that an ethic of virtue helps us to
liberate sexual morality from old heterosexist, marital, and procreative
norms—norms that are unconvincing, not because they are "old" but

because, when they are universally applied, such norms can be shown to artificially limit people's autonomy and happiness.

What is more, I have attempted to show that recreation, relational intimacy, and selective acts of procreation are "ends" of sexual virtue that make sense within a broad Christian framework. However, I have left the navigation of these ends to the prudential reflection of Christians themselves. To say that all people should pursue these ends would be too prescriptive. Indeed, on the basis of some people's religious convictions, keeping sexual relations to marriage, or open to procreation, allows them to practice sexual virtue in light of their understanding of God. I respect that. But I also want to encourage such Christians to accept that there are other valid ways of articulating sexual morality within a Christian framework; and that those who pursue recreational sex (well defined), or those who draw on contraceptives (whether in marriages or not) can do so and still realize valuable ends of sexual activity that contribute to our happiness as human beings.

Thus, my engagement with sexual virtue has been an attempt to show reasons why more inclusive definitions of sexual morality are justifiable. I do so with the real sense that advancing sexual liberation is important to human flourishing. Too often, and for too many people, the moral and religious restriction of human sexuality to the categories of "heterosexuality," or "marriage," or "procreation," has caused terrible distress—to LGBT people, to families struggling with disagreements over sexual morality, among friends who hold to opposing religious or moral views, and certainly across political lines too. While I accept that disagreements will abound on issues of sexual morality, those disagreements need not be as divisive as they are now, nor as painful.

But to alleviate that pain, we need to be more gracious with one another—to seek understanding first, and then to engage one another about why we hold to the positions that we do. Given that so many of our debates about sexual morality are religious in nature, I believe it is important to speak to religious concerns where we can. With respect to Christian perspectives on sexual morality, I have attempted to show that the principles of the Christian faith in no way forbid a person from pursuing sexual pleasures through the ends of sexual virtue that I have named. But to come to this conclusion requires letting go of fundamentalist and/or inconsistent "plain" readings of scripture. It requires engaging church teachings as particular theological perspectives, not final answers. And it requires being open to prudential reflection on data we have from the natural and social sciences, as well as to integrate our experiences into our moral vision. In my view, all of these sources can help the moral community to make better inferential judgments about living and doing well as sexual/human beings.

Of course, inasmuch as there will be critics who will conclude that my argument is too permissive, there will be others who will say that an appeal to virtue is itself an approach to sexual ethics that too easily becomes an authoritarian vessel, or is itself too prescriptive. I admit that virtue ethics certainly has been used to cast narrow views on sexual morality. But the point is: *it need not*. Reclaiming virtue, especially sexual virtue, is a way for us to embrace and take pride in sexual liberation as a movement of human excellence. It is not the only way, but it is one way that encourages people to free themselves of certain unnecessary social or religious shackles. What is more, virtue ethics also invites us to take seriously our moral commitments to one another. There will be give and take, and disagreements, even between like-minded people on these issues. But it is my hope that where we pursue virtue with generosity of thought and respect for human flourishing, we will eventually arrive at the world changed for the better, where our divisions are not as deeply entrenched as they are today, and freedom of sexual expression is praised as one part of living life to our human best.

Notes

Introduction

1. See: *Grindr*, or *Blendr*; Nearby Buddy Finder, LLC. *Grindr* was first launched March 25, 2009 (available on iOS, Blackberry OS, and Android platforms).

2. BDSM can stand for: bondage and discipline, dominance and submission; sadism and masochism. See, for example: Darren Langdridge, and Meg Barker, eds., *Safe, Sane, and Consensual: Contemporary Perspectives on Sadomasochism* (Houndmills, Basingstoke, Hampshire: Palgrave Macmillan, 2008).

3. Paul VI, Encyclical Letter, *Humanae vitae*, 25 July 1968.

4. Mark Jordan, *The Ethics of Sex* (Malden, MA: Blackwell, 2002).

5. Rosemary Radford Ruether, *Christianity and the Making of the Modern Family* (Boston: Beacon Press, 2000).

6. In many ways, the laws of modern society have already begun to transform the medieval patriarchal (male-privileged) and procreative frameworks for sexual morality (e.g., in the United States women have rights to reproductive choice, men and women have greater access to contraceptives, and gay and lesbian people no longer are under the penal threat of sodomy laws, etc.). However, cultural norms, sometimes expressed through certain religious teachings, do not always resonate with the aims of sexual liberation.

7. There is no "one" beginning to sexual liberation, per se. It, like all social movements, is the result of (poly) dependent origination: whether nineteenth-century first wave feminism; texts such as Betty Friedan's *Feminine Mystique* (1963); social-political movements like the one that emerged from the Stonewall riots (1969); or court cases such as *Roe v. Wade* (1973). We might even point to social "experimentations" with marriage and family in the nineteenth century among certain religious minorities. I do not mean to give a full history of sexual liberation, but I do mean to point toward the long arc of its egalitarian, nonpatriarchal goals.

8. See, for example: the Reform and Conservative branches of Judaism; The Universal Fellowship of Metropolitan Community Churches; The United Church of Christ, the Evangelical Lutheran Church in America, the Presbyterian Church (USA), the Episcopal Church; The Unitarian Universalist Association.

259

9. See: Sigmund Freud, *The Future of Illusion,* trans. and ed. James Strachey (New York/London: W. W. Norton, 1961), 47.

10. Beverly Wildung Harrison, "Sexuality and Social Policy," in *Sexuality and the Sacred,* ed. James Nelson and Sandra Longfellow (Louisville and London: Westminster/John Knox Press, 1994), 244–48.

11. See for example: Todd Salzman and Michael Lawler, *The Sexual Person: Toward A Renewed Catholic Anthropology* (Washington, DC: Georgetown University Press, 2008), especially chapter 4, "Unitive Sexual Morality: A Revised Foundational Principle and Anthropology." Also: Margaret Farley, *Just Love* (New York: Continuum. 2006).

12. For examples: Yoel Kahn, "Making Love as Making Justice," in *Sexuality,* ed. Karen Lebascqz (Cleveland: Pilgrim Press, 1999); Martha Nussbaum, *Sex and Social Justice* (Oxford and New York: Oxford University Press, 1999); and Farley, *Just Love.*

13. We do, however, have a number of analyses on sexual virtue (chastity) from theologians in the Catholic Church, as well as from scholars who analyze their teachings—but these largely explain why the church has maintained a marital and procreative norm as the definition of sexual virtue.

14. Diana Cates, *Choosing to Feel* (South Bend: University of Notre Dame Press, 1996).

15. Aristotle, *Nicomachean Ethics,* III.11.6ff.

16. Lyubomirksy, King, and Diener, "The Benefits of Frequent Positive Affect. Does Happiness Lead to Success?" *Psychological Bulletin* 131, no. 6 (2005): 808, 811, 829, 835.

17. Barry Moss and Andrew Schwebel, "Marriage and Romantic Relationships: Defining Intimacy in Romantic Relationships," *Family Relations* 42 (1993): 35.

18. *Summa Theologica* (ST) II–II.151.4.

19. Didi Herman, "(Il)legitimate Minorities: The American Christian Right's Anti-Gay-Rights Discourse," *Journal of Law and Society* 23, no. 3 (1996): 346–63.

20. In 2010, the U.S. Conference of Catholic Bishops condemned the scholarly book, *The Sexual Person: Toward a Renewed Catholic Anthropology.* The reader can find the bishops' full statement here: www.usccb.org/doctrine/Sexual_Person_2010-09-15.pdf. The authors of the text were fully defended by their academic institution.

21. Jimmy Creech, *Adam's Gift: A Memoir of a Pastor's Calling to Defy the Church's Persecution of Lesbians and Gays* (Durham and London: Duke University Press, 2011).

22. *National Gay and Lesbian Task Force.* See full report at: http://www.the-taskforce.org/downloads/reports/reports/HomelessYouth_ExecutiveSummary.pdf.

23. Mel White, *Stanger at the Gate* (New York: Plume/Penguin Group, 1994).

24. See, for example, the works of William Bennett, including: *The Book of Virtues* (1993); *Moral Compass* (1995); and *The Broken Hearth* (2003).

25. Salzman and Lawler, *The Sexual Person*, 4. They note, "In theological parlance . . . the disputed question, so beloved of the medieval Scholastics."

26. For example, consider Glenn Beck's 2010 "Restoring Honor" rally, the text of which waxed religious, moral, and political.

27. Martha Nussbaum, *Liberty of Conscience* (New York: Basic Books, 2008 (eBook edition), 75–76.

28. See: Jim Wallis, *God's Politics: Why the Right Gets It Wrong and the Left Doesn't Get It* (New York: HarperCollins, 2005).

Chapter One. Sexual Positions

1. Mel White, *Religion Gone Bad* (London: Jeremy P. Tarcher/Penguin, 2006).

2. Ruether, *Christianity and the Making of the Modern Family*.

3. Dale Martin, *Sex and the Single Savior: Gender and Sexuality in Biblical Interpretation* (Louisville: Westminster/John Knox Press, 2006), 65–76.

4. Phil Sherrard, "The Sexual Relationship in Christian Thought," *Studies in Comparative Religion* 5, no. 3 (1971): extracted June 12, 2012, from: www.studiesincomparativereligion.com/uploads/AriclePDFs/180.pdf.

5. Glenn T. Stanton, from *My Crazy Imperfect Christian Family* (NavPress, 2004). Extracted June 12, 2012, from: http://www.focusonthefamily.com/marriage/sex_and_intimacy/gods_design_for_sex.aspx.

6. Of course, neither *Focus on the Family* nor the Vatican are beholden to St. Gregory of Nyssa's teachings. The point is only that Christian views on sexuality can, and do, change.

7. 1 Corinthians 7.

8. Romans 1:18–2:1.

9. I draw on these dates for the Pauline texts from Raymond E. Brown, *An Introduction to the New Testament* (New York and London: Doubleday, 1997), 512, 560.

10. See Ruether, *Christianity and the Making of the Modern Family*, 38.

11. Ibid., 40.

12. Ibid.

13. See Elizabeth Clark, *St. Augustine on Marriage and Sexuality* (Washington, DC: The Catholic University of America Press, 1996).

14. Ruether notes that efforts to establish clerical celibacy began as early as the fourth century with the Council of Elvira. They were, apparently, unsuccessful. *Christianity and the Making of the Modern Family*, 47.

15. Ibid., 58.

16. *Summa Theologica* (ST) I–II.141.4.

17. *Theodosian* Code 9.7.3 and 9.7.6.

18. Jordan, *The Ethics of Sex*, 117–25.

19. Margaret Farley, "Sexual Ethics," in *Sexuality and the Sacred*, ed. James Nelson and Sandra Longfellow (Louisville and London: Westminster/John Knox Press, 1994), 65–66.

20. Leon Bouvier, "Catholics and Contraception," *Journal of Marriage and Family* 34, no. 3 (1972): 514–22.

21. Paul VI, *Humanae vitae*.

22. Ibid.

23. See for example: Pius XI, Encyclical Letter, *Casti connubii*, 31 December 1930; and, *Humanae vitae*. *Humanae vitae* was a direct response to those Catholic theologians who argued for contraceptive use; they are referenced in the encyclical.

24. *Humanae vitae*.

25. See Jo Freeman, *The Politics of Women's Liberation* (Lincoln, NE: iUniverse.com, 1975, 2000). And Byrne Fone, *Homophobia: A History* (New York: Picador/Pan Books, 2000).

26. Second-wave feminism.

27. Susan Archer Mann and Douglas Huffman, "The Decentering of Second Wave Feminism and the Rise of the Third Wave," *Science & Society* 69, no. 1 (2005): 56–91.

28. The LGBT community no longer speaks in terms of "gay rights" alone, as "gay" usually demarcates male homosexuality, not lesbians, bisexual people, the transgender community; the queer, etc.

29. See Mark Jordan, *Recruiting Young Love* (Chicago: University of Chicago Press, 2011); Maurine Waun, *More Than Welcome: Learning to Embrace Gay, Lesbian, Bisexual, and Transgendered Persons in the Church* (St. Louis: Chalice Press, 1999); Mel White, *Stranger at the Gate: To Be Gay and Christian in America* (New York: Plume, 1995).

30. For example, in a bibliographic survey on religion and sexuality collected by participants of the *Religion and Sexuality Symposium* at Emory University (June 2010), only nine of the texts collected were published before 1980; while seventy-six titles were published in 1990 or later. While not a complete portrait, it suggests that much of the work of religion and sexuality has been done in recent decades.

31. Joseph Ratzinger, *Letter to the Bishops of the Catholic Church on the Pastoral Care of Homosexual Persons*. 1986. See, in particular, Section 3.

32. Ibid., Section 10.

33. Mark Jordan, *The Silence of Sodom* (Chicago: University of Chicago Press, 2000), 37.

34. *Catechism of the Catholic Church* (Liguori, MO: Liguori Publications, 1994), § 2358, 566; emphasis mine.

35. Ruether, *Christianity and the Making of the Modern Family*, 156–80.

36. See for example the 2009 *Statement on Sexuality* by the Evangelical Lutheran Church in America.

37. See for example: John Boswell, *Christianity, Social Tolerance, and Homosexuality* (Chicago and London: University of Chicago Press, 1980). Also Patrick Cheng, *Radical Love: An Introduction to Queer Theology* (New York: Seabury Books, 2011).

Chapter Two. Sexual Ethics

1. As someone who engages in ethical inquiry within the field of Religious Studies, I draw on the work of theological ethicist, James Nelson, who defined sexuality this way: "[S]exuality is not the whole of our personhood, but it is a very basic dimension of our personhood. While our sexuality does not determine all of our feelings, thoughts, and actions, in ways both obvious and covert it permeates and affects them all. Sexuality is our self-understanding and way of being in the world as male and female. It includes our appropriation of attitudes and characteristics which have been culturally defined as masculine and feminine. It involves our affectional orientation towards those of the opposite and/or the same sex. It includes our attitudes about our own bodies and those of others. Because we are 'body-selves,' our sexuality constantly reminds each of us of our uniqueness and particularity: we look different and we feel differently from any other person. Sexuality is a sign, symbol, and a means of our call to communication and communion." James Nelson, *Embodiment* (Minneapolis: Augsburg Press, 1978), 17–18.

2. Diana Cates, *Aquinas on the Emotions* (Washington, DC: Georgetown University Press, 2009), 21–34.

3. Ibid., 31.

4. Ibid., 22.

5. Ibid.

6. Raymond Belliotti, *Good Sex: Perspectives on Sexual Ethics* (Lawrence: University Press of Kansas, 1993), 175–227.

7. Exodus 21.

8. Deuteronomy 22:23–29.

9. See Robert Firestone, Lisa Firestone, and Joyce Catlett, eds., *Sex and Love: In Intimate Relationships* (Washington, DC: American Psychological Association, 2005).

10. Jordan, *The Ethics of Sex*, 47–106.

11. Farley, *Just Love*, 188–89.

12. Ibid., 189.

13. A familiar proverb in many cultures—but with apparent origins in the Talmud.

14. See Introduction for review.

15. Jordan, *The Ethics of Sex*, 1.
16. Lisa Sowle Cahill, *Sex, Gender, and Christian Ethics* (Cambridge: Cambridge University Press, 1996), 46.
17. Ibid.
18. Judith Boss, *Analyzing Moral Issues*, 5th ed. (New York: McGraw-Hill, 2010), 3.
19. Cahill, *Sex, Gender, and Christian Ethics*, 56.
20. Nussbaum, *Sex and Social Justice*, 30.
21. Ibid.
22. Philip Hancock and Melissa Tyler, *Work, Postmodernism, and Organization: A Critical Introduction* (London and Thousand Oaks, CA: Sage, 2001), 166.
23. Belliotti, *Good Sex*, 175–227.
24. Ibid.
25. Cahill, *Sex, Gender, and Christian Ethics*, 29.
26. Ibid., 49.
27. Michael Warner, *The Trouble with Normal* (New York: The Free Press, 1999).
28. Ibid., 65–66.
29. Robert Goss, *Queering Christ: Beyond Jesus Acted Up* (Cleveland: The Pilgrim Press, 2002), 228–29, quoting Halperin, from *Saint Foucault: Towards a Gay Hagiography*.
30. Ibid.
31. Ibid., 228.
32. Cheng, *Radical Love*, 9.
33. Aristotle, *Nicomachean Ethics*, V.1.13.
34. Ibid., V.3.1–2.
35. See Deuteronomy 22 and 23.
36. See, for example, the United Church of Christ and the Evangelical Lutheran Church in America.
37. Farley *Just Love*, 216–32.
38. Carter Heyward, *Touching Our Strength: The Erotic as Power and the Love of God* (New York: Harper and Row, 1989), 95.
39. See chapter 1.
40. Christine Gudorf, *Body, Sex, and Pleasure: Reconstructing Christian Sexual Ethics* (Cleveland: Pilgrim Press, 1994), 90.
41. Gudorf says, "In philosophical terms, it should be clear that I am advocating a form of moral utilitarianism" (97).
42. Ibid., 90.
43. Ibid., 114.
44. Ibid., 115.
45. For new descriptions of sexual sins, I suggest Patrick Cheng, *From Sin to Amazing Grace* (New York: Seabury Books, 2012).
46. Gudorf, *Body, Sex, and Pleasure*, 117.

47. Return to the Introduction to recall the working definitions I provided for prudence and temperance.

48. Aristotle, *Nicomachean Ethics*, II.3.

Chapter Three. Virtue Ethics and Sexual Virtue

1. With respect to Buddhist thinkers, I am especially mindful of the Dalai Lama's comments about virtue. See *Ethics for the New Millennium* (New York: Riverhead Books, 1999).

2. See, for example, in Judaism, Maimonides (Moses ben Maimon), *Ethical Writings of Maimonides*, edited by Raymond L. Weiss and Charles Butterworth (New York: Dover, 1975). See especially "Laws Concerning Character Traits," chapter 1. For Christianity, see Thomas Aquinas, *The Summa Theologica*, translated by Fathers of the English Dominican Province (New York: Christian Classics/Benziger Brothers, 1948), esp. I–II.55–70. For Islamic commentary on Islamic scholarship on virtue, see Charles Butterworth, "Medieval Islamic Philosophy and the Virtue of Ethics," *Arabica* 34, no. 2 (1987): 221–50.

3. See for example the work of Jean Porter, starting with *Recovery of Virtue* (Louisville: Westminster/John Knox Press, 1990).

4. See for example David Cunningham, *Christian Ethics: The End of the Law* (London and New York: Routledge, 2008).

5. See J. Phillip Wogamann, *Christian Ethics* (Louisville: Westminster/John Knox Press, 1993).

6. Aristotle, *Nicomachean Ethics*, I.7.5.

7. Cates, *Choosing to Feel*, 4. Although here Cates emphasizes the activity of living and doing well, not the pleasure of doing so. I take it that *eudemonia* consists of living and doing well, and enjoying it.

8. Ibid., 7.

9. Aristotle, *Nicomachean Ethics*, Book 10.

10. An homage to Mark Jordan's concept of the rhetoric of repetition. See Mark Jordan, *The Silence of Sodom: Homosexuality in Modern Catholicism* (Chicago and London: University of Chicago Press, 2000), 1–17.

11. Recall queer theory (see chapter 2).

12. Cates, *Choosing to Feel*, 4–15.

13. Aristotle. *Nicomachean Ethics*. I.7.9–14.

14. Diana Cates explains that, for Aristotle, "[t]o choose as a person of practical wisdom would choose is to choose as the community's most experienced moral educators and exemplars have taught us to choose. It is to choose as the distinctive persons we are, in light of a well-deliberated vision of the good, with practiced attention to our own and relevant others' needs, capabilities, commitments, and desired ends, with carefully-honed sensitivities and attunements to shifting particulars." *Choosing to Feel*, 15.

15. Of course, we should be reflexive and consider our own proclivities for simple rhetoric.

16. Review chapter 2 on critical realism and moral relativism.

17. I am grateful for conversations with religious ethicist Laurie Jungling on the enterprise of normative ethics, especially at the intersection of religion and sexuality.

18. See http://www.itgetsbetter.org/.

19. David Myers and Letha Dawson Scanzoni, *What God Has Joined Together?* (New York: HarperSanFrancisco, 2005), 11–22.

20. Marilynne Robinson, *The Death of Adam: Essays on Modern Thought* (Boston and New York: Houghton Mifflin, 1998.

21. Bonnie Kent, "Habits and Virtues," in *The Ethics of Aquinas*, edited by Stephen Pope (Washington, DC: Georgetown University Press, 2002), 116–21.

22. Ibid.

23. Robert Fitterer, *Love and Objectivity in Virtue Ethics* (Toronto: University of Toronto Press, 2008), 17.

24. Unless the point of the critique is only to rehearse (again) moral relativism.

25. Lisa Cahill, *Sex, Gender, and Christian Ethics* (Cambridge and New York: Cambridge University Press, 1999), 56.

26. Salzman and Lawler have suggested we might best resist *relativism* with *perspectivism*. They say, "We prefer to speak of perspectivism rather than of relativism. . . . Where relativism has lost hope about the attainment of truth, perspectivism stresses the complexity of what the [scholar] is writing about . . . [and] whereas relativism concludes to the falsity of a judgment, perspectivism concludes to its *partial* truth." *The Sexual Person: Toward a Renewed Catholic Anthropology* (Washington, DC: Georgetown University Press, 2008), 53.

27. Aristotle, *Nicomachean Ethics*, I.7.15–20.

28. Examples drawn upon by Aristotle himself in ibid.

29. Ibid.

30. Ibid., II.8.

31. Aristotle says, "Among these three conditions, then, two are vices—one of excess, one of deficiency—and one, the mean is virtue." Ibid., II.8.1.

32. See   http://blogs.wsj.com/health/2008/08/13/the-michael-phelps-diet-dont-try-it-at-home/.

33. Aristotle considered only men capable of exercising reason perfectly. He also considered the deformed, unattractive, and the uneducated to be incapable of realizing true virtue. We can be more inclusive.

34. *Nicomachean Ethics*, III.1–4.

35. Ibid. VI.5.4. Aristotle says, "[P]rudence is a state grasping the truth, involving reason, concerned with action about things that are good or bad for a human being."

36. See my previous comments on "right reason." Just as Aristotle first described right reason, and then assigned prudence as its virtue, so too I followed the philosopher's rhetorical strategy.

37. Cates, *Choosing to Feel*, 15.

38. Patricia Jung and Aana Marie Vigen, eds., *God, Science, Sex, Gender: An Interdisciplinary Approach to Christian Ethics* (Chicago: University of Illinois Press, 2010), 9.

39. Christopher Ryan and Jethá Cacilda, *Sex at Dawn* (New York: HarperCollins, 2011), 285–88.

40. Ibid.

41. *Nicomachean Ethics*, IV.

42. Andrew Lester, *The Angry Christian* (Louisville and London: Westminster/John Knox Press, 2003), 19–34.

43. Cates *Choosing to Feel*, 25–27.

44. For example, see Aristotle, *Nicomachean Ethics*, Book VII, on moral incontinence.

45. Aristotle, *Nicomachean Ethics*, III.11.6, 7.

46. Gudorf, *Body, Sex, and Pleasure*, 81–138.

47. See chapter 2.

48. Aristotle, *Nicomachean Ethics*, II.3.

49. Ibid., VII.14.2.

50. Ibid., II.3.

51. Ibid., III.11.10–19.

52. See, for example: Salzman and Lawler, *The Sexual Person*.

53. Louis Crompton, *Homosexuality and Civilization* (Cambridge: The Belknap Press of Harvard University Press, 2003), 65–66.

54. For example, see: Richard Hamer, "Genetics and Male Sexual Orientation," *Science* 285, no. 5429 (1999): 803ff; Firestone, Firestone, and Catlett, *Sex and Love in Intimate Relationships*; L. A. Krudek, "Sexuality in Homosexual and Heterosexual Couples," in *Sexuality in Close Relationships*, edited by McKinney and Sprecher (Hillsdale, NJ: Erlbaum, 1991).

55. Firestone, Firestone, and Catlett. *Sex and Love in Intimate Relationships*, 45ff.

56. Ibid., 4.

57. See chapter 9 and the documented research.

58. Moss and Schwebel, "Marriage and Romantic Relationships": 36.

59. Firestone, Firestone, and Catlett, *Sex and Love in Intimate Relationships*, 13.

60. John McNeill, "Homosexuality: Challenging the Church to Grow," in *Homosexuality in the Church: Both Sides of the Debate*, edited by Jeffrey Siker (Louisville: Westminster/John Knox Press, 1994), 49–50, 52–53.

Chapter Four. Christian Virtue Ethics

1. Some Christian theologians and ethicists, such as John Wesley, have called these the quadrilateral sources of religious and moral authority.

2. For example, Protestant and Roman Catholic debates over the proper ordering of the authority and relationship between Scripture and Church teaching.

3. See: Søren Kierkegaard, *Works of Love*, translated by Howard V. Hong and Edna Hong (Princeton: Princeton University Press, 1995).

4. *Summa Theologica* (ST), I–II.4.5.

5. Ibid., I–II.3.2.

6. Ibid., I–II.62.

7. For example, members of the Religious Right have unapologetically claimed that American government is best run by Christian men (literally, Christians who are male). See Mel White, *Religion Gone Bad* (London: Jeremy P Tarcher/Penguin, 2006).

8. John McGreevy, *Catholicism and American Freedom* (New York and London: W. W. Norton, 2003), 91–126.

9. Ibid., 91.

10. Ibid., 92.

11. Mitt Romney. Extracted on Aug. 24, 2011, from http://www.thebostonchannel.com/r/14789305/detail.html.

12. Information extracted on May 28, 2012, from http://www.nomblog.com/wp-content/uploads/2011/08/Romney-Signed-Pledge.pdf.

13. Information extracted on May 28, 2012, from www.reuters.com/article/2012/05/08/us-usa-gaymarriage-poll-idUSBRE8471DW20120508.

14. ST I–II.5.5. and ST I–II.63.

15. Aquinas scholar Jean Porter says, "The natural end of human life, that is the attainment of specific perfection as a human being, is not rendered otiose or irrelevant by the fact that we are actually directed toward a supernatural end. The specific natural ideal of humanity remains the proximate norm of morality." *Recovery of Virtue*, 67.

16. See the entire *Summa Theologica*.

17. ST I–II.57.4.

18. ST I–II.58.1.

19. ST II–II.63.4.

20. Diana Cates, *Choosing to Feel*, 37–38.

21. Ibid.

22. ST II–II.141.4.

23. ST II–II.141.6. Aquinas calls the "need of life" the rule of temperance. To call the "need of life" a rule may mislead the reader. It is the rule, or exercise, of reason that properly cultivates virtue.

24. Ibid.

25. Ibid.

26. ST II–II.151.4.

27. Ibid.

28. John Giles Milhaven, "Thomas Aquinas on Sexual Pleasure," *The Journal of Religious Ethics* 5, no. 2 (1977): 157.

29. See Servais-Theodore Pinckaers, "The Sources of the Ethics of St. Thomas Aquinas," in *The Ethics of Aquinas*, edited by Stephen J. Pope (Washington, DC: Georgetown University Press, 2002).

30. Although the *Supplement* was constructed after Aquinas's death, most scholars agree that it is a compilation of the earlier scholarship of Aquinas. See, for example, Diana Cates, "The Virtue of Temperance," in *The Ethics of Aquinas*, edited by Stephen Pope (Washington, DC: Georgetown University Press, 2002), 331–32.

31. Richard McCarty, *An Ethical Analysis of Thomas Aquinas and the Virtue of Temperance: Revisiting Sexual Virtue* (Iowa City: The University of Iowa, 2008), 123–39.

32. Aquinas named this love charity; the practice of character friendship between moral equals. ST II–II.26 (especially, II–II.26).

33. ST I–II.94.2.

34. Diana Cates explains, "Thomas holds that each created being has within it certain ordering principles (or metaphysical causes). These principles determine the kind of being that the creature is, and these principles determine, accordingly, what it is for the creature to be a good specimen of its kind, to excel at being the particular creature that it is. . . . Thomas thinks it evident to reason that humans have been constituted in such a way that those who engage in sexual relations can do so humanly well in their relations only if they engage in them for the purpose of procreation. Intercourse for any reason other than the preservation of the human race reflects an impairment of natural human operations and a diminishment in the quality of life." "The Virtue of Temperance," 331.

35. ST II–II.154.1.

36. ST II–II.154.11.

37. ST II–II.154.1.

Chapter Five. Understanding Scripture

1. 2 Timothy 3:16 (from *The Inclusive Bible—The First Egalitarian Translation*).

2. From the prelude of the Book of Sirach. Apocryphal/Deuterocanonical Books, *New Revised Standard Version of the Bible* (NRSV).

3. For an accessible introduction to the Hebrew Bible see Michael Coogan, *The Old Testament* (New York and Oxford: Oxford University Press, 2006).

4. See Raymond Brown, *An Introduction to the New Testament* (New York: Doubleday, 1997), 3–15.

5. Bruce Shelley, *Church History in Plain Language* (Dallas: Word Publishing, 1995), 62–68.

6. See: *Biblia Hebraica Stuttgartensia* (1997), from the Deutsche Bibelge-sellschaft, and *The Greek New Testament*, 4th ed. United Bible Societies.

7. Gerard Sloyan, *Interpretation: John*, James Mays, Series Editor (Atlanta: John Knox Press, 1988), 95.

8. Bart Ehrman, *The Orthodox Corruption of Scripture* (New York and Oxford: Oxford University Press. 1993). For example, Acts 20:28 was changed from "the church of God, which he purchased with his own blood," to read "The church of the Lord, which he purchased with his own blood." It was changed so that Christians might not think that "God the Father" purchased the church with blood, but that Christ did. See also John 14:9, which distinguishes the Father and the Son as two persons, not one and the same (in order to refute modalism). Pp. 264–65.

9. For example, see Martin, *Sex and the Single Savior*.

10. See James Gustafson, *Ethics from a Theocentric Perspective*, vol. 1 and 2 (Chicago: University of Chicago Press, 1981).

11. I draw heavily in this section from my doctoral dissertation: "Sexual Virtue Revisited," in *An Ethical Analysis of Thomas Aquinas and the Virtue of Temperance: Sexual Virtue Re-Visited* (Iowa City: The University of Iowa. 2008), 177–214.

12. Ibid. But also Allen Verhey, "Scripture as Script and Scripted," in *Character Ethics and The New Testament; Moral Dimensions of Scripture*, edited by Robert L. Brawley (Louisville/London: Westminster/John Knox Press, 2007); and Dale Martin in *Sex and the Single Savior*.

13. Thomas Sheehan, "Historical Jesus," *Stanford Continuing Studies Program*. Creative Commons BY-NC-ND license. March 2007. (Available to the public without charge; available on iTunes.)

14. Mel White, *Religion Gone Bad* (New York: Tarcher/Penguin, 2006), xiii, xiv.

15. Brian McLaren, *Why Did Jesus, Moses, the Buddha, and Mohammed Cross the Road?* (New York: Jericho Books (eBook edition), 2012), 164.

16. Ibid., 169.

17. Ibid.

Chapter Six. Sex and Marriage

1. John Calvin, *Sermons on the Ten Commandments*, translated and edited by Benjamin Farley (Grand Rapids: Baker, 2000), 169–73, 178–80. And from *Sex, Marriage, and Family*, edited by Don S. Browning, M. Christian Green, and John Witte Jr. (New York: Columbia University Press, 2006), 132.

2. See John Calvin, *Commentary on Genesis*, Gen.38:8–10. (Baker's edition of Calvin's commentary deletes this line, oddly enough.)

3. John Calvin, *Institutes of the Christian Religion*, II.8.43–44.

4. See: John Witte and Eliza Ellison, eds. *Covenant Marriage in Comparative Perspective* (Grand Rapids: Eerdmans Press, 2005); Browning, Green, and Witte, eds., *Sex, Marriage, and Family in World Religions*; Kieran Scott and Michael Warren, eds., *Perspectives on Marriage* (New York: Oxford University Press, 2007); Ruether, *Christianity and the Making of the Modern Family*.

5. Raymond Lawrence, *Sexual Liberation* (Westport, CT: Praeger, 2007), 3.

6. Rachel Biale, "Sexuality and Marital Relations," in *Sexuality: A Reader*, edited by Karen Lebacqz (Cleveland: Pilgrim Press, 1999). According to traditional Judaism, God inspired the Oral Law in order to apply the written law. In its written form, the oral law is called Mishnah, with rabbinical commentary, Talmud.

7. See for example, Exodus 21:10 and Deuteronomy 21:15. Read also: Genesis 30:1–24.

8. Biale, "Sexuality and Marital Relations."

9. David Feldman, *Marital Relations, Birth Control, and Abortion in Jewish Law* (New York: Schocken, 1974), 46–59.

10. Michael Broyde, "The Covenant-Contract Dialectic in Jewish Marriage and Divorce Law," in *Covenant Marriage in Comparative Perspective*, edited by John Witte and Eliza Ellison (Grand Rapids: Eerdmans Press, 2005), 56.

11. Ibid., 57.

12. William Countryman, *Dirt, Greed, and Sex* (Philadelphia: Fortress Press, 1988), 147–67.

13. Broyde, "The Covenant-Contract Dialectic," 56.

14. Lawrence, *Sexual Liberation*, 4.

15. Luke 20:34–35 (NRSV); my emphasis.

16. Lawrence, *Sexual Liberation*, 5.

17. Matthew 19:3–9 (NRSV).

18. See the *Catechism of the Catholic Church* (Liguori, MO: Liguori Publications, 1994).

19. Many Christians are unfamiliar with the Dual Torah tradition in Judaism. According to Traditional Judaism, God gave not only the written Torah (Genesis-Deuteronomy) but also a set of instructions (the oral law) on how to interpret these laws. Jesus would have been familiar with both, and careful study of the gospels suggests that Jesus might have drawn on the idea of Oral Law in order to apply the Written Law in new ways (see for example, Matthew 5–7).

20. Although it should be noted that other biblical versions of this teaching do not contain the allowance of divorce for the sake of infidelity/adultery. In Mark 10:10–12, Jesus is *not* remembered as permitting divorce for adultery.

21. Countryman, *Dirt, Greed, and Sex*, 173–79.

22. See: Luke 14:25–27; Matthew 8:18–22; Matthew 10:34–39; Mark 3:31–35; Luke 20:34–36.

23. See Abraham Heschel, *The Prophets*, vol. 1 and 2 (New York: Harper Perennial Modern Classics, 2001).

24. See for example Zephaniah 1:2–18 and 3:8–13. In this text the prophet condemns the entire cosmos, but then offers words of restoration.

25. Luke 4:18–19.

26. Matthew 5:27–28.

27. Matthew 7:15–20.

28. Luke 11:37–41.

29. Lawrence, *Sexual Liberation*, 13.

30. Countryman, *Dirt, Greed, and Sex*, 263.

31. Ruether, *Christianity and the Making of the Modern Family*, 13–19.

32. Ibid.

33. Andrew Clarke, *First-Century Christians in the Graeco-Roman World—Serve the Community of the Church: Christians as Leaders and Ministers* (Grand Rapids: Eerdmans, 2000), 86.

34. Ruether, *Christianity and the Making of the Modern Family*, 13–19.

35. Clarke, *First-Century Christians*, 160.

36. Galatians 3:28. While Paul is discussing justification in this passage, the implications of justification speak to Christian ethics: how Christians regard each other in light of God's grace and impartiality.

37. Ruether, *Christianity and the Making of the Modern Family*, 13–19.

38. Luke 14:25–26.

39. Joyce Salisbury, *Perpetua's Passion: The Death and Memory of a Young Roman Woman* (New York: Routledge, 1997).

40. Ruether, *Christianity and the Making of the Modern Family*, 6.

41. Clarke, *First-Century Christians*, 79.

42. I Corinthians 11:2ff. In particular, as the father extends authority to the firstborn son in *pater familia*, so too God extends God's authority as "father" to Jesus as the "son." To the "father" and the "son" the rest of the "family" (the church) submits.

43. Ephesians 5:21–33.

44. James Brownson, *Bible, Gender, and Sexuality: Reframing the Church's Debate on Same-Sex Relationships* (Grand Rapids: Eerdmans, 2013), 79–80.

45. From the NRSV.

46. Martin, *Sex and the Single Savior*, 66.

47. Ibid., 67.

48. Brownson, *Bible, Gender, and Sexuality*, 129–40.

49. Ibid., 150–61, 163–65, 169, 179–80.

50. Ibid., 164.

51. Luke Timothy Johnson and Mark Jordan, "Christianity," in *Sex, Marriage, and Family in World Religions*, edited by Don Browning, M. Christian Green, and John Witte Jr. (New York: Columbia University Press, 2006), 82–83.

52. Ibid., 83.

53. Ibid., 82.

54. See Robert H. Von Thaden Jr., *Sex, Christ, and Embodied Cognition: Paul's Wisdom for Corinth*. Emory Studies in Early Christianity (16). Blandford Forum, UK: 2012.

Chapter Seven. The Bible and Homosexuality

1. Cardinal Ratzinger (now Pope Emeritus Benedict XVI) wrote in his *Letter to the Bishops of the Catholic Church on the Pastoral Care of Homosexual Persons* (1986), "Although the particular inclination of the homosexual person is not a sin, it is more or less strong tendency ordered toward an intrinsic moral evil; and thus the inclination itself must be seen as an objective disorder."

2. "For a sin to be mortal, three conditions must together be met: 'Mortal sin is sin whose object is grave matter and which is also committed with full knowledge and deliberate consent." *Catechism of the Catholic Church*, 45.

3. Cheng, *From Sin to Amazing Grace*, 41–43.

4. Ibid., 17.

5. Genesis 2:23 (NRSV).

6. Genesis 2:24 (NRSV).

7. Richard Hays, "Awaiting the Redemption of our Bodies," in *Homosexuality in the Church: Both Sides of the Debate*, edited by Jeffrey S. Siker (Louisville: Westminster/John Knox Press, 1994), 10.

8. Ibid.

9. *Catechism of the Catholic Church*, 560.

10. Salzman and Lawler, *The Sexual Person*, 127.

11. Ibid.

12. Jim Hill and Rand Cheadle, *The Bible Tells Me So: Uses and Abuses of Holy Scripture* (New York: Anchor Books/Doubleday, 1996), 10.

13. Brownson, *Bible, Gender, and Sexuality*, 88.

14. See chapter 2.

15. See chapter 6.

16. Recall that traditional Judaism did interpret a mandate to reproduce from the Genesis 1 and 2 passages, but they also believed that the reproduction of two children satisfied that requirement (see the previous chapter on Jewish marital practices).

17. In Hebrew, the world *angel* simply means "messenger," and therefore can be a human or a divine being.

18. Genesis 19:9 (NRSV).

19. There are, of course, some conservative biblical scholars and theologians who interpret the story of Sodom and Gomorrah as a "proof-text" against same-sex relationships. Cardinal Joseph Ratzinger (Pope Benedict XVI) is among them. But the reader may wish to compare their teachings on Genesis 19 with that of Richard Hays who, as a conservative evangelical and biblical scholar, argues the text is indeed about rape.

20. Judges 19:24 (*The Inclusive Bible: The First Egalitarian Translation*).

21. Judges 19:25 (TIB).

22. Phyllis Trible, *Texts of Terror: Literary-Feminist Readings of Biblical Narratives* (Minneapolis: Fortress Press, 1984).

23. Murray and Roscoe give a compelling description of the social shame men faced throughout the Ancient Near East, especially those who were known

to have been penetrated. See *Islamic Homosexualities: Culture, History, and Literature* (New York: New York University Press, 1997), 14–54.

24. See E. E. Pritchard, *Ancient Near Eastern Texts* (Princeton: Princeton University Press, 1969).

25. Extracted June 19, 2011, from http://www.hrw.org/en/news/2007/12/15/us-federal-statistics-show-widespread-prison-rape.

26. Carter Heyward, "Notes on Historical Grounding: Beyond Sexual Essentialism," in *Sexuality and the Sacred*, edited by James Nelson and Sandra Longfellow (Louisville and London: John Knox Press, 1994), 14; my emphasis.

27. Ezekiel 16:49–50.

28. http://www.hawaii.edu/hivandaids/Heterosexual_Anal_Intercourse__An_Understudied,_High-Risk_Sexual_Behavior.pdf.

29. See Leviticus 11–12 for a wide variety of examples of those things that are "detestable" and "abominations."

30. Countryman, *Dirt, Greed, and Sex*, 20–44.

31. Many Jewish scholars count the number of laws in the Torah as 613. This does not include rulings in the Oral Law (Halakah), which give explication to the written law; explaining how these laws ought to be lived out and the variety of ways in which that is possible.

32. According to traditional Judaism, the oral law was given to Moses by God, and shows Jewish people what it means to live according to the written law.

33. See Biale, "Sexuality and Marital Relations."

34. Traditional/Orthodox Jews still follow the holiness/purity codes today.

35. See Jewish theologian Yoel Kahn in his work, "Making Love as Making Justice," op. cit.

36. See: Leviticus 18:6–18. To date, twenty-five American states prohibit cousin marriage. And yet, there are more states that allow for first cousin marriage in the United States than there are (currently) states that allow for same-sex marriage.

37. Genesis 20:12.

38. Exodus 21:7–11 and Deuteronomy 20:15.

39. Countryman, *Dirt, Greed, and Sex*, 35–39.

40. For a brief review on same-sex relations in the Greco-Roman world, see Crompton, *Homosexuality and Civilization*, 1–31.

41. Ibid.

42. Plato. *Symposium*, edited by Alexander Nehamas and Paul Woodruff (Indianapolis and Cambridge: Hackett, 1989), 27.

43. Matthew 8:10.

44. Nancy Wilson, *Our Tribe: Queer Folks, God, Jesus, and the Bible* (San Francisco: HarperSanFrancisco, 1995).

45. For more discussion on this passage, see K. J. Dover, *Greek Homosexuality* (Cambridge: Harvard University Press, 1989); and Cheng, *From Sin to Amazing Grace*.

46. NRSV; my emphasis.

47. For example, see Myers and Scanzoni, *What God Has Joined Together?*, 96.

48. Waun, *More than Welcome*, esp. 3–90.

49. See the *American Psychological Association*.

50. Richard Hays, "Awaiting the Redemption of Our Bodies," in *Homosexuality in the Church: Both Sides of the Debate*, edited by Jeffrey S. Siker (Louisville: Westminster/John Knox Press, 1994), 7.

51. Martin, *Sex and the Single Savior*, 38.

52. Ibid.

53. Ibid., 38–39.

54. Ibid., 39.

55. Ibid., 41.

56. Ibid., 43.

57. Ibid., 43–47.

58. Jennifer Wright Knust, *Abandoned to Lust: Sexual Slander and Ancient Christianity* (New York: Columbia University Press, 2006), esp. chapters 1 and 2.

59. Romans 1:26–27, NRSV.

60. Knust, *Abandoned to Lust*, 6, 20.

61. Jack Rogers, *Jesus, The Bible, and Homosexuality* (Louisville: Westminster/John Knox Press, 2006), 77.

62. Conservative biblical scholar Richard Hays and progressive biblical scholar Dale Martin agree on at least this much.

63. Crompton, *Homosexuality and Civilization*, 1–110.

64. Brownson, *Bible, Gender, and Sexuality*, 157.

65. Jonathan Dudley, "My Take: Bible condemns a lot, so why focus on homosexuality?" Extracted from CNN.com June 30, 2011, at: http://religion.blogs.cnn.com/2011/06/21/my-take-bible-condemns-a-lot-so-why-focus-on-homosexuality/?iref=allsearch.

66. Ibid.

67. Ibid.

68. See chapter 2.

69. See the previous chapter.

Chapter Eight. Curious Interpretations of Nature

1. See chapter 4.

2. Jordan, *The Ethics of Sex*, 78.

3. Ibid., 78–79.

4. For example, see Mark Driscoll, *Real Marriage: The Truth About Sex, Friendship, and Life Together* (Nashville: Thomas Nelson, 2012).

5. Daniel Nelson, *The Priority of Prudence* (University Park: The Pennsylvania State University Press, 1992), 4–6. See also Jean Porter, *Natural and Divine Law* (Grand Rapids: Eerdmans, 2005), 66–75.

6. James Luther Adams, "The Law of Nature in Greco-Roman thought," *The Journal of Religion* 25, no. 2 (1945): 100.

7. Ibid.

8. See for example Jean Porter, *Nature as Reason* (Grand Rapids: Eerdmans, 2005).

9. The apostle Paul demonstrates familiarity with Greco-Roman philosophical thought (Acts 17:16–34); the second-century apologist Justin Martyr was well known for his sense that Greek philosophy prepared him for receiving the Gospel; later scholastic theologians (such as Aquinas) would incorporate Greek philosophy into their moral theologies. Additionally, Martha Nussbaum has argued that Protestantism owes much to Stoic philosophy.

10. See for example, the Gospel of John 1:1–14.

11. Porter, *Nature as Reason*, 8–14.

12. Boswell, *Christianity, Social Tolerance, and Homosexuality*, 318.

13. Ibid.

14. Ibid., 322.

15. Ibid.

16. Ibid., 328.

17. Ibid., 329.

18. Salzman and Lawler, *The Sexual Person*.

19. With respect to evolution, the religious ethicist Jean Porter responds to the evolutionary critique of natural law in her text *Nature as Reason*. She says, "The claim that species and higher taxa have real existence implies that recognizable kinds of creatures exhibit intelligible similarities, and relate to one another in orderly ways. . . . If this is so, then the diverse kinds of living creatures are not just a set of random groups—they constitute an ordered set of natural kinds. And it is difficult to see how this ordering can be entirely the result of random chance. Nor need this conclusion imply that the process is being directed 'from above,' so to speak, by God or by some other external agency. Rather, it implies that the order reflected in living creatures reflects causal forces intrinsic to the creatures themselves which operate in directed and intelligible ways" (97).

20. Salzman and Lawler, *The Sexual Person*, 93.

21. See Nelson, *The Priority of Prudence*.

22. *Catechism of the Catholic Church*, § 2332–35.

23. See chapter 2.

24. For example, Protestants who do not draw on natural law as a religious authority still turn to the Bible in order to speculate on sexual nature, before and after the "fall" of humankind into sin. (I bracket the concept of the "fall" in quotations, as there is no agreement in Christianity on this doctrine, and it is absent in Judaism.)

25. Nelson, *Embodiment*, 52.

26. Ibid., 55; see also the introduction.

27. See chapter 1.

28. "St. Ambrose," *Catholic Encyclopedia*. Extracted July 16, 2012, from http://www.newadvent.org/cathen/01383c.htm.

29. Nelson, *Embodiment*, 52.

30. Ibid.

31. James Turner Johnson, "Marriage as Covenant in Early Protestant Thought," in *Covenant Marriage in Comparative Perspective*, edited by John Witte Jr. and Eliza Ellison (Grand Rapids: Eerdmans, 2005), 127.

32. Nelson, *Embodiment*, 55.

33. Extracted July 16, 2012, from: https://www.rca.org/SSLPage.aspx?pid=501.

34. The American Psychological Association notes that "lesbian, gay, and bisexual orientations are not disorders. Research has found no inherent association between any of these sexual orientations and psychopathology. Both heterosexual behavior and homosexual behavior are normal aspects of human sexuality." Extracted July 17, 2012, from: http://www.apa.org/helpcenter/sexual-orientation.aspx.

35. Ibid.

36. https://www.rca.org/SSLPage.aspx?pid=501.

37. *Human Sexuality: Gift and Trust* (February 19, 2009). Extracted July 16, 2012, from: http://www.elca.org/What-We-Believe/Social-Issues/Social-Statements/JTF-Human-Sexuality.

38. Ibid.

39. Ibid.

40. See: the American Psychological Association on homosexuality: http://www.apa.org/helpcenter/sexual-orientation.aspx.

41. C. J. Wysocki and Y. Martins et al., "Preference for Human Body Odors Is Influenced by Gender and Sexual Orientation," *Psychological Science* 16, no. 9 (2005): 694–701.

42. Rowland Miller, *Intimate Relationships*, 6th ed. (New York: McGraw-Hill, 2012), 70–71.

43. Ibid., 77–84.

44. While there have been proposed changes in the fifth edition of the *DSM* (*Diagnostic and Statistical Manual on Mental Disorder*) about pedophilia, these have largely sought to clarify the difference between active and nonactive pedophiles, as well as their treatment by specialists. These changes in the *DSM* have not reversed the conclusion that an adult who engages in sex with children does, in fact, harm those children.

45. Ryan and Cacilda, *Sex at Dawn*, 85.

46. Ibid., 94.

47. Ibid., 236.

48. Ibid.

49. Ibid., 255–68.

50. Daniel Siegel, *The Developing Mind: How Relationships and the Brain Interact to Shape Who We Are* (New York: Mind Your Brain, 2012).

51. Ibid., 280–312.

52. Christian/fundamentalist teachings on dinosaur bones as a "test of faith" can be found, for example, at: http://www.antievolution.org/cgi-bin/ikonboard/ikonboard.cgi?act=ST;f=2;t=5004;st=0.

53. On STD demons, see Amy DeRogatis, "Born Again Is a Sexual Term: Demons, STDs, and God's Healing Sperm," *Journal of the American Academy of Religion* 77, no. 2 (2009): 275–302.

Chapter Nine. Church Teachings Revisited

1. The Roman Catholic Church allows for "natural family planning" (NFP, or the "rhythm method, according to ovulation cycles)—however, such is still considered "open" to procreation.

2. See The Presbyterian Church (USA) and the Evangelical Lutheran Church in America.

3. Diana Butler Bass, *Christianity After Religion: The End of Church and the Birth of a New Spiritual Awakening* (New York: HarperCollins, 2012), 47; my emphasis.

4. Roger Finke and Rodney Stark, *The Churching of America, 1776–1990: Winners and Losers in our Religious Economy* (New Brunswick: Rutgers University Press, 1992), 235–75.

5. See: http://www.pewforum.org/Unaffiliated/nones-on-the-rise.aspx.

6. Elizabeth Drescher, "None Means None (Not Atheist, Agnostic, Unbeliever . . .), *Religion Dispatches*, January 8, 2013. Accessed from http://www.religiondispatches.org/archive/atheologies/6749/none_means_none__not_atheist__agnostic__unbeliever_.

7. Bass, *Christianity After Religion*, 103–98; my emphasis.

8. Ibid., 68.

9. Fran Ferder and John Heagle, "Tender Fires: The Spiritual Promise of Sexuality," in *Human Sexuality in the Catholic Tradition* (Lanham and Boulder: Rowman and Littlefield, 2007), 23.

10. Waun, *More than Welcome*, 91–92.

11. Bass, *Christianity After Religion*, 113–14.

12. In some churches, rejecting ideas about sexual morality is, in effect, "accepting sin" and rejecting "God's will."

13. http://pewresearch.org/assets/pdf/gun-control-2011.pdf.

14. http://pewresearch.org/pubs/1755/poll-gay-marriage-gains-acceptance-gays-in-the-military.

15. John Barrett, Faith Adams Johnson, and Judith Frediani, eds., *Sexuality and Our Faith: A Companion to Our Whole Lives* (Boston: Unitarian Universalist Association and United Church Board for Homeland Ministries, 2000), 50.

16. Ibid.

17. Bass, *Christianity After Religion*, 115–16.

18. Romans 7:21–25 (NRSV).

19. Waun, *More than Welcome*, 95–96.

20. See Nussbaum, *Sex and Social Justice*.

21. James Tunstead Burtchaell, "Community Experience as a Source of Christian Ethics," in *From Christ to the World: Introductory Readings in Christian Ethics*, edited by Wayne Boulton, Thomas Kennedy, and Allen Verhey (Grand Rapids: Eerdmans, 1994), 65.

22. Ibid.

Chapter Ten. Recreational Sex

1. Heyward, "Notes on Historical Grounding," 9–16.

2. Dossie Easton and Janet Hardy, *The Ethical Slut*, 2nd ed. (Berkeley: Celestial Arts, 2009), 12.

3. Anthony G. Greenwald and Mahzarin R. Banaji, "Implicit Social Cognition: Attitudes, Self-Esteem, and Stereotypes," *Psychological Review* 102, no. 1 (1995): 4–27.

4. *Catechism of the Catholic Church*, 564.

5. Ibid., 546–66.

6. DeRogatis, "Born Again Is a Sexual Term": 275–302.

7. J. R. Kelly, M. W. Steinkamp, and J. R. Kelly, "Later-Life Satisfaction: Does Leisure Contribute?" *Leisure Sciences* 9 (1987): 189–200.

8. C. Gordon, C. M. Gaitz, and J. Scott, "Leisure and Lives: Personal Expressivity across the Life Span," in *Handbook of Aging and the Social Sciences*, edited by R. H. Binstock and E. Shanas (New York: Van Nostrand Reinhold, 1976), 310–41. Accessed from Robert V. Kail and John C. Cavanaugh, *Human Development* (Pacific Grove: Brooks/Cole, 1996), 400.

9. Lyubomirksy, King, and Diener. "The Benefits of Frequent Positive Affect. Does Happiness Lead to Success?" *Psychological Bulletin* 131, no. 6 (2005): 803.

10. Rex Skidmore, "The Protestant Church and Recreation—An Example of Social Change," *Social Forces* 20, no. 3 (1942): 364.

11. H. B. Rodgers, "The Demand for Recreation," *The Geographical Journal* 139, no. 3 (1973): 467.

12. Skidmore, "The Protestant Church and Recreation": 364.

13. Ibid., 365.

14. Lyubomirksy, King, and Diener, "The Benefits of Frequent Positive Affect": 803.

15. Ibid., 808, 811, 829, 835.

16. Ibid., 808, 811, 829.

17. Farley, *Just Love*, 216.

18. Ibid., 217.

19. Ibid., 218.

20. Ibid., 220.

21. Ibid., 223.

22. Ibid.

23. For example, see: http://www.truthwinsout.org/blog/2012/06/26605/.

24. Farley, *Just Love*, 223.

25. Ibid., 225.

26. Heyward, *Touching Our Strength*, 110.

27. Ibid.

28. Ibid., 112.

29. Ibid., 128.

30. Gene Outka, *Agape* (London: Yale University Press, 1977).

31. Farley, *Just Love*, 226–28.

32. For example: Matthew 5:43–48.

33. Easton and Hardy, *The Ethical Slut*.

34. Ibid., 78.

35. Ibid., 78, 79.

36. Cheng, *From Sin to Amazing Grace*, 73.

37. Richard Wasserstrom, "Is Adultery Immoral," in *Analyzing Moral Issues*, 5th ed., edited by Judith Boss (McGraw-Hill, 2010), 373. Reprinted from *Today's Moral Problems* (1975).

38. Ibid.

39. Gurdorf, *Body, Sex, and Pleasure*, 210.

40. Matthew 22:37–40.

41. Galatians 5:22–23 (NRSV).

42. Ibid.

Chapter Eleven. Relational Intimacy

1. Miller, *Intimate Relationships*, 280–82.

2. Ibid., 273–304.

3. *Geddes and Garner v. State of Texas*, 15, 16.

4. *Vatican Council II*, Vol. 2. (New Revised Edition), Section 7: The Synod of Bishops on "the Christian Family," Austin Flannery, O.P., general ed. (Northport, NY: Costello, 1988), 840–41.

5. For example, even the *Catechism of the Catholic Church* draws on psychological data for talking about emotional and sexual intimacy (see: "The Sixth Commandment"); as does the Evangelical Lutheran Church in America, in their document, *Sexuality: Gift and Trust* (9–10).

6. Moss and Schwebel, "Marriage and Romantic Relationships": 42.

7. Ibid., 33.

8. Ibid.

9. Ibid.

10. Ibid.

11. Ibid.

12. Ibid.

13. I draw extensively in the following analysis on relational intimacy from "Sexual Virtue Revisited," 177–214.

14. See: McKinney, K. and Sprecher, S. eds. *Sexuality in Close Relationships* (Hillsdale, NJ: Erlbuam, 1991).

15. For a review of the evidence see the following studies: A. Aron and L. Henkemeyer, "Marital Satisfaction and Passionate Love," *Journal of Social and Personal Relationships* 12 (1995): 139–46; N. K. Grote and I. H. Frieze, "Remembrance of Things Past: Perceptions of Marital Love from its Beginning to Present," *Journal of Social and Personal Relationships* 15 (1998): 91–109; P. J. Marston, M. L. Hecht, M. L. Manke, S. McDaniel, and H. Reeder, "The Subjective Experience of Intimacy, Passion, and Commitment in Heterosexual Loving Relationships," *Personal Relationships* 5 (1998): 15–30; S. Sprecher and P. C. Regan, "Passionate and Compassionate Love in Courting and Young Married Couples," *Sociological Inquiry* 68 (1998): 163–85; D. H. Henderson-King and J. Veroff, "Sexual Satisfaction and Marital Well-Being in the First Years of Marriages," *Journal of Social and Personal Relationships* 11 (1994): 509–34; L.A. Kurdek, "Sexuality in Homosexual and Heterosexual Couples," in *Sexuality in Close Relationships*, edited by McKinney and Sprecher (Hillsdale, NJ: Erlabum, 1991), 177–91.

16. Firestone, Firestone, and Catlett, *Sex and Love in Intimate Relationships*.

17. Ibid., 17, 18.

18. McCarty, "Sexual Virtue Revisited," 177–214.

19. Ibid.

20. However, in a 2010 statement by Benedict XVI, the pontiff opened the door for the use of condoms as an aid against transmitting HIV. Even so, this allowance in no way condones the use of condoms for birth control. See chapter 12.

21. McCarty, "Sexual Virtue Revisited," 177–214.

22. Ibid.

23. Kahn, "Making Love as Making Justice," 584.

24. McCarty, "Sexual Virtue Revisited," 177–214.

25. Ibid.

26. Ibid.

Chapter Twelve. Selective Acts of Procreation

1. Genesis 1:31.

2. Paul VI, *Humanae vitae*,§ 13.

3. "Nuns on the Bus Meet Tea Party Protests in Ohio," *Huffington Post*, October 17, 2012. Accessed July 11, 2013, at: http://www.huffingtonpost.com/2012/10/17/nuns-on-the-bus-tea-party-protests-ohio_n_1973766.html.

4. McCarty, "Sexual Virtue Revisited," 177–214.

5. See again: Farley, *Just Love*, 207–70.

6. See, for examples, Harold Coward, "New Theology on Population, Consumption, and Ecology," *Journal of the American Academy of Religion* 65, no. 2 (1997): 259–73; Daniel Callahan, "Ethics and Population Limits," *Science* 175.4021 (1972): 487–94.

7. McCarty, "Sexual Virtue Revisited," 177–214.

8. Extracted August 10, 2010, from: http://www.who.int/child-adolescent-health/OVERVIEW/CHILD_HEALTH/map_00-03_world.jpg.

9. Ibid.

10. Ibid.

11. Extracted August 10, 2010, from http://www.cathnews.com/news/310/53.php.

12. See Benedict's interview in Peter Seewald's *Light of the World* (Ignatius Press, 2010).

13. For example, Phyllis Zagano, "It's Not Just About Male Prostitutes," *Natural Catholic Reporter*, November 24, 2010.

14. McCarty, "Sexual Virtue Revisited," 177–214.

15. Ibid.

16. Ibid.

17. See also Firestone, Firestone, and Catlett, *Sex and Love in Intimate Relationships*.

18. *Song of Solomon* 5:2, 4, 5 (NRSV).

19. Phyllis Trible, "Love's Lyrics Redeemed," in *A Feminist Companion to the Song of Songs*, edited by Athalya Brenner (Sheffield, UK: Sheffield Academic Press, 1993), 100–120.

20. Biale, "Sexuality and Marital Relations"; see also David Novak, "Some Aspects of Sex, Society, and God in Judaism," in *Contemporary Jewish Ethics and Morality*, edited by Elliot Dorff and Louis E. Newman (Oxford and New York: Oxford University Press, 1995).

21. McCarty, "Sexual Virtue Revisited," 177–214.

Conclusion

1. See: http://www.independent.co.uk/news/world/europe/cardinal-carlo-maria-martini-his-final-interview-and-a-damning-critique-that-has-rocked-the--catholic-church-8101498.html.

2. See: http://politics.blogs.foxnews.com/2012/08/31/koch-brother-breaks-gop-supports-gay-marriage.

Bibliography

Adams, James Luther. "The Law of Nature in Greco-Roman thought," *The Journal of Religion* 25, no. 2 (1945).

Aquinas, Thomas. *Summa Theologica*. Translated by Fathers of the English Dominican Province. Notre Dame, IN: Christian Classics/Ave Maria Press, 1981.

Aristotle. *Nicomachean Ethics*. Translated by Terence Irwin. Indianapolis and Cambridge: Hackett, 1999.

Barrett, John, Faith Adams Johnson, and Judith Frediani, eds. *Sexuality and Our Faith: A Companion to Our Whole Lives*. Boston: Unitarian Universalist Association and United Church Board for Homeland Ministries, 2000.

Bass, Diana Butler. *Christianity After Religion: The End of Church and the Birth of a New Spiritual Awakening*. New York: HarperCollins, 2012.

Belliotti, Raymond. *Good Sex: Perspectives on Sexual Ethics*. Lawrence: University Press of Kansas, 1993.

Biale, Rachel. "Sexuality and Marital Relations." In *Sexuality: A Reader*, edited by Karen Lebacqz. Cleveland: Pilgrim Press, 1999.

Boss, Judith. *Analyzing Moral Issues*. 5th Ed. New York: McGraw-Hill, 2010.

Boswell, John. *Christianity, Social Tolerance, and Homosexuality*. Chicago and London: University of Chicago Press, 1980.

Bouvier, Leon. "Catholics and Contraception." *Journal of Marriage and Family* 34, no. 3 (1972): 514–22.

Brown, Raymond E. *An Introduction to the New Testament*. New York and London: Doubleday, 1997.

Browning, Don S., M. Christian Green, and John Witte Jr., eds. *Sex, Marriage, and Family*. New York: Columbia University Press, 2006.

Brownson, James. *Bible, Gender, and Sexuality: Reframing the Church's Debate on Same-Sex Relationships*. Grand Rapids,: Eerdmans, 2013.

Burtchaell, James Tunstead. "Community Experience as a Source of Christian Ethics." In *From Christ to the World: Introductory Readings in Christian Ethics*, edited by Wayne Boulton, Thomas Kennedy, and Allen Verhey. Grand Rapids: Eerdmans, 1994.

Butterworth, Charles. "Medieval Islamic Philosophy and the Virtue of Ethics." *Arabica* 34, no. 2 (1987): 221–50.

Cahill, Lisa Sowle. *Sex, Gender, and Christian Ethics*. Cambridge: Cambridge University Press, 1996.

Calvin, John. *Sermons on the Ten Commandments*. Translated and edited by Benjamin Farley. Grand Rapids: Baker, 2000.

Catechism of the Catholic Church. Liguori, MO: Liguori Publications, 1994.

Cates, Diana. *Aquinas on the Emotions*. Washington, DC: Georgetown University Press, 2009.

———. *Choosing to Feel*. South Bend: The University of Notre Dame Press, 1996.

———. "The Virtue of Temperance." In *The Ethics of Aquinas*, edited by Stephen Pope. Washington, DC: Georgetown University Press, 2002.

Cheng, Patrick. *From Sin to Amazing Grace*. New York: Seabury Books, 2012.

———. *Radical Love: An Introduction to Queer Theology*. New York: Seabury Books, 2011.

Clark, Elizabeth. *St. Augustine on Marriage and Sexuality*. Washington, DC: The Catholic University of America Press, 1996.

Clarke, Andrew. *First-Century Christians in the Graeco-Roman World—Serve the Community of the Church: Christians as Leaders and Ministers*. Grand Rapids: Eerdmans, 2000.

Coogan, Michael. *The Old Testament*. New York and Oxford: Oxford University Press, 2006.

Countryman, William. *Dirt, Greed, and Sex*. Philadelphia: Fortress Press, 1988.

Coward, Harold. "New Theology on Population, Consumption, and Ecology." *Journal of the American Academy of Religion* 65, no. 2 (1997): 259–73.

Creech, Jimmy. *Adam's Gift: A Memoir of a Pastor's Calling to Defy the Church's Persecution of Lesbians and Gays*. Durham and London: Duke University Press, 2011.

Crompton, Louis. *Homosexuality and Civilization*. Cambridge: The Belknap Press of Harvard University Press, 2003.

Cunningham, David. *Christian Ethics: The End of the Law*. London and New York: Routledge, 2008.

DeRogatis, Amy. "Born Again Is a Sexual Term: Demons, STDs, and God's Healing Sperm." *Journal of the American Academy of Religion* 77, no. 2 (2009): 275–302.

Driscoll, Mark. *Real Marriage: The Truth About Sex, Friendship, and Life Together*. Nashville: Thomas Nelson, 2012.

Easton, Dossie, and Janet Hardy. *The Ethical Slut*. 2nd Ed. Berkeley: Celestial Arts, 2009.

Ehrman, Bart. *The Orthodox Corruption of Scripture*. New York and Oxford: Oxford University Press. 1993.

Feldman, David. *Marital Relations, Birth Control, and Abortion in Jewish Law*. New York: Schocken, 1974.

Ferder, Fran, and John Heagle. "Tender Fires: The Spiritual Promise of Sexuality" In *Human Sexuality in the Catholic Tradition*. Lanham and Boulder: Rowman and Littlefiled, 2007.

Finke, Roger, and Rodney Stark. *The Churching of America, 1776–1990: Winners and Losers in our Religious Economy*. New Brunswick: Rutgers University Press, 1992.

Firestone, Robert, Lisa Firestone, and Joyce Catlett, eds. *Sex and Love: In Intimate Relationships*. Washington, DC: American Psychological Association, 2005.

Freud, Sigmund. *The Future of Illusion*. Translated and edited by James Strachey. New York/London: W. W. Norton, 1961.

Greenwald, Anthony G., and Mahzarin R. Banaji. "Implicit Social Cognition: Attitudes, Self-Esteem, and Stereotypes." *Psychological Review* 102, no. 1 (1995): 4–27.

Gustafson, James. *Ethics from a Theocentric Perspective*. Volumes 1 and 2. Chicago: University of Chicago Press, 1981.

Hamer, Richard. "Genetics and Male Sexual Orientation." *Science* 285, no. 5429 (1999).

Hancock, Philip, and Melissa Tyler. *Work, Postmodernism, and Organization: A Critical Introduction*. London and Thousand Oaks, CA: Sage, 2001.

Harrison, Beverly Wildung. "Sexuality and Social Policy." In *Sexuality and the Sacred*, edited by James Nelson and Sandra Longfellow. Louisville and London, Westminster/John Knox Press, 1994.

Herman, Didi. "(Il)legitimate Minorities: The American Christian Right's Anti-Gay-Rights Discourse." *Journal of Law and Society* 23, no. 3 (1996): 346–63.

Heschel, Abraham. *The Prophets*. Vol. 1 and 2. New York: Harper Perennial Modern Classics, 2001.

Heyward, Carter. *Touching Our Strength: The Erotic as Power and the Love of God*. New York: Harper and Row, 1989.

Farley, Margaret. *Just Love: A Framework for Christian Sexual Ethics*. New York: Continuum. 2006.

———. "Sexual Ethics." In *Sexuality and the Sacred*, edited by James Nelson and Sandra Longfellow. Louisville and London: Westminster/John Knox Press, 1994.

Fitterer, Robert. *Love and Objectivity in Virtue Ethics*. Toronto: University of Toronto Press, 2008.

Fone, Byrne. *Homophobia: A History*. New York: Picador/Pan Books, 2000.

Freeman, Jo. *The Politics of Women's Liberation*. Lincoln, NE: iUniverse.com, Inc., 1975, 2000.

Goss, Robert. *Queering Christ: Beyond Jesus Acted Up*. Cleveland: Pilgrim Press, 2002.

Gudorf, Christine. *Body, Sex, and Pleasure: Reconstructing Christian Sexual Ethics*. Cleveland: Pilgrim Press, 1994.

Hays, Richard. "Awaiting the Redemption of Our Bodies." In *Homosexuality in the Church: Both Sides of the Debate*, edited by Jeffrey S. Siker. Louisville: Westminster/John Knox Press, 1994.

Hill, Jim, and Rand Cheadle. *The Bible Tells Me So: Uses and Abuses of Holy Scripture*. New York: Anchor Books/Doubleday, 1996.

Jordan, Mark. *The Ethics of Sex*. Malden, MA: Blackwell, 2002.

———. *Recruiting Young Love*. Chicago: University of Chicago Press, 2011.

———. *The Silence of Sodom*. Chicago: University of Chicago Press, 2000.

Jung, Patricia, and Aana Marie Vigen, eds. *God, Science, Sex, Gender: An Interdisciplinary Approach to Christian Ethics*. Chicago: University of Illinois Press, 2010.

Kahn, Yoel. "Making Love as Making Justice." In *Sexuality*, edited by Karen Lebascqz. Cleveland: Pilgrim Press, 1999.

Kent, Bonnie. "Habits and Virtues." In *The Ethics of Aquinas*, edited by Stephen Pope. Washington, DC: Georgetown University Press, 2002.

Kierkegaard, Søren. *Works of Love*. Translated by Howard V. Hong and Edna Hong. Princeton: Princeton University Press, 1995.

Knust, Jennifer Wright. *Abandoned to Lust: Sexual Slander and Ancient Christianity*. New York: Columbia University Press, 2006.

Krudek, L. A. "Sexuality in Homosexual and Heterosexual Couples." In *Sexuality in Close Relationships*, edited by McKinney and Sprecher. Hillsdale, NJ. Erlbaum, 1991.

Langdridge, Darren, and Meg Barker, eds. *Safe, Sane, and Consensual: Contemporary Perspectives on Sadomasochism*. Houndmills, Basingstoke, Hampshire: Palgrave Macmillan, 2008.

Lawrence, Ryamond. *Sexual Liberation*. Westport, CT: Praeger, 2007.

Lester, Andrew. *The Angry Christian*. Louisville and London: Westminster/John Knox Press, 2003.

Lyubomirksy, King, and Diener. "The Benefits of Frequent Positive Affect. Does Happiness Lead to Success?" *Psychological Bulletin* 131, no. 6 (2005): 803–55.

Maimonides (Moses ben Maimon). *Ethical Writings of Maimonides*. Edited by Raymond L. Weiss and Charles Butterworth. New York: Dover, 1975.

Mann, Susan Archer, and Douglas Huffman. "The Decentering of Second Wave Feminism and the Rise of the Third Wave." *Science & Society* 69, no. 1 (2005): 56–91.

Martin, Dale. *Sex and the Single Savior: Gender and Sexuality in Biblical Interpretation*. Louisville: Westminster/John Knox Press, 2006.

McCarty, Richard. *An Ethical Analysis of Thomas Aquinas and the Virtue of Temperance: Revisiting Sexual Virtue*. Iowa City: The University of Iowa, 2008.

McGreevy, John. *Catholicism and American Freedom*. New York and London: W.W. Norton, 2003.

McKinney, K., and S. Sprecher, eds. *Sexuality in Close Relationships*. Hillsdale, NJ: Erlbuam, 1991.

McLaren, Brian. *Why Did Jesus, Moses, the Buddha, and Mohammed Cross the Road?* New York: Jericho Books, 2012.

McNeill, John. "Homosexuality: Challenging the Church to Grow" In *Homosexuality in the Church: Both Sides of the Debate*, edited by Jeffrey Siker. Louisville: Westminster/John Knox Press, 1994.

Milhaven, John Giles. "Thomas Aquinas on Sexual Pleasure." *The Journal of Religious Ethics* 5, no. 2. (1977).

Miller, Rowland. *Intimate Relationships*. 6th ed. New York: McGraw-Hill, 2012.

Moss, Barry, and Andrew Schwebel. "Marriage and Romantic Relationships: Defining Intimacy in Romantic Relationships." *Family Relations* 42 (1993).

Myers, David, and Letha Dawson Scanzoni. *What God Has Joined Together?* San Francisco: HarperSanFrancisco, 2005.

Nelson, Daniel. *The Priority of Prudence*. University Park: The Pennsylvania State University Press, 1992.

Nelson, James. *Embodiment*. Minneapolis: Augsburg Press, 1978.

Novak, David. "Some Aspects of Sex, Society, and God in Judaism." In *Contemporary Jewish Ethics and Morality*, edited by Elliot Dorff and Louis E. Newman. Oxford and New York: Oxford University Press, 1995.

Nussbaum, Martha. *Liberty of Conscience*. New York: Basic Books, 2008.

———. *Sex and Social Justice*. Oxford and New York: Oxford University Press, 1999.

Outka, Gene. *Agape*. London: Yale University Press, 1977.

Paul VI. Encyclical Letter: *Humanae vitae*. July 25, 1968.

Pinckaers, Servais-Theodore. "The Sources of the Ethics of St. Thomas Aquinas." In *The Ethics of Aquinas*, edited by Stephen J. Pope. Washington, DC: Georgetown University Press, 2002.

Pius XI. Encyclical Letter: *Casti connubii*. December 31, 1930.

Plato. *Symposium*. Edited by Alexander Nehamas and Paul Woodruff. Indianapolis and Cambridge: Hackett, 1989.

Porter, Jean. *Natural and Divine Law*. Grand Rapids: Eerdmans, 2005.

———. *Recovery of Virtue*. Louisville: Westminster/John Knox Press, 1990.

Pritchard, E. E. *Ancient Near Eastern Texts*. Princeton: Princeton University Press, 1969.

Ratzinger, Joseph (Pope Emeritus Benedict XVI). *Letter to the Bishops of the Catholic Church on the Pastoral Care of Homosexual Persons*. 1986.

Robinson, Marilynne. *The Death of Adam: Essays on Modern Thought*. Boston and New York: Houghton Mifflin, 1998.

Rogers, Jack. *Jesus, The Bible, and Homosexuality*. Louisville: Westminster/John Knox Press, 2006.

Ruether, Rosemary Radford. *Christianity and the Making of the Modern Family: Ruling Ideologies, Diverse Realities*. Boston: Beacon Press, 2000.

Ryan, Christopher, and Jethá Cacilda. *Sex at Dawn: The Prehistoric Origins of Modern Sexuality*. New York: HarperCollins, 2011.

Salisbury, Joyce. *Perpetua's Passion: The Death and Memory of a Young Roman Woman*. New York: Routledge, 1997.

Salzman, Todd, and Michael Lawler. *The Sexual Person: Toward A Renewed Catholic Anthropology*. Washington, DC: Georgetown University Press, 2008.

Shelley, Bruce. *Church History in Plain Language*. Dallas: Word Publishing, 1995.

Sherrard, Phil. "The Sexual Relationship in Christian Thought." *Studies in Comparative Religion* 5, no. 3 (1971).

Siegel, Daniel. *The Developing Mind: How Relationships and the Brain Interact to Shape Who We Are.* New York: Mind Your Brain, 2012.

Sloyan, Gerard. *Interpretation: John.* Series editor James Mays. Atlanta: John Knox Press, 1988.

Stanton, Glenn T. *From: My Crazy Imperfect Christian Family.* NavPress, 2004.

Trible, Phyllis. *Texts of Terror: Literary-Feminist Readings of Biblical Narratives.* Fortress Press, 1984.

Verhey, Allen. "Scripture as Script and Scripted." In *Character Ethics and The New Testament; Moral Dimensions of Scripture,* edited by Robert L. Brawley. Louisville/London: Westminster/John Knox Press, 2007.

Von Thaden Jr., Robert H. *Sex, Christ, and Embodied Cognition: Paul's Wisdom for Corinth.* Emory Studies in Early Christianity (16). Blandford Forum, UK: 2012.

Wallis, Jim. *God's Politics: Why the Right Gets It Wrong and the Left Doesn't Get It.* New York: HarperCollins, 2005.

Warner, Michael. *The Trouble with Normal.* New York: The Free Press, 1999.

Waun, Maurine. *More Than Welcome: Learning to Embrace Gay, Lesbian, Bisexual, and Transgendered Persons in the Church.* St. Louis: Chalice Press, 1999.

White, Mel. *Religion Gone Bad.* London: Jeremy P. Tarcher/Penguin, 2006.

———. *Stranger at the Gate.* New York: Plume/Penguin Group, 1994.

Witte, John, and Eliza Ellison, eds. *Covenant Marriage in Comparative Perspective.* Grand Rapids: Eerdmans, 2005.

Wogamann, J. Phillip. *Christian Ethics.* Louisville: Westminster/John Knox Press, 1993.

Wysocki, C. J., Y. Martins et al. "Preference for Human Body Odors Is Influenced by Gender and Sexual Orientation." *Psychological Science* 16, no. 9 (2005): 694–701.

Index

Made in the USA
San Bernardino, CA
23 July 2015